Also by Paul Salsini

Fiction:

The Fearless Flag Thrower of Lucca: Nine Stories of 1990s Tuscany

A Piazza for Sant'Antonio: Five Novellas of 1980s Tuscany

The Temptation of Father Lorenzo: Ten Stories of 1970s Tuscany

Dino's Story: A Novel of 1960s Tuscany

Sparrow's Revenge: A Novel of Postwar Tuscany

The Cielo: A Novel of Wartime Tuscany

Nonfiction:

Second Start: Stories of Second-Career Priests

For Children:

Stefano and the Christmas Miracles

THE GHOSTS OF THE GARFAGNANA

Seven Strange Stories from Haunted Tuscany

Cover Photo by Ivano Stefani: The Village
of Vergemoli in the Garfagnana.

PAUL SALSINI

THE GHOSTS OF THE GARFAGNANA
SEVEN STRANGE STORIES FROM HAUNTED TUSCANY

Copyright © 2019 Paul Salsini.

All rights reserved. No part of this book may be used or reproduced by any means, graphic, electronic, or mechanical, including photocopying, recording, taping or by any information storage retrieval system without the written permission of the author except in the case of brief quotations embodied in critical articles and reviews.

iUniverse books may be ordered through booksellers or by contacting:

iUniverse
1663 Liberty Drive
Bloomington, IN 47403
www.iuniverse.com
1-800-Authors (1-800-288-4677)

Because of the dynamic nature of the Internet, any web addresses or links contained in this book may have changed since publication and may no longer be valid. The views expressed in this work are solely those of the author and do not necessarily reflect the views of the publisher, and the publisher hereby disclaims any responsibility for them.

ISBN: 978-1-5320-7492-9 (sc)
ISBN: 978-1-5320-7493-6 (e)

Library of Congress Control Number: 2019906148

Print information available on the last page.

iUniverse rev. date: 05/07/2019

For Barbara,
Jim, Laura and Jack

AUTHOR'S NOTE

DURING THE COURSE of writing the six volumes—novels and collections of short stories—that make up what I call "A Tuscan Series," I would often drive north from the area around Lucca, where those books were set. Although I was still in Tuscany, I found a region, stretching between the Apennines to the east/northeast and the Apuan Alps to the west, different from any other I had encountered in Italy. The towering mountains were either in brilliant shades of white or densely covered with chestnut trees. Tiny villages nestled on bubbling streams. Exotic flowers covered great stretches. And unaccountable fog and mist sometimes hid the landscape.

The region, which I was told was called the Garfagnana, seemed both mysterious and threatening. My curiosity was raised when I heard tales about happenings there. A bridge that was built by the devil. An underground grotto where voices can be heard. A witches' coven on a mountain. A spooky ghost carrying a scythe. A village that had been flooded by a power company but whose church bells could be heard on cold winter nights—even though the bells had been removed before the inundation.

Here, in this land of the supernatural, were ideas for a new collection of stories. The reader will quickly find that although the tales may be strange, they are not scary. After all, one of the ghosts is even called "gentle." Enjoy.

CONTENTS

The First Miracle   1

The Second Miracle   15

The Miraculous Statue   57

A Friendship Shawl   75

The Crystal Ball   99

The Village That Went to Sleep   143

Behind the Curtain   201

THE FIRST MIRACLE

Anno Domini 1225

KNOWING THAT THEY HAD only an hour's break from their vow of silence, the monks tried to make good use of it. They had not spoken to each other for a day, and they mainly whispered.

"What do you think it means?" Brother Antimo wondered.

"Why would he call a meeting now?" Brother Frediano asked.

"Something terrible must have happened," Brother Corinado said. "I am sure it has something to do with that terrible smell from the cistern."

The monks were gathered in the courtyard, in groups of three or four, enjoying the hot sun on this brilliant August day. From this vantage point they could see the craggy white cliffs and the green valleys, the forested hills and the vast plains. But they were too high to observe the farmers tilling their fields and gathering their beans and cabbage and onions, too far away to see women washing clothes in the creeks that dribbled down from the mountains.

From north to south, from east to west, barns and farmhouses with thatched roofs sprinkled the plains like stars in the heaven. Occasional bell towers spiked the sky. Tiny lakes lay like deep cerulean jewels. Chestnut trees blanketed mushroom patches. Fields of sunflowers swept into the horizon.

An eagle swooped overhead, circled and then vanished. Rabbits chased each other up and down the nearby hills.

A few tiny villages, not much more than clusters of houses, scattered the valley. The closest was Castelnuovo di Garfagnana, where farmers brought their produce to market every week.

The Garfagnana region of Tuscany had never looked so much like an extraordinary creation of God.

The meeting called by Abbot Domenico would be held that evening, and the monks knew that it was highly unusual for the abbot to gather all of them in the Villa of Saint Gaudentius of Novara. For one thing, there wasn't a room big enough to adequately hold all seventy-two men who were now in residence.

There had been only five Benedictines when the villa was given to them in 1152 by the estate of Count Emilio Santucci, who had died without heirs. The count had been in ill health for many years, and it took decades of muscle and sweat for the monks to make repairs to the building. Soon there were twenty monks, then forty, then sixty. With crowding came the inevitable grumbling and griping.

It seemed as though whenever one monk would die there would be two or three others ready to take his place. Becoming a monk was a popular career choice in the twelfth and thirteenth centuries.

Just after Vespers the congregation of the Villa of Saint Gaudentius crowded into the refectory, which normally served meals on a staggered basis. The younger oblates crunched in the back, allowing the monks to sit elbow to elbow at the long tables. Since this was a meeting of the entire group, everyone was permitted to speak. A few of the older monks complained about leg pains, foot pains, back pains, pains in places they never knew existed. A couple of the corpulent monks compared notes on the meals for the last few days, deciding that it was time for a new cook.

"The pork is always undercooked," one said. "I don't know if I should eat it."

"But you do," his neighbor observed.

The younger monks confessed to being distracted during prayer, especially the early morning Lauds.

"I can't stay awake for that long," one complained. "I've tried. It's impossible." Three others agreed.

When everyone had gathered, Abbot Domenico entered slowly, leaning firmly on his wooden cane. Looking more frail by the day, he took naps frequently now, and the other monks worried. He was, after all, sixty-eight years old. His tonsure, once brown, was now a wispy white, looking remarkably like a halo in a certain light.

Abbot Domenico was followed by a tall man whose silver hair fell to his shoulders. His long royal blue tunic, trimmed in scarlet at the neck and wrists, was in stark contrast to the abbot's simple black Benedictine habit. A pendant adorned with jewels hung on a gold chain on the visitor's broad chest.

As usual, the meeting began with the reading of a section from the Rule of Saint Benedict, followed by a short sermon on the need to accept God's will in all things. Then Abbot Domenico stood behind the lectern, coughed into his sleeve and began.

"*Pace,* my brothers. You probably wonder why I called you all here. I can assure you that it was not to praise our kitchen on the wonderful dinner of fresh beans and cauliflower that we had last night."

The abbot's attempts to lighten the proceedings were always feeble.

"No, it is because I have some exciting news for you. I could hardly keep this to myself for the last few weeks."

With trembling hands, he paused to wipe his forehead and take a sip of water from the metal mug.

"As you know, God has rewarded our congregation with more and more men who are willing to accept the rule of our saintly founder. Please thank God for this blessing."

Everyone in the room murmured "Amen."

"In fact, He may have been too generous. I remember when I came here forty-two years ago in 1183 there were only thirty-three of us in residence. Now that number has more than doubled. We have indeed been blessed."

"Amen."

"But, as you can see, we can barely fit into this room, and that is the situation throughout the villa. It was, after all, built more than a hundred years ago as a palazzo and given to us by the Santucci family, but it has never quite filled our needs. We have had to knock down a few walls and build two extensions. Now, every time we make one repair there are four or five others waiting."

He stopped to catch his breath and take another sip of water.

"And as you are quite aware, our chapel is so small that we must schedule prayers and services over several hours. The infirmary is turning away our brothers with minor illnesses because we don't have enough beds. Several of you are sleeping in makeshift spaces in the dormitory or in the hallways. We will not, of course, allow more than one man to a cell."

Everyone nodded.

"We have, in short, outgrown this villa. It is a good problem to have, but we must resolve the problem. We must! And quickly! So I have this grand announcement. We are going to build a monastery! Yes, a real monastery where we will have room to work and study and, most of all, to pray, in solitude and without interruption. It will be the finest monastery in all of the Garfagnana, in all of Tuscany, and indeed, in all of Italy."

His face red, the abbot attempted to raise his arms in praise.

"Amen! Amen!" The cheer might have been heard by the cows and horses in the barns across the fields.

"And so I would like to introduce Count Adolfo Benini, an architect whose family goes back hundreds of years and has built some of the most famous and most beautiful monasteries in Italy. In fact, they have also built monasteries in Germany, in France and even in England. Everywhere their work has received the highest accolades. We are so honored that Count Benini, the newest member to this heritage, has accepted our invitation to do this work. Count Benini, please."

As the abbot slowly lowered himself into the wooden chair, the count stood and acknowledged the loud applause.

"Thank you, Abbot Domenico. It is I who am honored to be given this challenging task, and it is my pleasure to share with you the plans that we have developed for your beautiful monastery. It will indeed be the most outstanding monastery in all of the Garfagnana. And, let me say, beyond."

He pulled a heavy scroll out of a long wooden tube and attached it to the rear wall. The Benedictines leaned forward.

"If you can look closely, you will see the drawing for the edifice." He picked up a long stick as a pointer. "I will go through this quickly and you can ask questions later. First, of course, over here will be the chapel, a large chapel with several altars and spaces for prayer and reflection. So big and beautiful some might even call it a cathedral. Next to it will be the bell tower, so tall that the glorious sounds will be heard for miles around.

"Then, here in the middle is the central court, the cloister, where you can walk quietly in prayer or meditation. Over here is the refectory with the kitchen to the rear. You will all be able to eat together! Then here is the dormitory with individual cells, larger than you have now, and there's room over here for expansion. Here's the infirmary, big enough for all your patients. And here is the chapter house so that you can hold real meetings there instead of in the refectory."

He paused to let the Benedictines smile and whisper among themselves.

"And here," the count continued, "is the library, big enough to store all the books that are now in crates. And next to it something new, a *scriptorium* where you can copy precious manuscripts. There is a great demand for books now and I know you must have very talented people here who can do this work."

Abbot Domenico interrupted. "Praise be to God! It has always been my dream to have a *scriptorium*. I think that years from now, our monastery, indeed all monasteries from this time, will be remembered for the beautiful books they have written and copied."

Count Benini continued. "I should also mention some basics. Here, a *lavatorium* where you will be able to wash your hands before meals. Also a *garderobe*, a privy that will have a hole where waste will drop into a cesspit."

He went on to other features of the complex.

"Now, just beyond the main buildings will be the barns and bakeries, laundries and workshops. The present buildings there will be rebuilt and expanded. And all of this will be surrounded by a high wall. We know there are marauders traveling the countryside and you need to be protected.

"And finally—this may not ever be necessary, but it is a standard feature in the monasteries we have been building—a separate small hut called the *misericord,* where monks can be disciplined for violations of your order's rule."

"We hope that is never needed," Abbot Domenico interjected.

The monks nodded. They had never heard of a *misericord.*

The count paused to let all this sink in. The good Benedictines were overwhelmed and speechless. They could not imagine that their humble and deteriorating quarters would be replaced by such a magnificent monastery. Of course, they also knew that none of them would live to see it completed, or in some cases even barely begun.

Abbot Domenico rose again. He gripped the lectern, thanked the architect, praised the plans and asked if there were any questions. The room fell silent.

"Well, you may be too polite to ask this, but I know you must be wondering who is going to provide the funds for this costly venture. As you know, we Benedictines live a simple life. Just as an example, the rule of our founder says:

"Let those who receive new clothes always return the old ones, to be put away in the wardrobe for the poor. For it is sufficient for a monk to have two tunics and two cowls, for wearing at night and for washing."

"If we are allowed only two tunics as our only possessions, how could we afford this? We thank God first of all. And we thank also Our Holy Roman Emperor, Frederick II. As you know, he has long been a patron of the arts, including architecture, and, as it happens, Count Benini's father is a friend of Frederick's tutor, Walter of Palearia. His father told Signor Walter, who told Frederick of our desires, and he agreed to finance the entire project. We thank Our Holy Roman Emperor, too!"

"Amen!"

"Now, I wonder if there are any other questions."

Heads were turned, eyebrows were raised, but no one could think of anything. Then Brother Antimo raised his hand.

Abbot Domenico smiled. "Yes, Antimo?"

"If I may ask," he began nervously, "I wonder where this beautiful monastery will be built."

"That is a good question," Count Benini said. "You are now sitting on top of this gorgeous mountaintop. Your villa is of a generous size, but it cannot be seen from very far. Let me assure you that we want the monastery to be a sign of God's presence from everywhere in this entire region. We will build it right next to the villa, just to the east, so that you will not be disrupted during the construction, but it will be many times the size."

"Amen!" everyone said.

Brother Frediano raised his hand.

"Signor," he said, "just east of our villa is the burial ground. What will happen to that?"

"We will build a beautiful cemetery on the west end of the property, one where monks for centuries to come will rest in peace and dignity.

Obviously, we will move the good monks who are resting in the present cemetery to the new one."

Abbot Domenico rose again.

"I know I will not see the completion of this magnificent monastery, and I assume none of you will either. We will watch the construction in the glory of God's heavens."

As they walked back to their cells, Brother Antimo was jubilant. "I can't imagine living in a big place like that."

"We'll be lost," Brother Frediano said.

Brother Corinado shrugged. "We don't have to worry about it. We'll never see it. Maybe we won't even see them dig the first hole."

"Just as well," Brother Antimo said. "I just have a feeling that strange things may happen in that new monastery."

"Why do you say that?"

"I don't know. I just do."

WHILE COUNT BELLINI and his staff drew more detailed plans for the monastery, the present burial ground had to be cleared and the caskets interred in the new site. First, a tall iron fence was constructed to surround the new cemetery, and a white statue of the Virgin Mary, her hands outstretched in supplication, placed in the middle. There were twenty-six caskets to be moved.

Since none of the monks volunteered for the job, Abbot Domenico appointed a crew of twelve. He gave the leader, Brother Massimo, a sheet of parchment that had been carefully stored in the vault in his office. It contained the list of all the deceased by number and the dates of their birth and death. The cemetery was democratic; abbots rested with the other monks with no distinction made for rank.

The digging began in the far northwest corner with the oldest. Each grave was also numbered.

Brother Massimo led the diggers to the first grave and read from the parchment.

I: "Brother Cirillo. Born 1122, died 1156."

"You're the first," Brother Massimo said to the small marker. "And I hope you're the first in Heaven."

The ground was hard and their shovels were old and rusty. They took turns digging until they heard the clunk against the wooden casket. Disintegrated and barely held together by the ropes, it was lifted to the surface. The monks covered their faces with handkerchiefs, bowed their heads and said a short prayer but did not look inside. Then the remains were loaded onto an oxcart and carried to the new site, where other monks had already prepared a grave.

Sweat pouring down from their tonsured heads and into their cowls, the monks began digging the next grave.

The ground seemed even harder in this area. One shovel broke and another bent out of shape. No one noticed the murmured curses that were uttered.

II. "Brother Enrico," Brother Massimo read. "Born 1134, died 1161."

"I wish we knew something about these brothers," another monk said. "They all seem so anonymous."

"They won't be anonymous in Heaven. Think of it. We'll be able to meet all our brothers."

Brother Enrico's coffin had deteriorated even more than the first. Unspeakable creatures had invaded it and the monks knew that little of the corpse remained. They did not look, and it was quickly carted off.

They turned to the third grave.

III: "Brother Giacomo. Born 1145, died 1167," Brother Massimo read. "Only twenty-two years old. Poor boy. He died so young."

"So that's Brother Giacomo!" another monk said. "I often wondered where exactly his body was."

"As opposed to his spirit, you know."

"What are you talking about?" Brother Zito asked. He had entered the order as an oblate just eight months ago and still had much to learn.

"Well," Brother Massimo said, "Brother Giacomo is somewhat of a legend here. He was, as you can see, only twenty-two years old when he died."

"Only twenty-two? I'm twenty-one."

"He was the kindest, most generous monk who ever lived here," Brother Massimo said. "That's what people said anyway. He helped other young monks learn the Rule. He helped older monks who had trouble getting around. He would do any kind of chore. When he prayed it seemed that his face radiated with joy. People called him a saint even then."

"Why did he die so young?"

"He didn't just die, he was murdered. At least everyone believes that. Even though everyone else in the congregation loved him, one monk hated him, Brother Fausto. This was a monk who believed that we must punish ourselves for our sins. Which may be true, but he carried it to the extreme. Brother Fausto fasted so much that he was just skin and bones. He didn't participate in the communal time when the monks would share a few jokes and even a glass of wine. Instead, he lay prostrate on the floor of the chapel. And worse, he beat himself with a whip."

Brother Zito cringed.

"The other monks ignored him, but Brother Giacomo tried to help. He tried to reason with him, but Brother Fausto wouldn't listen. He just got worse and worse and then he began to take it out on Brother Giacomo. He would go to his cell and castigate him, tell him that he should be the one who should whip himself. One night, Brother Giacomo told Brother Fausto that he would pray for him. That was the last straw. Brother Fausto threatened him, and Brother Giacomo went to the abbot. The next morning, Brother Giacomo was found dead. Strangled. There were marks around his neck that indicated that a leather whip was used. Brother Fausto was nowhere to be found, just vanished. The order tried to hush it up and there was no investigation. Brother Giacomo was buried here within a few hours."

Brother Zito shuddered. "I can't believe this."

"He was a martyr, pure and simple," Brother Massimo said. "He died for his faith. If the order hadn't wanted to hush it all up, he would have been declared a saint."

Brother Massimo added that it was fairly easy to be declared a saint in those days, and even a bishop could do it.

The young monk, who had much to learn about life and its consequences, was still puzzled. "Did you say something about his spirit?"

"There were reports," Brother Massimo said, "that Brother Giacomo often said he loved it here so much that after he died he would like to come back to visit. So every once in a while people claim that they actually see him. He's not threatening. He just stands there and then he floats away."

"Really? What does he look like?"

"Slim, not too tall, kind of handsome. And he has red hair, what's left of it after his tonsure. Oh, also, he has ears that stick out. Everybody agrees about that."

"Aren't people scared?"

"Only those who have something to be scared about. There are stories that he has appeared to people who haven't been, well, very good. One monk was known to filch things from the kitchen and Giacomo stood in the door as he tried to get out. You can imagine how fast the monk put everything back. But otherwise, he's just a friendly ghost."

The young monk stared down at Brother Giacomo's casket. "You sound nice to me. It's all right if you come to see us."

"All right, all right," Brother Massimo said. "Let's stop gossiping and get this finished."

The monks gingerly brought the casket to the surface.

"Doesn't it seem lighter than the others?" one asked.

"Don't let your imagination run wild," Brother Massimo said. "He was just a young man. Take a look if you want."

"No, thank you."

The casket was taken to the new burial site and the remains transferred to another wooden coffin.

The monks were able to dig up only five coffins that first day. By the time they were carried to the new site and buried, the sun was mercifully setting.

The next day, five more.

"Only sixteen more," Brother Massimo said, looking at his list as they returned to the villa.

The next day, five more. Nine left.

Then another five.

On the last day, they dug up the remaining four, completing their task in darkness. The last to be returned to the surface was the twenty-sixth, Brother Paolo.

XXVI. "Brother Paolo. Born 1157, died 1224."

"I remember him," Brother Massimo said. "He died just last August. Very quiet. I didn't know him very well. I don't think anyone did."

"He was a nice man," another said. "I always had the feeling that he'd had a hard life and that's why he entered the order."

Before they returned to the villa they stopped at Brother Giacomo's empty grave.

"I wonder if he will visit the new monastery when it's completed," one of the monks said. "It would be nice for the monks there to see him."

WITH THE OLD BURIAL GROUND CLEARED, Abbot Domenico led the monks to the site for a blessing and prayer to formally begin construction of what everyone agreed would be the most beautiful monastery in all of the Garfagnana.

"Oh, God, bless the work that we are about to begin. May this monastery be a sign of Your goodness and a place where generations of Benedictines will share Your blessings. May it also be a place for pilgrims to rest and contemplate the beauty of Your kingdom."

"Amen."

Brother Massimo picked up a shovel tied with a golden ribbon and helped Abbot Domenico dig into the ancient earth.

Two days later, Count Bellini arrived and the long, arduous, backbreaking work began. The slogging efforts went slowly, and then weeks turned into months, and months into years. It took seven years just to dig the foundation with strong-armed workers using axes and metal-tipped ploughs from the monks' own farm and borrowed from farms outside Castelnuovo di Garfagnana. Peasants from miles around earned modest sums by helping throughout the construction.

With the huge rectangular hole dug, the crews traveled to a quarry at the base of the mountain to carve out stones. A parade of oxcarts lugged the heavy loads up the mountain to the site. After a partial wall was built, stones were measured and cut, and a floor laid. Another thirty-eight years.

Count Benini, who had supervised the construction almost daily, had died by then and was succeeded by his son. The son knew somebody who knew somebody and that person was able to acquire a new device that would greatly simplify the construction of the walls. The device, called a treadwheel crane, was a complicated, awkward machine consisting of a wooden wheel turning around a central shaft. The wheel used human power. Two monks, stepping side by side, turned the wheel and, with ropes attached to a pulley, the machine could lift heavy stones to complete the walls. It took five months alone for the two monks, the biggest men in the congregation, to learn how to tread in sync. Then they could maneuver the machine and start on the walls.

That process took another forty-two years and Count Benini's son was succeeded by his grandson who was eventually succeeded by his great-grandson. The two Benedictines who originally operated the treadmill died, separately—perhaps from fatigue—and were succeeded and succeeded again by other massive monks.

When the walls were connected by the immense tie beams of the roof, the crane lifted more stones to complete the task. Another twenty-two years.

For the chapel, oxcarts traveled even farther into Tuscany to bring back marble from distant quarries. Finally, the newest Count Benini commissioned stained glass windows to be made in Florence. These were installed in the chapel, and paintings, including that of Saint Gaudentius of Novara, were hung. Finally, a stately pipe organ, the biggest in all of Tuscany, was installed.

Remarkably, construction of the monastery exceeded expectations, completed in record time in August of 1378, only one hundred and fifty-three years. It might have taken even less time, but the Black Death, roughly from 1346 to 1353, stopped all activity as Italy, indeed all of Europe, cared for the sick and dying.

During the course of the construction there were unconfirmed reports that Giacomo the Ghost was observed at least a dozen times.

"Look, there he is again!" was the usual cry.

"It's him! Red hair!"

"Ears sticking out!"

The shouts apparently scared the transparent visitor away.

The longest apparitions supposedly took place during the operation of the treadmill cranes. The visitor seemed to be fascinated by this unusual machine, even getting close to it. The two monks on the treadmill became so unnerved when they looked over and saw the figure of a young man all in white staring at them that they lost their balance, got out of sync and had trouble starting again.

Giacomo was also said to have been seen during the installation of the organ, standing very near as the resident organist attempted to practice.

"He must have liked my music," the organist said later. "I offered to let him play, but I guess he was too shy and he vanished."

He was also seen floating in the kitchen late at night, surprising a monk who was trying to snitch some bakery.

There was one notable exception. In 1350, during the height of the Black Death, six monks were gravely ill. There was no one to help them, and they languished in the infirmary. One of them thought to pray to Giacomo. He promised that if he and the others recovered, they would establish a hospital to care for others infected by the plague. In a dream, the monk saw a young man all in white who stretched out his arms and said, "God loves you." He pointed to the village of Castelnuovo di Garfagnana not far away. In two days, the monk had recovered completely and the others within a week. They went to the village and found an old villa to use as a hospital. Miraculously, vials of medicine were found in a storeroom, and these were used to treat the people in the village who had been stricken by the plague. Many of them recovered.

When the abbot at that time, Nazario, heard about this, he immediately ordered an investigation. Clearly, Giacomo was responsible, and this was a miracle. A delegation interviewed the monks who had been cured and they went to the villa in Castelnuovo di Garfagnana to talk to the people there. Then they traveled to the Vatican to present the evidence, and after a lengthy investigation, the Holy See declared that this was indeed a true miracle for sainthood.

Since then, however, no other miracle occurred, and ghost tales became greatly exaggerated. If a plate fell off a table, Giacomo was blamed. If a candle suddenly went out, surely it was Giacomo's breath that did it. If a tree fell during a storm, it was obvious that Giacomo had something to do with it. Along the way, someone added "gentle" to his name since the young ghost never harmed anyone.

"There will be another miracle," one of the monks predicted as they sat around and tried to scare the young oblates with ghost stories. "It is just a matter of time."

THE SECOND MIRACLE

Anno Domini 1378

ALTHOUGH THE MONASTERY would not be dedicated until the following January 22, the feast of Saint Gaudentius of Novara, it would be occupied and used as soon as the last stone was polished in August of 1378.

There was some discussion about whether the monastery should be renamed in honor of another, more well-known saint, but the congregation agreed that Saint Gaudentius' name should be retained. The saint had been the first bishop in Novara, in the Piedmont, and was known for his piety.

Also, as one monk pointed out, "there's the legend that after he died his head continued to speak so that his sermons could be repeated."

"Nobody believes that," another said.

"Some people don't believe that Giacomo comes to visit us every once in a while either," a third monk said, and the others tried to be amused.

There had been six abbots during the years of construction, the first, Abbot Domenico, dying in 1234, and the last, Abbot Nazario, in 1372. Their bodies, in wooden caskets, were buried in the new cemetery.

The present abbot, Nicolo, was a young forty-four. He was well over six feet tall, with a ruddy face, wide shoulders and big hands. If it were not for his tonsure, he would have had curly black hair. He was strong enough to help the workmen lift the marble top onto the new altar.

More important, he knew every monk by his name, his family history and his personal problems and desires. He was both respected and loved.

Nicolo had originally planned to become a doctor, and when he entered the order he used his natural talents to use herbs to heal the sick. Herbal remedies, combined with prayer, had become an increasingly common practice in monasteries, and they were successful. For example, he found that a mixture of radish, bishop's wort, garlic, wormwood, helenium, crop leek and hollow leek was especially useful for joint pains.

Nicolo also translated old Latin texts on herbal remedies, adding information on new herbs that were found, and he looked forward to establishing a garden only for herbs outside the new monastery. The books were stored in the new library.

Abbot Nicolo now had ninety-five monks in his flock, the oldest seventy-four and the youngest twenty-three. After being squeezed even more tightly in the old palazzo, they couldn't wait to move into new quarters.

When the last floor was swept, when the last window was washed and when the last bench was put in place in the refectory, the monastery was declared completed. On a warm August day, Abbot Nicolo and the newest Count Benini led the monks from the villa to the monastery for a tour.

The first stop was the kitchen. Brother Rocco, whose ample girth required frequent adjustments of his habit, was first in line. "I can't wait," he said as he nudged another monk aside.

"I know some of you are more interested in this than in the chapel," the abbot sighed.

The kitchen was dominated by a central hearth with four additional fireplaces on the sides. One was for baking and the others for smoking and roasting. Spits for roasting meats were ready for the lambs, cattle, pigs and fowl that were in pens outside. Large iron cauldrons hung in two of the fireplaces.

"Can you just smell the soups and stews that we'll be having?" the abbot asked.

"I can!" Brother Rocco replied.

"This kitchen is large enough to roast a whole ox at a time," Count Benini said. "Maybe two!"

Three long tables stood in the middle of the room, and pots, pans, kettles, skillets and cauldrons hung from the walls. Chests contained knives, ladles, meat forks and scissors.

"And here," Abbot Nicolo said, "we have something essential. Mortar and pestle so that our cooks can use nuts and spices in their recipes."

Count Benini also pointed out the sink, because the monastery now had its own water supply from nearby Lake Venito.

With coaxing, Brother Rocco was edged out of the kitchen, and the tour continued: A buttery for storing beverages such as ale, a bottlery for wines, and a pantry for perishable food products.

After inspecting these, the monks were split into small groups and given tours of the chapter house, the infirmary and their cells, which were nicely furnished with a small bed, a simple chair and a table.

Then they came to the *scriptorium*.

"At last," Abbot Nicolo said, "we'll be able to follow the rule of our beloved founder."

The Rule of Saint Benedict, written in the seventh century, specifically called for monks to have ready access to books. They were to read for two hours every day and in Lent each monk was to read an entire book. The villa had housed a small library, but it did not contain nearly enough books for the entire congregation.

"The only way we can acquire a large quantity of books," Abbot Nicolo said, "is to copy them, and that's what we'll do here in the *scriptorium*."

"I remember," Count Benini said, "my grandfather quoting his father who quoted the abbot who was in charge when construction was started—I believe his name was Abbot Domenico—that it had been his dream to have a *scriptorium*. Now we are fulfilling that dream."

The spacious room was filled with light from windows stretching almost from marble floor to vaulted ceiling. Sixteen writing desks were lined against the windows. Shelves underneath contained pens and colored inks.

Count Benini also pointed out the library next door, and Abbot Nicolo promised that it would soon be filled with books produced right here.

"We are going to be the most famous *scriptorium* in all of Italy!" he said. "Our books will not only be read, but they will also be on display in museums around the world."

Brother Marco, the oldest monk in the congregation, was the last to leave the area. There was nothing that made him happier than having a book in his hands, and he couldn't wait to begin his new assignment of copying them himself. He walked slowly around the room, running his hands over the desks and shelves.

"Thank You, God," he whispered.

The final stop on the tour was the chapel, and the monks instantly stopped their chatter. As the original architect had promised, it could be compared to a cathedral. Besides the main altar, there were two side altars, each in a separate niche. And besides the central aisle, there were two side aisles with a row of arches on the ground floor topped by a row on the second, which was itself topped by beautiful stained glass windows.

"Notice the story in the windows," Abbot Nicolo said. "Here at the end we have the angel announcing to Mary that she will bear a child. Then we have Mary's visit to Anna. Then the birth in the stable. Jesus growing up. And on and on. John the Baptist. The sermons. The wedding at Cana. Lazarus. And finally, over here, the crucifixion and the resurrection."

Count Benini added, "We found the best artists in Florence to do this work. Notice how alive all the people are with the sun shining through. Yes, they were expensive, but we had the money and it was worth it."

Since there were only a few benches, the monks easily walked throughout the building, examining the marble columns, the marble pulpit, the baptistery.

Finally, exhausted, they followed the abbot and the architect out into the darkening night and back to the villa. Fast-moving clouds played hide-and-seek with the full moon, and the tall pines shivered in the gusty winds.

"Looks like a good night for ghosts," one of the older monks said as they traipsed back to the villa.

"You mean like Giacomo the Gentle Ghost? Like over there?" said another, pointing to a light in the distance. "I knew he'd want to come to see all this. I wonder if he wishes he lived here now."

The light could have been a glimmer of moonlight on a small tree. Or it could have been something else.

Although most of the monks hurried back to their cells, a few lingered, hoping to have a conversation with the visitor. But soon the light vanished.

ALONE IN HIS STUDY at the far end of the complex, Abbot Nicolo poured himself a goblet of the fine red wine produced by the exceptional grape harvest three years ago and looked out the window. He could see the roof of the new monastery and the bell tower silhouetted in the moonlight. He was exhausted, but pleased. Despite all the crises over the years, the monastery had turned out to be as fine as anyone could have expected. Even finer. He paused to say a prayer.

"Thank You, Almighty Father, for all Your blessings. May we always live in Your service."

Then, remembering petty disputes over the years, he added, "And may we always live in peace and harmony."

Now there was more mundane work to do. Ordering supplies for the kitchen. Replenishing candles for the altar. Getting new sheets for the infirmary. Hiring workers from nearby farms to help take care of the animals and the gardens. Preparing the *scriptorium*. With Brother Marco's help, he couldn't wait to do that.

But there were two duties for tomorrow. He pulled out a sheaf of papers from a drawer in his wooden desk and began to go through them. Because the Monastery of Saint Gaudentius now had more space, Benedictines from other, much more crowded monasteries had been sending in applications to transfer. Abbot Nicolo agreed to take in five monks from the Abbey of Monte Casino and, after a long journey across Italy by horse, mule and foot, they had just arrived.

Tomorrow he would interview them, and then assign all the monks to their new cells in the monastery.

Perhaps because he had so much on his mind, Abbot Nicolo slept sporadically and was awake long before Lauds. As usual, he skipped breakfast and settled in his office to greet the new residents.

Brother Arnaldo, who was in his late forties, was the first.

"Welcome, Brother," the abbot said. "You have come from perhaps the most famous monastery in the world, the one that our own founder established. Sometime, I would like to talk to you about living in such an extraordinary place. It must have been such a rewarding spiritual experience. I can't imagine wanting to leave."

Brother Arnaldo began to sob.

"What's the matter, Brother? What did I say?"

"You don't understand, Father, how crowded we were at Monte Casino. We could hardly breathe. We just couldn't…"

"It's all right, Brother," the abbot said. "You're here now. Welcome!"

Brother Santino, on the other hand, seemed to think the Monastery of Saint Gaudentius of Novara was fortunate to have him as a new member, and he recited all of his accomplishments at Monte Casino.

"I'm sure, Brother Santino," Abbot Nicolo said, "you will enjoy meeting the other monks here as you clean the cisterns."

Brother Silvano wanted to know if he could spend more time in the chapel, and Brother Flavio asked if he could assist in the kitchen.

Last to enter the study was Brother Ludovico, who slid in so silently that Abbot Nicolo wasn't aware he was there until the monk coughed. He was a small man, but wiry. He had thick eyebrows, a pointed noise and bad teeth that unfortunately resulted in an unsavory breath.

Abbot Nicolo wondered why he didn't sit back on the chair, but assumed it was because of nervousness.

"Welcome, Brother Ludovico. All of us at the Monastery of Saint Gaudentius are pleased that you are joining us."

"I didn't ask to come here."

"But you are here."

"The abbot at Monte Casino told me to come. He said I might be happier here."

"You were unhappy there?"

"He said I might be happier here."

Abbot Nicolo smiled. "Well, we hope you are. We are pleased to have you. Now, do you have any questions?"

"I like to be alone as much as possible."

"Well, that's fine. It's good to say our prayers in solitude. But of course we have communal prayer, and reflection, and dining. And we enjoy the hour of free time every evening together. It helps us to get to know one another."

"I don't like free time," Brother Ludovico said. "I don't want to know about the other monks. I don't care if they know anything about me. I will spend such time in my cell. In prayer!"

"That's your prerogative, but I think you might enjoy the company of your other brothers."

"I doubt that."

"It's up to you."

Staring at the floor, Brother Ludovico had not looked up once during the conversation.

"Well," Abbot Nicolo said, "today I am assigning all our monks to their new cells in the monastery and I will let you know about yours."

"I want to be at the end of the hall. It's quieter there."

Abbot Nicolo's smile was tight. "I'll see what I can do."

As Brother Ludovico turned to leave, the abbot said, "Brother, I do hope you are happy here."

The brother made no response. Abbot Nicolo watched the little monk shuffle off and sighed. "Thank you, Monte Casino. We all appreciate that you sent this new addition to our congregation."

He turned to the task of assigning cells. Although all the cells in the new monastery were identical, some monks had seemed to see differences on their tour, and had let Abbot Nicolo know.

"I think the bed is too close to the wall for me and I'll be able to hear the brother next door," one monk observed, ignoring the fact that the walls were of thick stones.

"I wish my cell was on the east side," another said. "The setting sun will keep me awake at night."

"I'm a cook so I need to be near the kitchen," a third monk said.

Tired of the grumbling, Abbot Nicolo decided to assign the monks in the only fair way possible, by alphabet. There were four long rows of cells, each cell opposite the other along two corridors.

In the first, Abbot Nicolo assigned Brother Alessio at the end, then Brother Angelico, then Brother Arnaldo, then Brother Biaggio, and so on. The second row started with Brother Flavio, then Brother Franco, then Brother Geronimo, and more.

Then the third row. Brother Ludovico, Brother...

"Brother Ludovico? He's getting his wish to be at the end. I wish I knew why he wanted this solitude. Oh well."

In the cell next to him was Brother Marco, the monk Abbot Nicolo respected most of all. He sat back and thought about the saintly monk.

As private and sullen as Brother Ludovico was, Brother Marco was just the opposite. He arrived at the Benedictines' door when he was just fourteen years old and had come from a large family. He had actually asked to join the order. Unusually bright and studious, he had decided that he would devote his life to the Church as a monk. His parents reluctantly agreed, believing that it was a blessing that would reflect on them.

With other boys his age, Marco first became an oblate and lived in a kind of dormitory. Some of the boys were coaxed into disobedience in this atmosphere, but it was always Marco who broke up arguments and calmed them down until a senior monk could provide discipline.

When he was twenty, Marco became a novice, and when he was twenty-two, he took his final vows. His parents, his six brothers and five sisters all wept with joy even though they knew they would probably never see him again.

More than any other monk in the monastery, Brother Marco relished the religious life. Praying and working were all the same to him, gifts from God. He quickly became a mentor for new oblates and novices, teaching them about the Benedictine Rule and their role in monastic life. Boys soon found that he would listen to their problems and offer comforting advice. He spent hours reading before he went to bed at night.

"He always has a smile on his face," a monk told Abbot Nicolo. "How can he be so happy all the time?"

"God's grace," the abbot replied.

At seventy-four, he was the senior monk in the monastery, esteemed by all.

Next to him would be Brother Pietro. The youngest monk in the congregation at twenty-three, Brother Pietro had been brought to the congregation by his family when he was ten because they could no longer afford to care for him and his nine siblings after their father died. The family was especially hit hard by the Black Death, and the farm fields they so desperately needed were now mostly barren.

Perhaps because he came from such a large family, all of whom had somehow inherited red hair, Pietro was extremely shy and spoke only when someone spoke to him. He was also very self-conscious about his protruding ears.

Brother Marco came upon Brother Pietro one day and found the young man sobbing.

"Brother Pietro! What's the matter?"

After a long hesitation, the young monk confessed that he had been afflicted by impure thoughts.

Brother Marco put his hand on his shoulder. "Is that all? Brother Pietro, we all have impure thoughts, some more than others. What did you do then?"

"I took out the Rule and began to read."

"Did that help?"

"Yes, they went away."

"Brother Pietro, you are just fine. You're a fine example of a true Benedictine monk. I predict you're going to have a long and happy life with us."

From that day, Brother Pietro often called on the older man for advice. They talked about life before the monastery, life in the monastery, and especially life after life. No matter how occupied Brother Marco was, he always made time for Brother Pietro.

As for the monk in the fourth cell, Brother Rocco, Abbot Nicolo sighed. The man was incorrigible but somehow lovable at the same time. How could anyone object when he told funny jokes, especially on himself? He was always playing tricks, hiding things from other monks and getting into trouble. He was as generous of girth as he was in spirit; it seemed the word "jolly" was invented for a monk just like him.

Brother Rocco was not easily admitted to the Benedictines. The oldest son of a peasant family that seemed quite willing to see him leave, he failed to impress the admitting monks when he wondered if he really needed to have his hair cut because "it looks good on me long." He struggled with learning the Rule of Saint Benedict and sometimes had trouble staying awake during its reading before meals. He had no trouble during the meals, however, and usually asked for a second helping. Although he asked to work in the kitchen, the abbot thought otherwise, and assigned him to cutting wood in the nearby forest. He did not chop wood well. Although he attempted to refine his language, his childhood had taught him certain barnyard words that could not be forgotten and were always a surprise to his fellow monks.

Despite his faults, or perhaps because of them, he was immensely popular with most of the other monks. Perhaps putting him near Brother Marco, Abbot Nicolo thought, might tame him.

TWO DAYS LATER, the monks moved in, and it was truly an amazing sight. Ninety-nine black-robed Benedictines—their ranks swelled by five with the arrival of those from Monte Casino—wove their way from the old villa to the new monastery. They laughed, they sang, a few (even the older ones) danced a little. Each carried their extra habits, books, big and small crucifixes, candles, anything they could hold. Most would return to get more things.

At the entrance, Abbot Nicolo again said a prayer and the multitude quieted down for a few minutes. Then they were off to find their new homes. Each cell had a stone marker with the initials of the resident monk, and even though the names were alphabetical, there was much confusion.

Amidst all this, Brother Ludovico pushed others aside to find his cell. Except for his extra habit and underclothing, the only thing he brought was a long black leather bag that he placed under his bed. He closed the door tightly, knelt on the hard stone floor besides the bed, closed his eyes and prayed.

"Who's he?" one monk wondered.

"A new one. Came from Monte Casino."

"Seems a little strange, don't you think?"

"Yes, not like the rest of us, who are perfectly normal."

A few minutes later, Brother Rocco dropped his clothes on the bed in his cell and went immediately to the new kitchen to see what he could coax from the cooks making dinner.

Then young Brother Pietro moved in, with the only extra articles the bound Rule of Saint Benedict, which he studied nightly, and a string of rosary beads. This was a new form of prayer for the Benedictines. The custom of saying prayers while counting beads on a string had existed for centuries, and people firmly believed that the first rosary was given by the Blessed Mother herself to Saint Dominic in 1214. Since Dominic founded another order, the Dominicans, the Benedictines at first declined to adopt the practice, simply on principle. But gradually, they recognized the rosary's comforting benefits.

Brother Marco greeted the others as he moved in. Although he had taken a vow of poverty, he had accumulated several precious books, a small wooden statue of the Virgin Mary that his mother had given him long ago and a wooden crucifix that he placed on his desk next to his Book of

Psalms. He smiled at his new surroundings. He thought, incorrectly, that they were so much bigger than his cell in the villa.

For the rest of the day, a boisterous group of men who on another day would be praying or studying or working in the fields filled the halls with noise and laughter. They had to inspect each other's cells, had to test the mattresses and, of course, had to open the bottles that each had brought. Some brought more than one.

"To our new life," Abbot Nicolo led the toast as they gathered in the refectory. "May we all be filled with peace."

It was then that someone noticed that Brother Ludovico had stayed in his room all this time with the door closed.

"He is very strange," the monks concurred.

As they rearranged themselves for dinner, the monks noticed something odd at the end of a hall. Some thought it was just a light. A few said it was a shadow. But others were sure of who it was.

"He's going to join us!" they whispered to each other.

BY LATE SEPTEMBER, the old villa had been torn down and the monks had settled into their new quarters and to the routine of the expansive monastery. Silence times were again strictly observed, workers in the farms produced bountiful harvests, the meals in the refectory were especially varied, the infirmary had fewer patients, the *scriptorium* was almost fully staffed, and, best of all, prayer life had improved with more space for solitude.

Brother Marco now spent every minute of his free time—and there weren't many—in the *scriptorium*. He had a natural talent for copying the texts and, especially, for illuminating the Biblical figures and scenes with brilliant colors. Pages from his books were truly works of art, and he spent time instructing the other eager monks to become proficient.

Brother Rocco instantly became acquainted with the cook who, easily complimented, showed him where leftover desserts were stored.

Young Brother Pietro, although congenitally nervous, was now known to smile occasionally.

The new monastery also fostered a better sense of community. The monks laughed more, cared for each other more, prayed for each other more often. And, yes, they enjoyed their nightly glass of wine, or two, during their common hour.

Except for one. Brother Ludovico declined to take part in any communal activity and rarely even spoke to another monk. He ate by himself in a corner, stayed at the far end of the bench in the chapel and worked alone in his daily assignment to clean the stables. While the other monks enjoyed their nightly permission to talk and joke, Brother Ludovico lay prostrate in the chapel, his face against the cold stones and his arms outstretched. One night, a monk who was preparing the altar tripped over him and shattered an ankle.

The abbot and the other monks shook their heads and tried to ignore this odd creature. Until some things happened that could not be ignored.

A week after they all moved in, Brother Marco had made himself as comfortable as possible on his straight-back wooden chair, picked up his Psalms and started to read one of his favorite passages.

Our mouths were filled with laughter, our tongues with songs of joy. Then it was said among the nations, "The Lord has done great things for them...."

Lost in meditation, he was not at first aware of strange noises coming from the next cell.

Since the old villa where he had lived had long been overrun by rats, he was only too familiar with the sounds the furry creatures made. He had heard them every night. The noises now, he realized, were not rats next door.

When the noises became louder, and were interspersed with muffled cries, Brother Marco listened with his ear against the stone wall. Eventually, the noises stopped, and the elderly cleric tried, unsuccessfully, to read again about joy.

Three nights later, the same noises came back, only this time the cries were louder. Brother Marco tried in vain not to listen.

When they resumed again the following night, he went next door and knocked.

"Brother Ludovico! Are you all right?"

A murmured whisper. "Go away."

"It's Brother Marco. From next door."

"Go away."

"Should I call for help?"

"Go away."

Brother Marco returned to his cell and tried to concentrate on a Psalm. *The Lord is my light and my salvation—whom shall I fear? The Lord is the stronghold of my life—of whom shall I be afraid?*

The noises next door made meditating impossible, and although they eventually ceased, he didn't sleep at all that night.

The following week, he heard the noises again, this time with more cries. In the nights that followed, the noises and cries became louder. Brother Marco was now distraught.

"Brother Ludovico!" he shouted after not getting a response when he pounded on the door. "Please. I just want to help you."

"Go away!"

This went on for three weeks and then, in the middle of the night, Brother Marco, sleepless, sat up in bed. He knew what was going on, and he also knew he had to see Abbot Nicolo right after Lauds.

PREOCCUPIED WITH DETAILS of the dedication ceremony only months away, Abbot Nicolo was not in a mood to be disturbed with minor matters involving monks. But he was shocked, and at first disbelieving, when he heard Brother Marco's story.

"A Flagellant? Are you certain?"

"I can't imagine anything else," Brother Marco said. "The sounds of the whips. His moans. His cries. I have tried to intercede, but he refuses to see me."

"I thought we'd seen the last of the Flagellants."

"Apparently not."

Abbot Nicolo sighed. "Leave this to me."

Having read many books on the subject, Abbot Nicolo knew the whole history of Flagellantism, going back to the cult of Isis in Egypt and to the Dionysian cult in Greece. While some individuals, especially those who had given their lives to God, had practiced whipping themselves to atone for their sins for ages, it was, in fact, a Benedictine, Peter Damian in the eleventh century, who had introduced the practice to the order. He had followed the example of the zealot Dominicus Loricatus, who reportedly repeated the entire Book of Psalms twenty times each week, accompanying each Psalm with a hundred lashes to his back.

If the practice had been confined to monasteries, that might have been tolerated. But in the thirteenth century the self-mortification became public—and widespread. People of all ages, adults and children, priests and laity, marched through cities in Italy telling people they had to repent. They stripped to the waist and scourged themselves with leather thongs until the blood ran. They went into churches and prostrated themselves before altars. There was mass hysteria.

People came out to see them, sobbing in sympathy as the Flagellants pleaded to Christ to have mercy for their sins. They even began to perform twice a day in church squares. The abbot grimaced as he remembered that the male followers were forbidden to bathe, shave, change their clothes, sleep in beds, talk or have intercourse with women without permission from a "master," although he doubted if all of these strictures were followed.

Abbot Nicolo knew, of course, of the legendary incident in Perugia in 1259, after an outbreak of an epidemic. Thousands took part in a march with crosses and banners, singing and whipping themselves. The movement spread, and as many as ten thousand people processed in Modena, Bologna, Reggio and Parma, although some authorities refused the Flagellant processions entry to their churches.

The movement took on an anti-Church offensive. The Flagellants disrupted services, looted altars and ridiculed the Eucharist. When the Flagellants preached that mere participation in their processions cleansed sins, Pope Alexander IV finally censured the movement in 1261.

Despite that, Flagellantism not only continued but also spread to other countries in Europe, and it was especially powerful during the Black Death. Meeting little resistance, the Flagellants blamed the Jews for the plague and invaded their ghettos and killed them.

Now, in the fourteenth century, the Church became more concerned when the group disparaged the need for the Sacraments and claimed to work miracles. In 1349, the movement was officially condemned by Pope Clement VI, who issued a decree, which he called a bull, that ordered Church leaders to denounce the practice.

It was known, however, that individuals, especially monks, continued the custom privately and secretly.

"No wonder Monte Casino wanted to get rid of him," Abbot Nicolo thought.

The sun had barely risen the next morning when Brother Ludovico reported to the abbot.

"Brother Ludovico," the abbot began, "I have become aware that you might be continuing the practice of Flagellantism, and I'd like to discuss this abhorrent practice with you."

Brother Ludovico sat on the edge of the chair again, apparently unwilling to lean back.

"I have known about the movement for a long time," Abbot Nicolo continued. "My uncle was a follower. God rest his soul."

"You were fortunate to have a member in your family. He must be a saint. You must pray to him."

"But, Ludovico, the Flagellants went far beyond their original practices. They were known to kill Jews during the plague. They even killed priests who opposed them."

"But, Father, remember that our own famous Benedictine monk Peter Damian called this a public form of penance. I want to be just like him. He became a cardinal, and some day he'll be called a saint."

"Not because of Flagellantism, Ludovico. For other reasons. Don't you know that the Church has condemned it?"

"Yes."

"That doesn't discourage you to stop?"

"The Pope condemned public flagellation. I do it in private."

"Not so private that others don't hear you."

"Who? What others?"

"Never mind. I just know."

"Brother Marco, right?"

Abbot Nicolo folded his hands in prayer. "Ludovico, is this the reason why Monte Casino asked you to leave?"

"They said I would be happier here."

"Are you?"

"It is the same as before."

The abbot stared out the window, painfully aware of the contrast between the snowy white mountains in the distance and the dark conversation he was having in this room. "I hate to ask this, Ludovico, but do you use a leather whip?"

"I have two. One is embedded with nails."

"Oh my God!" Abbot Nicolo covered his eyes. "I'm told that sometimes you cry out."

"Who said that?"

"Never mind. Do you cry out?"

"I have a gag, but sometimes it falls out."

The abbot cringed. "But, Brother, why don't you show signs of this during the day?"

"I have great self-discipline. I am fine in the morning."

"And your habit? And your bed sheets? Don't they show signs of blood?"

"Since I work in the stables, my garments are always filled with dirt and stains. If they get too black, I find some thick lye soap in the laundry and am able to keep my clothing clean and without stains."

Abbot Nicolo threw up his hands. "Ludovico, Ludovico. Now, I could order you to stop this malevolent practice, but I won't. Not entirely. At least not yet, but I very well may do that in the future. I understand that it is your way of doing penance, and we all must do penance for our sins. But at this point I am ordering you to limit this practice. You may use a whip only ten times a night. Is that clear?"

"Ten? Ten?"

"Ten."

"But…"

"Ten. At the most. Ludovico, you must learn to understand that this is a dangerous practice. Do you understand?"

Brother Ludovico showed no reaction. "I have taken a vow of obedience."

Abbot Nicolo helped Brother Ludovico up from his chair and guided him to the door. "You know, years and years ago, long before any of us was born, there was another monk in our order who beat himself. This was centuries before the Flagellant movement became popular. He simply did it in his cell. Like you. In due course, a young monk became concerned about this strange habit. He worried about him and tried to convince him that this was extreme. When he did not, he told his abbot about this. Shortly after, the young monk died. Everyone said he was murdered."

"Sometimes it is better not to report on other monks' activities," Brother Ludovico said. "Perhaps he should not have gone to the abbot. There might be consequences."

"Ludovico, of course he should have gone to the abbot. This was a terrible practice."

"The saintly monk who was threatened by this young monk was suspected for this deed, I suppose."

"The story is that the monk disappeared and was never seen again."

"I am sure there is a reasonable explanation for all this. And it has nothing to do with me."

"I thought you would want to know this."

"I see no need."

Even though Abbot Nicolo put his hand gently on Brother Ludovico's back, the monk flinched. "There is just one more thing you should know. The young monk supposedly visits us every once in a while. He has been reported occasionally for many years. He is called Giacomo the Gentle Ghost. I'm sure you'll hear about him."

"I don't believe in ghosts."

"Fine. But if you continue to disturb others, then I will have to order you to stop this practice entirely."

"As I said, I have taken a vow of obedience," Brother Ludovico repeated.

"Go back to your cell and may God have mercy on you."

Although he was still under the rule of silence when he returned, Brother Ludovico pounded on the door of the adjoining cell.

"It's Brother Ludovico. Let me in!"

Brother Marco opened the door. "Yes?"

"Look, I don't care how everyone around here likes you and I don't care how you go around being so pious, you had no right to go to the abbot and…"

"Dear Brother Ludovico. I was only concerned about your well-being."

"Well, don't be. This is my practice."

"Brother, I can sympathize with your need to punish yourself. We all need to do that."

"You haven't heard the end of this!"

Brother Marco held his hand out but Brother Ludovico pushed it away. "Let me alone!" he shouted. "You're going to regret this!"

He went back to his cell. There was no flagellation that night.

Since their cells were next to each other, they found themselves meeting in the hall on the way to the chapel or refectory, but Brother Ludovico never acknowledged Brother Marco. The older monk's smiles and gestures were ignored.

THROUGHOUT HISTORY, researchers have been fascinated by the psychology of revenge. The Bible reports that Moses led the Israelites in a holy war against the Midianites because they had committed hideous, violent acts against them. In the Middle Ages, wars were fought when one city-state battled another because of a real or perceived grievance. Many a knight charged another who had made disparaging remarks about his lady fair, often with fatal results.

Researchers have also studied cases in which a person becomes obsessed with retaliation. Some unknown factor in the brain suddenly clicks off, they have found, and the drive to achieve vengeance becomes overwhelming. Revenge takes over their lives. They will do anything to wreak damage on the object of their revenge.

Brother Ludovico of the Monastery of Saint Gaudentius of Novara in the Garfagnana would have made a good case study.

When Brother Ludovico had returned to his cell after being admonished by Abbot Nicolo, he ignored his duties and prayer schedule for the day and lay on his bed—on his side—seething. Only ten times a night? He was used to forty or fifty. He had so many sins, he needed to punish himself. Unconscionable!

He got up and paced the room, smacking the wall, the top of his table. He threw his breviary on the floor. He picked up his whips and kissed them. He wanted to scream and yell, but that would only arouse the attention of that old monk in the next cell.

That old monk. Yes, he was to blame. He was the one who reported him to the abbot. So now he had to suffer.

Still raging in the days that followed, Brother Ludovico forced himself to obey the abbot's restrictions on his flagellation, but he drew out each lash stroke longer and harder. And with every stroke, instead of thinking about his sins, he thought about Brother Marco. Although he lashed himself, he imagined that he was flogging the monk next door.

He had to find a way to retaliate, and it consumed his thoughts so much that he became even more feared in the monastery. When they saw him approaching, his black eyes fixed in the distance, the other monks turned and went the other way. If they cared at all about him, they would have worried about this strange behavior. They didn't care.

Aware of what was happening, Abbot Nicolo called Brother Ludovico into his office again.

"Brother, are you obeying my instructions about flagellation?"

"Of course."

"You are not adding to the number?"

"No. I have taken a vow of obedience."

"You have seemed preoccupied lately. Is something wrong?"

"Nothing is wrong. I must go, Father."

Before returning to his cell, Brother Ludovico passed Brother Marco's door. He knew Brother Marco was in the *scriptorium*, so he entered. Looking around the room, he saw the small statue of the Virgin Mary on the desk. He took out the knife he always concealed in his robes and was about to slash it.

"No, that isn't good enough."

He saw the Book of Psalms on the chair. He could rip out pages and tear them up. "No, not good enough either."

Brother Ludovico was not going to let this rest. The need for revenge had grown like a cancer. At night, when he pulled his two whips out of their black bag, he stroked and caressed them. He had given them names, Lucifer for the one with the metal studs, and Beelzebub for the other.

"How can I use you for my purpose?" he wondered. He kissed their handles.

After finishing the flogging one night, he tried to think of a punishment using his whips that would severely torment his neighbor. Then something came into his demented brain.

"The abbot told me ten lashes. He didn't say they had to be all at one time."

Brother Ludovico laughed out loud. And then another idea.

"He said I could use the whip ten times. He didn't say where I could use it."

He laughed even harder.

THE DEDICATION CEREMONY on January 22 went off precisely as planned. Although Pope Urban VI himself was unable to attend because of various wars and threats to his control, he sent a delegation of four cardinals from the Holy See. Count Bellini's great-great-great-great-grandson, wearing black and looking strikingly similar to the architect of the monastery, walked with Abbot Nicolo.

With a brilliant mid-January sun overhead, Abbot Nicolo led the cardinals, twenty-two archbishops, thirty-eight bishops and various other clergy from the villa to the monastery. Symbolically, he rapped three times on the door of the monastery before entering.

"Saint Gaudentius of Novara!" he declared. "On this, your feast day, we dedicate our abbey to you."

They swept through the cloister and to the chapel, which, as large as it was, could barely hold all the dignitaries and the resident monks, who were assigned to the side altars.

With two cardinals flanking him, Abbot Nicolo said the Mass. When it came time for the incense, he not only went around the chapel but also into every room, every nook and every cranny in the monastery itself. Followed by the youngest of the monks, including Brother Pietro, he traveled through the cloister, the refectory, the kitchen, the dormitory, the infirmary and, last, the *scriptorium*. The thurible had to be refilled with more coals two dozen times.

Although six priests distributed Communion, the lines stretched through the nave, outside the church and into the rest of the monastery. That alone took forty-five minutes.

After more than five hours, Abbot Nicolo said the benediction. Everyone was famished and the movement to the refectory was far from orderly. Because of all the guests, mealtime was staggered: first the visiting hierarchy, then the visiting clergy, and finally the Benedictine monks themselves.

Needless to say, there was grumbling in the ranks, and needless to say, Brother Rocco was first in line.

But the meal was worth waiting for. Suspending the vow of poverty, the abbot ordered a feast that could have been served in Frederick II's palace itself. Cooks were hired from neighboring farms, and a whole delegation came from Castelnuovo di Garfagnana. Servers brought out golden plates filled with vegetables, venison, wild boar, suckling pigs, beef and poultry, and finally cheeses and fruit.

As always, Brother Marco ate sparingly, moving vegetables and slices of ham over to Brother Pietro's plate.

"Eat! Eat! You're too thin."

"Wouldn't someone else like this?" the young monk asked.

"Brother Pietro, eat!"

If anyone noticed that Brother Ludovico was absent the entire day, no one thought to mention it.

Satiated both gastronomically and spiritually, the monks drifted back to their cells. Early Lauds would arrive soon enough the next morning.

Near the entrance to their dormitory, several of the monks stopped short.

"It's Giacomo!"

"It is!"

The figure, clad in white, hovered near the entrance for more than a minute, then faded into the background.

"Good bye!" one monk called. "Hope to see you soon."

When he arrived at his cell, Brother Rocco had to ease himself into his bed. He knew he had eaten too much, but he gladly endured the stomach pains that came in spasms.

In the next cell, Brother Pietro prayed on his beads, worrying that he might have offended another monk with a comment, that he might have not been attentive enough at Mass, that he took a second helping of the pie for dessert. Brother Pietro knew that he worried too much, but he couldn't help it.

Meanwhile, Brother Marco attempted to meditate on a Psalm but kept interrupting himself by thinking that he heard noises next door. As fearsome as Brother Ludovico was, Brother Marco couldn't help feeling sorry for him. Everyone had to make recompense for their sins, and Brother

Ludovico was simply taking things too far. Brother Marco couldn't justify the way the Flagellants beat themselves, but he could understand how a movement such as this could lead to excesses. He tried to find a Psalm that he could concentrate on.

Brother Ludovico paced the floor in his cell. Would Brother Marco ever stop walking around and begin meditating? Hearing no sounds, he pulled Lucifer out of the bag and kissed the leather and the handle.

"All right. Do your duty."

He swung the whip around his head, turned around three times, and with all his strength—which was considerable for a small man—he crashed it on the wall that separated the cells. Then he moaned a little.

In the next cell, Brother Marco dropped his Psalm book and stared at the wall.

"My God, what's he doing?"

But then there was nothing. Brother Marco waited, then went back to his Psalms.

If clocks had existed then, they would have recorded that thirty-two minutes had elapsed before another crash of the whip hit the wall. Brother Ludovico moaned louder.

Startled, Brother Marco got up from his chair. "What is he doing? Why is he flogging the wall?"

Quiet. Brother Marco tried to concentrate on his reading again but he was so conscious of what might happen next door that he closed his eyes and put his book down. A half hour later, it happened again. Then silence for forty minutes.

And again. And silence.

And again. Silence.

Thus it went through the night. Brother Ludovico flogged the wall intermittently, varying the times in between, sometimes for as much as two hours. Drunk with his new plan, he could hardly stifle his glee. He held a handkerchief over his mouth so that his shrieks and howls of joy were muffled.

Meanwhile, Brother Marco finally gave up any thought of sleep, and sat in his chair all night, occasionally dozing off but jolting awake whenever there was a new smash on the wall. The tenth occurred just before the morning Lauds.

Bleary-eyed, he stumbled into the hallway, where Brother Ludovico slapped him on the shoulder and leered in his face. "Did you have a nice night?"

Somehow, Brother Marco got through the day. "I'm going to be seventy-five in two months. I hope I can get some sleep tonight."

The noises didn't happen the next night, but Brother Marco stayed awake for hours waiting for the sounds. It was only minutes before Lauds that he dozed into a fitful slumber.

The next night was noise-free as well. Brother Marco managed two hours of sleep.

Then, they started again. Night after night, Brother Ludovico tormented the old man with crashing noises that came haphazardly at odd times. Brother Marco didn't close his eyes for six nights.

He gave up on his attempts to read the Psalms. He would read a line or two and try to concentrate, but then his eyes would wander to the wall and he wondered when the next crash would occur. Instead, he took to picking up his rosary beads and reciting, over and over, the Our Father and the Hail Mary. Praying by rote, Brother Marco realized, could be mesmerizing. After four or five Hail Marys he realized that he hadn't concentrated on a single word, and he started all over again.

Many nights, he simply put the rosary beads down, closed his eyes and tried to meditate on the mercies of God, only to startle himself awake by listening to a wall.

"I can't go on like this. It's got to end."

One morning, young Brother Pietro found him with his oatmeal untouched at breakfast. His hands were at his sides.

"Brother Marco! Are you ill? You're so pale."

"No, nothing. I guess I didn't sleep very well last night."

Brother Rocco joined them. "Marco, you look like hell. What's going on?"

"Nothing, nothing. I need to get to the *scriptorium*. Excuse me."

"Something," Brother Rocco told Brother Pietro, "is definitely going on."

Something was also going on with Brother Ludovico. Now, he smiled, or rather smirked, when he walked down the hall, although he always seemed preoccupied. There was a little gossip about this changed personality, but mostly the other monks ignored him.

Lacking sleep, Brother Marco lost his appetite and after almost three weeks he not only was pale but also had lost weight. Brother Pietro and Brother Rocco became more concerned.

"Brother, if you are not well, you must tell us," Brother Rocco said. "We are very worried."

Brother Pietro had tears in his eyes. "I can't see you like this. Please."

"I'm fine," Brother Marco said. "Don't worry about me."

"Look," Brother Rocco said, "if you don't get some (expletive deleted) help soon, we're going to take you to the infirmary ourselves."

"Just give me a few more days. I'll be fine."

Abbot Nicolo also became worried, and asked if Brother Ludovico was the cause, but Brother Marco refused to discuss his tormentor.

The nights became more excruciating, and five weeks after Brother Ludovico's onslaught began, Brother Marco collapsed during evening prayer. Dozens of brothers crowded around him.

"Give him air, give him air," Brother Rocco shouted.

They lifted him up and after he assured everyone that he was fine, they escorted him back to his cell. Brother Ludovico mercifully didn't take out his whips that night. But when Brother Marco was unable to get up the following morning, he received a visit from Abbot Nicolo.

"Marco, I want you to go to the infirmary so that the staff there can determine what is going on with you."

"Father, it's nothing, really. I'm fine."

"Then why are you unable to get up? Why are you so pale? Why aren't you eating better? Why aren't you taking part in our prayers, and why aren't you doing more in the *scriptorium*? You have always liked that work."

"Just age, I suppose."

"Brother Marco, you know that's not true."

"Sometimes it's difficult for me to get to sleep lately."

"Lately? Why is that?"

"I'd rather not discuss it."

"So Brother Ludovico is the cause. I knew it."

"I'd rather not discuss it."

"Well, then the only thing I can do is order you to go to the infirmary. All right?"

"All right."

BROTHER PIETRO AND BROTHER ROCCO received permission to leave their assignments—the former in the chapel and the latter in the woods—and found Brother Marco in the infirmary the following morning. The many successors of Count Bellini had seen to it that the infirmary would be better equipped and more comfortable than in any other monastery they had built. The walls were whitewashed but decorated with colorful paintings of the saints. The beds, lined in four rows, had enough separation to allow both privacy and the needs of the monks who served as nurses. A formidable desk at the end allowed the monks to keep track of the patients and their medications. Since the room was in a long separate wing, large windows on both sides allowed the patients to behold not only the rise of the sun but its setting as well.

Other monks bustled around on that morning, delivering herbs and medicines, washing faces and emptying bedpans. Some of the patients slept, but some were alert, talking quietly and sipping orange juice.

Not Brother Marco. He lay motionless with his eyes closed. His face was almost as white as his pillow and his wispy hair. His cheeks were sunken. His hands were folded on his chest. His visitors thought he was dead.

"Brother Marco!" Brother Rocco cried. He put his hand on the old man's shoulder.

Brother Marco opened his eyes.

"Oh, thank God," Brother Rocco said. "We thought, well, we thought you had left us."

"No, no, I'm still here." Brother Marco's voice was barely above a whisper. "I guess God doesn't want me quite yet."

"And He won't for a long time." Brother Rocco adjusted the pillow and smoothed the sheets. "Did you sleep well?"

"Like a baby. The first time in weeks."

Brother Pietro was again almost in tears. "Brother Marco, what can we do? What can we bring you? Would you like a book? Would you be able to read? Brother, we are all so worried."

Brother Marco lifted a thin hand lined with veins. "Don't worry, Brother. I'm fine. I just need to get some rest."

A nurse arrived to wipe the patient's forehead. When the nurse shook his head, Brother Marco's visitors were alarmed. Brother Rocco followed him back to the nurses' desk.

"What's wrong?"

"He's very weak. I'm afraid this is going to take a long time."

"What can you do?"

"Let him get a lot of rest. See that he eats well. That's about all we can do."

"God bless you."

As Brother Rocco turned away, the nurse called him back.

"What might help," he said, "is for something really nice to happen to him, something to cheer him up. I think that besides his other problems, he's suffering from melancholy."

"Melancholy? Really?"

"It's not uncommon. When the body becomes frail, the mind does, too. You're his friends. Perhaps you can think of something."

"Hmmm. We'll see what we can do. Thank you, Brother."

Knowing that Brother Marco needed his rest, Brother Pietro and Brother Rocco didn't stay long, and went back to Brother Rocco's cell. Although they knew they were violating the order's rule for silence, they thought that Saint Benedict would forgive them.

"How can we cheer him up?" Brother Pietro asked. "I don't know. I just don't know."

Brother Rocco thought for a while. "We can't bring him something to eat. The nurses wouldn't allow it."

"Perhaps a book? The Psalms!"

"I don't think he's up to reading. He looks like he needs a lot of rest."

"Many of the Psalms wouldn't be very cheerful anyway," Brother Pietro said.

For the next three days, the monks visited Brother Marco each morning, finding him a little better physically each day, although his mind was still in a place far away. On the fourth, they tried a little humor, basic as it was.

"Brother Marco," Brother Pietro said, "I have a joke. Would you like to hear it?"

"Of course, Pietro. Go ahead."

"Why do dragons sleep during the day?"

"I guess I don't know."

"Because they're afraid of knights! Isn't that funny?"

Brother Marco managed a small smile.

"Here's another one," Brother Rocco said. "When a knight in armor was killed in battle, what sign did they put on his grave? I'll tell you: Rust in peace!"

This did not even bring a small smile.

"All right," Brother Rocco said, "one more. A knight returned to the king's castle with prisoners, bags of gold and other riches from his victories. 'Tell me of your battles,' the king said. 'Well, sire,' the knight said, 'I have been robbing and stealing on your behalf for weeks, and I have been burning all of the villages of your enemies in the north.' The king was horrified. 'But I have no enemies in the north,' he said. 'Well,' the knight said, 'you do now.'"

Brother Rocco guffawed. "You do now! Get it? He didn't have any enemies in the north! But he does now!"

"I know," Brother Marco said. "Thank you for trying. I think I'll get a little sleep now."

As they returned to Brother Rocco's cell they encountered Brother Ludovico coming out of his, leering as usual.

"Brother Ludovico!" Brother Rocco said. "You look so cheerful. Are you having a pleasant day?"

"Of course! Everything is going very well."

"We're so pleased to hear that. You must have a good life."

"Yes, a wonderful life."

"No worries? No problems?"

"No, nothing."

"And there's nothing on your conscience?"

"My conscience? No, of course not."

"You may be interested in knowing that we just came from seeing your neighbor, Brother Marco. I'm afraid he's not doing well."

"I am so sorry to hear that!" His leer grew even broader as he fled down the hall.

"Bastard!" Brother Rocco yelled after him.

"Brother Rocco!" Brother Pietro cried.

"I don't care. He's a mean, mean man. I'm sure he has something to do with Brother Marco being in the infirmary."

"Really?"

"Of course! I don't know why or how, but he must be the cause. Pietro, we have to do something about him."

"But what?"

"I don't know."

They sat in Brother Rocco's cell, Rocco on the bed, Pietro on the chair. They could hear the other monks' chants from the chapel, and they knew they were late.

> "*Respice in me, et miserere mei, quoniam unicus et pauper sum ego.*
> "*Tribulationes cordis mei dilatate sunt, et de necessitatibus meis eripe me.*"

"If only…" Brother Rocco said.

"If only what?"

"If only Giacomo were here to help us."

ALTHOUGH SEVERAL MONKS told tales of seeing Giacomo lately, no one was absolutely certain that the gentle ghost had been encountered since the day of the dedication. As usual, some monks told tales of sightings, but they were only in jest or attempts to frighten their naïve brethren.

"I wish there was some way we could get him here," Brother Rocco said.

"Why?" Brother Pietro wondered. "What would he do? How could he help us?"

"I'm thinking off the top of my head, but what if Giacomo made an appearance before our dearly beloved Brother Ludovico? Wouldn't that scare the, well, hell out of him?"

Brother Pietro couldn't help smiling. "That would be fun. I wish we could just wish it and he would appear."

The young monk got up and stood in front of the window. The morning sunlight seemed to cast a golden halo around him, but also accentuated his protruding ears. He returned to his chair.

"Pietro, go stand in front of the window again."

"Why?"

"Just do it."

He did.

"Brother Rocco, why are you staring at me like that?"

"Just stand there."

"Why?"

"Just stand there. I'm thinking."

"Brother Rocco, I don't like this."

"Just stand there."

Brother Pietro began to fidget.

"You know," Brother Rocco said, "you're about the same height, the same size, as Giacomo."

"So?"

"And your ears stick out."

"Thanks."

"In a certain light, or maybe dark, someone might think that you were Giacomo."

"That I was dead?"

"No, just a little...alive."

"Brother Rocco, I'm not that stupid. I know what you're thinking, but you can't be serious. He'd never believe it. And we could get in trouble."

"Oh, Brother Pietro, you're afraid of your own shadow. Oh, that was a good one, afraid of your shadow. That's exactly what we want, Brother Ludovico afraid of a shadow. We won't get caught, and even if we do, everyone, including the abbot, will be glad we did it. Nobody likes Brother Ludovico around here, you know."

Brother Pietro went back to the chair. "I don't like this. I don't like this at all. What are you suggesting?"

"Tonight, when it's dark, we'll go outside his window. Bring a sheet. And I'll find some chalk in the *scriptorium*."

Brother Pietro had a hard time concentrating for the rest of the day.

With a full moon that night, Brother Pietro was still nervous about this whole undertaking, but he dutifully followed along behind Brother Rocco, a sheet draped over his shoulder.

"We're not supposed to take sheets out of the monastery, you know," he said.

"I'm ignoring that. Look at that moon. It's perfect. God Himself must be approving."

"I doubt that. Come on, let's do whatever we're going to do."

Because of its fragrant white flowers, the shrub *carissa bispinosa* had been planted all along the outside walls of the dormitory. The small flowers were gorgeous and the ripe fruit glowed a bright red. Their thorns, however, were long and sharp, something the landscapers had considered to keep intruders from entering the monks' cells. Or, perhaps, to prevent any disgruntled monk from escaping.

"Ouch!" Brother Pietro cried as a thorn pierced his bare ankle just above his sandal.

"Shhh!" Brother Rocco whispered.

As they neared the cell's window, they saw a single candle providing the only illumination inside. Brother Ludovico was pacing the floor. Occasionally, he raised his arms, apparently in anger.

"What's he doing?" Brother Pietro asked.

"He's not only mean, he's crazy," his companion said. "He looks like he's out of his mind. Here, put that sheet around you and let me whiten your face with this chalk. Now just stand there under that tree so that you're sort of in the shadows. There, that's right. I'll go back over here. Ouch! Damn thorns."

Brother Rocco hopped back over a bush, a clumsy move considering his weight, while Brother Pietro established firm footing thirty paces in front of the window. Inside, Brother Ludovico continued pacing and waving his arms, not noticing anything strange outside. They waited a while, and then to get his attention, Brother Rocco threw a pebble at the window. Brother Ludovico turned and looked out the window. He didn't see anything.

"Pietro," Brother Rocco said, "get a little closer."

He threw a bigger pebble at the window. This time, Brother Ludovico saw the ghostly figure under the tree.

"Holy shit!"

Brother Pietro crouched down, but Brother Rocco saw the fiendish monk crawl under his bed.

"Let's go!"

It was good that the other monks were asleep so that no one saw an overweight middle-aged monk and a thin young monk running back to their cells, a sheet flying in the wind, and laughing so loud the horses in the barn started to neigh.

Back in Brother Rocco's cell, it took a while for the older monk to catch his breath, but they congratulated themselves and planned another excursion the next night.

They were so excited, they hardly slept and it was difficult getting through the day. The other monks wondered why the two exchanged knowing glances during what was supposed to be a quiet prayer time. They also wondered why sweat covered Brother Ludovico's forehead all day and why his hands trembled.

Since the cells did not have shutters—darkness would have encouraged more sleep—Brother Pietro was again a hazy figure in the moonlight the next night. This time, he raised his hands under the sheet, a move interpreted by the captive occupant in the cell as threatening, and he again fled under the bed.

The conniving monks continued their escapades for three nights, each time becoming more audacious. On the third night, Brother Pietro's sheet slipped when he raised his hand and his black habit was briefly visible. Still, Brother Ludovico darted for safety.

"I think he recognized me," the young monk said as they ran back to their cells.

"That's all right. Giacomo had big ears, too, you know."

"Thanks."

Lacking sleep and frightened by the nightly apparitions, Brother Ludovico had another change of personality. He became inattentive and sluggish. His demonic leer disappeared. He jumped at sudden noises. He was afraid to stay in his cell, and took to hiding in a barn. No one seemed to care. The abbot did not call him in for a conversation. "Let's let well enough alone," he thought.

The plotters took two nights off, and when they resumed their adventures they tried new tactics. Wearing black gloves, Brother Rocco carried a lighted candle back and forth a few yards from the window, making it appear that it was floating in midair. Brother Pietro took to moaning, first quietly and then louder and louder. The young monk could also be seen running through the cornfields near the dormitory, darting in and out between the cornstalks.

Another night, the brothers tossed a horseshoe back and forth so that Brother Ludovico only saw metal gleaming in the moonlight. They found a can of putrid grease in the kitchen and let its awful smell drift into the cell. Standing far back, Brother Rocco howled like a wolf for a half hour.

This went on for three weeks.

The conspirators took another few days off, allowing Brother Ludovico to assume that the danger was over. It was not. On their next visit, in the middle of the night, just as Brother Ludovico had dozed off, Brother Pietro picked his way through the *carissa bispinosa* and stood concealed under the window. He began to moan, softly at first but then so loudly it was almost a shriek. Brother Ludovico tried to see the source, but the *carissa bispinosa* effectively concealed the moaner. He went back to bed. An hour later, the same thing. Again, an hour after that, and it was time for Lauds.

Brother Rocco and Brother Pietro weren't getting much sleep either, but this adventure had so energized them that they didn't mind.

"How long are we going to keep this up?" Brother Pietro wondered.

"As long as necessary."

Now when Brother Rocco and Brother Pietro visited Brother Marco in the infirmary they found him looking, and feeling, better. Nurses took him for short walks in the halls.

"Is everything still the same out there?" he asked.

Brother Rocco glanced at Brother Pietro. "Oh yes, everything is just fine. Better than fine, actually."

"There isn't anything new happening?"

"No, no, nothing to speak of."

"What about Brother Ludovico? Is he the same? Sometime I worry about him."

"No need to worry," Brother Rocco said. "I would say that Brother Ludovico is encountering some new adventures. Well, we must be going."

BROTHER MARCO WAS IN THE INFIRMARY for more than a month. After he was released, he only gradually resumed the schedule of a Benedictine monk, at first with prayers and meditation, and then he returned for a few tasks in his beloved *scriptorium*. He had been copying the Gospel of Luke and had just finished the section where a woman had perfumed Jesus' head with oil and Jesus explained that this was a sign of his coming death. Brother Marco was always consumed by this story and couldn't wait to get back at it. He knew exactly what blues and reds he would use to illuminate the initial letter.

Brother Marco was grateful to be back in his cell and also for the silence next door. Strange, he thought, he hadn't heard nor seen Brother Ludovico since he'd been back.

Pleased that Brother Marco was well again, Abbot Nicolo decided to have a little party to which every monk in the monastery was invited. The party was held in the abbot's large reception room, and all the monks came up to shake Brother Marco's hand and to tell him that they missed him. Brother Marco had never known how much the other monks admired him.

"By the way," he said to Brother Rocco, who had brought him a glass of sherry, "I don't see Brother Ludovico here, and I haven't seen him since I've returned. Is he all right?"

"Brother Marco, this sherry is really good. Please try it."

"But I wonder…"

"Everyone is so pleased that you're back. Did you sleep well last night?"

"Yes, I did, but I was asking about…"

"Oh, I see Brother Roberto over there. I need to ask him something. Excuse me, Brother."

Across the room, Brother Pietro hesitated, then approached Brother Marco.

"Don't be afraid," the elder monk said. "I'm perfectly fine, just have to get my bearings every once in a while. How have you been?"

"Um, fine."

"Are you spending some time in prayer?"

"Yes! I have been reading the Psalms!"

"Wonderful! You will discover so many things, mostly about yourself. By the way, have you seen Brother Ludovico lately?"

"Um, Brother Marco, I think I see Brother Sebastian over there. Yes, there he is. Perhaps we can talk later?"

"Yes, of course."

Finding Brother Marco alone, Abbot Nicolo sat down next to the guest of honor, who thanked the abbot for the party and for his prayers and care.

"We've missed you," the abbot said. "This place needs your presence. You bring a sense of peace to us."

"I've missed being here, too. I didn't realize how much until I was away. Thank God I'm feeling better now. But I was wondering about Brother Ludovico. I don't see him here and I haven't heard him in his cell. Is he well?"

The abbot sighed. "Well, I'm afraid there's a reason he's not here."

"I'm sorry."

His superior lowered his voice. "Not everyone knows this, but I felt it necessary that Brother Ludovico have some time and space to himself. He has been in the *misericord* for a week."

"The *misericord?* Isn't that the hut where monks who commit some sort of misdeed are punished? I've never heard of anyone being sent there."

"Indeed. No one has been sent there during my tenure, and I don't think anyone by the last two or three abbots."

"It must have been serious."

Abbot Nicolo took a long sip of his own sherry and set the glass down.

"Normally, I wouldn't discuss this with anyone, but I know you have been concerned about Brother Ludovico. This was not a decision I made lightly, but it reached a point where it was the right thing to do."

"What? What happened?"

"Over the last couple of months we noticed some abrupt changes in his behavior. For a while, he seemed overly jubilant, smiling at everyone. Well, at least more than smiling. Some might even call it leering. We didn't know why. Then—I believe you were in the infirmary by that time—he changed. He began to look frightened all the time. He kept looking around as if someone were following him. He was shaking and very nervous. The other monks had nothing to do with him."

"I'm afraid none of the other monks liked him. I always felt a little sorry for him."

"Also, he seemed angry all the time. He began to lash out at other monks, verbally at first but then physically as well."

"Oh, the poor man."

"I talked to him several times, but he wouldn't discuss anything about his behavior. He wouldn't answer any question I had. I told him about the *misericord*, but that didn't seem to faze him."

"He knew what it was?"

"Oh, yes. He started hallucinating. He'd go around shouting 'Stay away from me! Stay away from me!' But there was no one near him. Last week, Brother Antonio—as you know, a kind and gentle man, one of the smallest monks in the abbey—happened to walk past him and Brother Ludovico struck him on the back. Very hard. For no reason. Brother Antonio reported this to me, and I called Brother Ludovico in. I asked him about his behavior, but he wouldn't answer. He just sat cringing on the chair.

"Well, I had to do something. So I put him in the *misericord*. I told him he had to stay there for two months so that he could pray and consider the goodness of God. It was for his own good, and for the safety of others, as well."

"And that's where he is now?"

"Yes. We've given him the Bible to read. We bring him food, but he isn't eating much. Frankly, I'm worried about him. The only thing we can do for him is pray."

Brother Marco looked down at his thin hands. "The poor man. I didn't know any of this. I tried to get some answers from Brother Rocco and Brother Pietro, but they wouldn't answer me."

"I wonder why."

"I don't know. In fact, they were rather evasive."

"Evasive?"

"Yes, as if they knew something but weren't going to tell me."

"Hmmm. I think, Brother Marco, you have confirmed my suspicions."

TWO VERY NERVOUS MONKS, their quivering hands clasped behind their backs, stood before Abbot Nicolo's desk the next morning.

"All right, I know you two have somehow been behind Brother Ludovico's strange behavior lately. I've heard about how you are out in the middle of the night. I've heard about how you linger at Brother Ludovico's cell. People tell me. These are all infractions of our rule, but I've let it go."

"Brother Ludovico?" Brother Rocco said. "I hardly know the man. Do you know Brother Ludovico, Brother Pietro?"

Brother Pietro was not good at lying. "Um, is he the one with the bad breath?"

Abbot Nicolo intervened. "All right. Enough of that. I don't know exactly what you've been doing, but I am certain that you are somehow responsible for Brother Ludovico's condition right now. And if you don't want to end up in *misericord* with him, you'd better see that he returns to normal. Now!"

"But..." Brother Rocco said.

"But..." Brother Pietro said.

"Now! Or the *misericord*!"

Abbot Nicolo shuffled some papers on his desk while the two monks hustled out.

"What do you think he knows?" Brother Rocco whispered in the hall.

"Probably everything."

"I don't think so. I think he's bluffing us."

"But we can't take a chance."

The two monks pondered the alternatives as they walked back to their cells. There weren't many. They could agree on only one thing: Giacomo must return. Tonight.

The *misericord* was in a separate small building, a hut, really, just beyond the cemetery. The space was big enough for only a cot and a chair. A small window, with bars, let in a little sunlight for an hour or so in the afternoon. There were no candles, so after the sun set it was completely dark until dawn. A monk from the kitchen brought a meal and emptied the chamber pot once a day. The door locked from the outside.

The same *carissa bispinosa* that surrounded the dormitory encircled the walls so that no one could go easily in or out.

After everyone else in the monastery had extinguished their candles and settled in for the brief time they had to sleep, Brother Rocco and Brother Pietro rushed out of the dormitory and toward the cemetery. Brother Pietro carried a sheet.

"I don't know what we're doing," he whispered after they arrived at the hut. "Why are we even here?"

"Just go up to the window. Remember, you're Giacomo the Gentle Ghost. The Gentle Ghost. Not scary, gentle!"

Stepping carefully over the *carissa bispinosa*, Brother Pietro moved to the front of the bars on the window. Brother Ludovico lay on the cot, or rather convulsing so violently that he kept slipping onto the floor and back again. He was whimpering.

Attempting to get his attention, Brother Pietro began to moan a little. Instantly, Brother Ludovico sprang to his feet and to the window.

"What are you doing here?" he shrieked.

Brother Pietro smiled, but of course that couldn't be seen under the sheet.

"Go away! You've ruined my life enough."

He crawled to a corner and cowered, his cowl pulled over his head.

Brother Pietro looked at Brother Rocco for guidance, but received only a shrug. "Be gentle," he whispered.

Not knowing what else to do, Brother Pietro began to hum a hymn that he was certain Brother Ludovico would recognize.

> "*O splendor of God's glory bright,*
> "*Who bringest forth the light from Light…*"

Brother Ludovico looked up, wiped his eyes and settled back down in the corner.

Still humming, Brother Pietro edged away through the bushes, and with his partner fled back to the dormitory, leaving the stricken monk in the cell to wonder what had just happened.

Shortly after midnight the next night, Giacomo's lookalike again appeared near the window of the *misericord*. He stood back and began to hum the same hymn again. Inside, Brother Ludovico sat in the corner, listening.

They waited a while, humming and listening.

"All right," Brother Rocco said, "enough for tonight."

Each night, they gradually increased their vigilance, and Brother Ludovico became less fearful. One night he got up the courage to stand and look at the apparition in the window. The ghost of Giacomo stood silently, then disappeared in the bushes.

A few nights later, Brother Ludovico fearfully approached the window and gripped the bars. Brother Pietro gently touched his hands. Brother Ludovico pulled his hands away. Brother Pietro tried to make a comforting sound. Brother Ludovico recoiled. Brother Pietro reached in, his small white hand outstretched. Brother Ludovico hesitated, then touched it gently.

"Mmmmmmmm," Brother Pietro murmured.

"No!" Brother Ludovico cried and plunged into the corner, where he stayed.

"All right," Brother Rocco whispered. "Let's go back. We're making good progress."

"I wish I could say something to him."

"No. Ghosts can't talk. They can only hum and sing."

They mulled over this dilemma.

"Well," Brother Pietro said, "maybe we can write something."

"There's an obvious problem with that."

The next day they visited Brother Marco in the *scriptorium*.

"We need to give a message to someone," Brother Rocco said, "but there's a problem. We can't write. Can you do us a favor?"

"I suppose I should ask questions, but I won't," Brother Marco said. He took a piece of parchment from a shelf and a quill pen from the desktop.

"Just write," Brother Rocco said, "'God Loves You.'"

"That's all?" Brother Marco dutifully wrote the words down. "Believe it."

Late that night, Brother Pietro stood outside Brother Ludovico's small window. With a gentle hand, he beckoned the prisoner to come closer. He handed over the note.

Brother Ludovico looked at the parchment and with shaking hands took it. He looked at the white figure outside the window and sat down on his bed.

"All right, that worked," Brother Rocco said. "Let's go. We'll ask Brother Marco to write some more messages."

The succeeding parchments contained such advice as "Don't Be Afraid," "God Is Good," "Love Yourself" and "God Forgives You."

A week passed. Then another. And another. Unless they were committed to something else, like choir practice, Brother Rocco and Brother Pietro visited their captive brother every night, and as this ghostly Giacomo became more friendly, Brother Ludovico became less frightened and more benign. Sometimes, he was waiting at the window for the nightly visits and even greeted the gentle ghost warmly. Brother Rocco and Brother Pietro now found him praying or lying peacefully on his bed when they visited at night. Sometimes he was reading the Bible. They gave him a rosary.

The cook from the kitchen noticed that he was eating more, and brought additional helpings.

At the end of two months it was time for Abbot Nicolo to visit. He found Brother Ludovico kneeling on the floor next to his bed, deep in prayer. There was barely room for both of them in the hut and so they both stood, the abbot towering over the little monk. After a long conversation, the abbot put his hand on Brother Ludovico's shoulder and left.

An hour later, he called Brother Rocco and Brother Pietro into his office, where they stood nervously before his desk.

"I wanted you to know that I had a long talk with Brother Ludovico this morning."

His visitors tried not to show their panic, but the abbot took his time.

"As you know, he has been in a separate place for a while, the *misericord*. It is a place where he could pray and meditate."

"We're pleased," Brother Rocco said.

"Now, something has happened, and he is feeling better. In fact, much better."

The brothers smiled awkwardly and the abbot continued.

"Brother Ludovico said he had had time to think while he was in seclusion and has made some decisions."

The brothers waited.

"He knows that we must punish ourselves for our sins, but realizes now that he was carrying his own punishment too far. Once he started, he couldn't stop. But now he has renounced Flagellantism. He knows that was extreme. He will never whip himself again."

Abbot Nicolo paused. He let his visitors wait for more.

"Last night, he also decided that he does not want to return to the monastery. He knows that his behavior has created disturbances and he is very repentant. He said he would like to apologize personally to Brother Marco."

Another long pause.

"He has also made another big decision. He has asked, and I agreed, that he be sent out to the countryside to care for the poor and preach the Gospel. I have heard about another monk who did this. His name was Francis and he came from a town called Assisi. He went about talking to the poor and telling them about Jesus. He even acquired followers. Perhaps Brother Ludovico will have followers."

Brother Rocco and Brother Pietro didn't know what to say.

"I suppose you wonder what brought about the changes," the abbot said.

"Well, yes," the brothers aid together.

"Well, it seems Brother Ludovico was actually visited every night by Giacomo, our old friendly ghost who has been with us for almost as long as our congregation has existed. Imagine, a visit almost every night from this friendly spirit."

The abbot looked for signs of recognition from the two monks in front of him, but their faces were blank—and increasingly flushed.

"Are you all right?" the abbot asked. "You look nervous."

"Fine," Brother Rocco said. "We're just fine."

"Fine," Brother Pietro said. "We're fine."

"Are you surprised that Giacomo would visit him so regularly?" the abbot asked.

Brother Rocco stammered, "Um. No. Well, yes. Well, no."

Smiling, Abbot Nicolo continued. "Each night this saintly ghost calmed Brother Ludovico down and helped him to understand God's mercy. Also, that it was not necessary to punish oneself so grievously for one's sins."

The brothers tried not to show any emotion.

"Tuesday night was especially good," the abbot said. "He and Giacomo were together for a long time, and our friend from Heaven helped Brother Ludovico realize how he had to change his life. With the help of Giacomo Tuesday night, he decided to leave the monastery and accept the life of a monk who will preach to the poor."

After standing still for so long, Brother Rocco and Brother Pietro began to fidget. Their hands were sweating. Smiling, the abbot continued.

"So I think we must have a new understanding of Giacomo. He is not just a monk who decides to visit us once in a while. I think he comes with a purpose. We have thought of him as just a gentle ghost, but think about it. Other saints have appeared on Earth. Many times. The Blessed Mother comes often. And I think that Giacomo has been visiting us these many years as a saint, not just as a ghost. He just hasn't been canonized. At least not yet.

"And what he did for Brother Ludovico is truly a miracle. In a way, the transformation that has occurred in Brother Ludovico is almost as miraculous as the cures that Giacomo brought to the sick in the plague more than twenty-five years ago. I'm convinced of this. In fact, I am going to have a report written, and I will need your assistance, and that of Brother Marco, of course. I will go to the Vatican myself and present all this evidence, and I hope they agree that this is the second miracle needed to declare Giacomo truly a saint. Brothers, we are going to have a saint among us!"

Again, the abbot tried to see if these two monks would admit to knowing anything about this. They remained silent, their faces blank but entirely crimson.

"You can go now. God bless you, and, oh, yes, thank you for all you have done."

When they were almost out the door, Abbot Nicolo called them back. "And I'm sure Giacomo thanks you, too. I encourage you to pray to him."

When Brother Rocco and Brother Pietro were safely back in the dormitory, they had a hasty discussion.

"Do you think we should confess, tell the abbot that it was really us who calmed Brother Ludovico down?" Brother Pietro asked.

"Then," Brother Rocco said, "we would have to tell him it was us who scared Brother Ludovico in the first place. Can we do that? Why don't we just let him believe it was Giacomo all the time? No harm done."

"Still, is it right that we should deceive him?"

"Let's think about it."

They thought, which may have been a bad idea.

"Wait," Brother Rocco said. "I just realized something. Abbot Nicolo said that Brother Ludovico was especially changed by his visit from Giacomo Tuesday night."

"Yes."

"Pietro, we weren't there Tuesday night!"

"That's right! It was the first night we missed. We had to practice in the choir for Easter Mass, and Brother Sandro made us stay all night until Lauds because we sang so bad."

"Yes! Then who?"

They stared at each other.

"Well, of course," Brother Rocco said.

"Saint Giacomo!"

THE MIRACULOUS STATUE

1379-1760

ABBOT NICOLO soon realized that the Vatican would take months, if not years, to declare Giacomo a saint, and he wished the Holy See had abided by its old rules. Until more than a century ago, the process was simple, and even local bishops could verify that someone was responsible for the miracles that sainthood required. In practice, bishops sometimes abused their privileges. The abbot had heard of the scandal in Sweden when a local church canonized—as a martyr, in fact—a drunken monk who had been in a brawl.

But in 1234, Pope Gregory IX established strict procedures to investigate the life of a candidate for sainthood and any miracles that were claimed.

Since Giacomo had lived so long ago and, except for the manner of his death, so little was known about his twenty-two years of life that the burden of the investigation was on his two miracles. Abbot Nicolo knew that the first was in 1350 during the height of the Black Death, when monks in the abbey were gravely ill and one of them prayed to Giacomo, promising to establish a hospital if they were cured. In a dream, the monk saw a young man dressed in white who pointed to the village of Castelnuovo di Garfagnana not far away. The monks recovered, went to the village and turned an old villa into a hospital. With medicine miraculously found in a storeroom, they treated villagers who had been infected. The monks were certain that the young man was Giacomo himself.

The other case was earlier this year, 1379, when Abbot Nicolo was certain that Giacomo had transformed the heretical Brother Ludovico into a saintly preacher to the poor.

Convinced that these were certifiable miracles, even the one with Brother Ludovico, Abbot Nicolo was not willing to wait for the Vatican. Besides, he wasn't getting any younger. On his own, he declared Giacomo a saint and went ahead with plans to turn a side altar into the chapel that would contain the young monk's body. A lovely statue would be sculpted to represent him.

A week after Brother Ludovico said his farewells and packed up his things—ceremoniously burning his whips in a bonfire while the other monks cheered—the abbot summoned the current Count Bellini.

"I know you are acquainted with all the great artists of Florence," he said. "I want the finest sculptor there to come and create a statue of our beloved Giacomo. Spare no expense."

Count Bellini looked confused. "I know I can find the sculptor, but how will he know how to do this? How would he know what this Giacomo looked like?"

Abbot Nicolo hadn't thought about that problem.

"Well, he's certainly been seen many times. But I suppose not very clearly, and not for very long. Could we just imagine what he looked like?"

"I suppose so, but it wouldn't be very authentic."

The abbot got up and looked out the window. It was another beautiful October day in the Garfagnana. Trees in the valley had put on cloaks of red, purple, orange and all the shades in between. The white marble mountains glistened under wisps of floating clouds. The shallow streams and rivers gurgled on their way south.

Dozens of monks were crossing the grass and the fields as they went to their chores after another fine repast in the refectory. The abbot noticed a young one, Brother Pietro, helping an elderly one, Brother Marco, along a pebbled path.

"Brother Pietro! Everyone always said that he looked like the ghost of Giacomo. Slightly built, red hair, ears that stick out. There was a time during that ugly affair with Brother Ludovico when I thought that perhaps Brother Pietro could fool someone into thinking he actually was Giacomo's ghost, but that was such a preposterous idea that I put it out of my mind. But, yes, Brother Pietro could be the model for Giacomo. Of course!"

Three weeks later, Giovanni Balduccio, highly recommended by Count Bellini, arrived from Florence. His horse was sweating after the long climb to the monastery, and the artist was not in a benevolent mood. Abbot Nicolo plied him with tender veal from the farm, vegetables fresh from the gardens, and red wine from the cellar.

After a good night's rest in the monastery's most un-monk-like guest room, Balduccio was ready for work. In a sunlit room off the library, Brother Pietro was introduced to the famous sculptor from Florence. That itself was enough to make the young monk even more nervous.

Florentine art was going through a transition at this time, breaking from the Byzantine styles of, say, Cimabue, to a more naturalistic look. This was true in paintings, but also in sculptures, where the figures now often showed strong emotions. Some figures, who wore gracefully draped robes, even smiled. Balduccio was especially known for carving figures of angels and younger saints, and his most recent work was on a side altar in Saint Maria Novella.

Rather than hauling a multi-ton, six-foot-long piece of marble up to the monastery, the sculptor planned to draw the figure on a piece of parchment first and do the actual work in his studio in Florence.

Squinting in the sunlight, Brother Pietro didn't know what to do and clasped his shaking hands behind his back.

"Don't be nervous," Balduccio said, adjusting the parchment on his easel. "This isn't going to hurt."

"Not much," Brother Pietro thought, but he dutifully tried to relax.

"Just stand on this little platform, put your hands together like you're in prayer, and look over my shoulder as if you're seeing God."

Brother Pietro tried, but all he could see was Brother Rocco urging him on as he stood outside Brother Ludovico's window of the *misericord*.

He thought that standing there in the same numbing position would be short and simple, taking an hour at most, but Giovanni Balduccio was meticulous. He had almost completed a drawing when he decided he didn't like it, tore it up and went to the *scriptorium* for more parchment.

And another.

And another.

Three days later, Balduccio was satisfied, and Brother Pietro tried to get the blood flowing in his hands and feet again.

"Thank you, Brother, thank you! *Grazie!*" The sculptor shook the young monk's numbed hand. "I think everyone will be most pleased with the statue. Especially you. You will think you are looking in a mirror."

That was exactly what Brother Pietro didn't want to hear, and he anxiously told all this to Brother Rocco that night.

"People will know!" he said. "People will know that I played the ghost of Giacomo to Brother Ludovico!"

"Don't be ridiculous. Anyway, who really knows what Giacomo looked like?"

While Balduccio began his work in Florence, Abbot Nicolo supervised the transfer of Giacomo's body to the side altar. The wooden casket had been buried in what was a new cemetery in 1225 and had gone little noticed for more than one hundred and fifty years. But it was marked with a small white cross and easily found.

Slowly, four monks dug deep into the solid soil and lifted what was left of the casket to the surface. The coffin was in pieces, and what little remained of the saint's remains were gently transferred to a polished walnut coffin. A team of oxen, followed by a dozen monks reciting the rosary, brought it to the chapel. Abbot Nicolo decided not to have a ceremony, and the casket was simply inserted below the altar stone of a side chapel.

Less than five months later, Giovanni Balduccio again rode up the hills to the monastery, but this time he led a mule-drawn cart that carried a long wooden box. Inside the entrance, eight monks, chosen for their strength, lifted the box, carried it to the chapel, tore off the ropes and ties, and lifted the statue into place.

No longer a slight, ghostly presence that so many had observed over the years, Giacomo stood before them in solid glimmering white marble. His hands were folded in prayer, his face and robes shone, his tonsure was delicately etched and he wore a slight smile. Since no one knew of a proper symbol to attach to him, Balduccio placed a white dove, the sign of peace, next to his sandaled feet.

There were gasps.

"So that's what he looked like!"

"He's younger than I imagined."

"He's very handsome."

"And saintly."

Brother Pietro stood in the back with Brother Rocco.

"I can't look," he said.

"Pietro, it's beautiful. It looks just like you. And Brother Giacomo, too!"

"That's exactly what I feared."

A High Mass a week later celebrated the dedication of the statue. The local bishop and clergy helped to officiate, with places reserved for relatives of people from Castelnuovo di Garfagnana who had been miraculously cured by Giacomo during the Black Death. Ancient hymns were sung and there was plenty of incense and holy water. As the eldest in the congregation, Brother Marco lit a row of candles in front of the statue and everyone knelt and recited the rosary.

As they were leaving, they couldn't help but notice a small monk at the very back. He had a long beard and his black robe was dirty and torn. Next to him were three other monks looking similarly impoverished.

"My God," Brother Rocco said to Brother Pietro. "It's Ludovico!"

"And those must be his followers."

Hesitating, they approached the visitors, and Brother Ludovico stepped forward.

"God love you," he said, embracing Brother Rocco and then Brother Pietro. "And blessings on you. If it were not for you, I would not be granted the privilege of serving the poor. God bless you!"

He introduced his three brethren, but said he had to leave. "God calls us to the valley. God bless you again!"

And then they were gone.

"What?" Brother Rocco said after they left. "What was that?"

"A saint?" Brother Pietro replied.

"I thought we'd never see him again."

Meanwhile, Abbot Nicolo was inspecting the statue and was especially pleased to see the inscription that Giovanni Balduccio had carved on the base: Saint Giacomo of Castelnuovo di Garfagnana.

As they were leaving, one monk was heard to whisper to another, "Isn't it odd? Saint Giacomo looks a little like Brother Pietro."

ALTHOUGH ABBOT NICOLO had already taken the action, Pope Urban VI, in a formal document in 1381, declared Giacomo of Castelnuovo di Garfagnana a saint of the Roman Catholic Church. This resulted in another elaborate Mass, more singing, more incense and another fine meal in the refectory.

Now that it was official, the monastery experienced additional visitors, some coming from as far away as Lucca and Pisa. The story of the young saint resonated especially with young people, and over the years entire families arrived to pray before what became known as the Giacomo Altar. Their large donations, placed in easily accessible collection baskets, swelled the monastery's coffers and warmed Abbot Nicolo's heart.

Then something happened that was totally unexpected. A fourteen-year-old girl, Natalia Stantucci from nearby Castiglione di Garfagnana, had suffered from a palsied left leg since early childhood. She walked with crutches, sometimes painfully, had other problems. She had trouble eating and sleeping, and shyly kept to herself most of the time.

With her parents and two older brothers, she visited the Giacomo Altar on May 15, 1385. Dozens of other visitors were present, and they cleared a path so that the girl, slightly built and small for her age, could kneel before the altar. Her father Luca began to recite the rosary and the rest of the family responded. Soon, everyone joined in.

After the entire rosary had been recited, Luca Stantucci reached out and touched the foot of the statue. "Oh, Saint Giacomo, my daughter has been in pain so much. She has so many problems. And as you can see, her left leg is shorter than the other. She is a good girl. Please intercede with God to make her whole again."

No one spoke. Then soft organ music was heard. Except that no one was playing the organ. Then what sounded like a distant choir could be heard singing an ancient Latin hymn. But there was no choir around. And then a light shone on Saint Giacomo's statue. Everyone knelt and bowed.

These events were incredible enough, but then something even more remarkable happened. Slowly, the hands of the statue, which had been clasped together, separated. The arms stretched out, as if comforting the crowd. The smile on the saint's lips grew wider. The organ music and the choir's hymn grew louder.

A minute later, it was over. The music stopped, the light flickered out and the statue resumed its original position. The crowd began to shout. "What happened?" "Did you hear that?" "Did you see that? The statue moved! I swear it! I saw it!"

Luca Stantucci helped his daughter to her feet. Suddenly, she didn't need his help. Without her crutches, she walked into his arms and then her mother's. Her legs were exactly the same length.

When the crowd realized what had happened, everyone knelt again. It was indeed a miracle. Someone ran to tell Abbot Nicolo, who had been counting up the food expenses for the last month and arrived in the chapel out of breath.

The abbot summoned other monks, who searched the choir loft for evidence of a recent organ player and of an invisible choir. A few other monks inspected all candles to make certain they hadn't recently been lit. The abbot himself examined the statue. Nothing indicated a change.

He then took the Stantucci family into his study and interviewed them all carefully. Little Natalia, trying out her new legs, skipped and hopped among the abbot's books. Normally shy, she answered his questions loudly and clearly, declaring, "Saint Giacomo cured me!"

The crowd waited patiently until the abbot stood before them.

"This does indeed appear to be a miracle. I will notify the Holy See at once."

Three investigators from the Vatican, along with a medical doctor, arrived soon after. They interrogated the abbot and other monks. They summoned the sculptor Giovanni Balduccio from Florence, who examined the statue and found no faults in the marble. And they sat down with little Natalia's physician and nurses and the little girl herself.

They came to the same conclusion and went back to Rome.

There were no newspapers in the fourteenth century, of course, but the story spread, from house to house and then from village to village: "*Miraculo a Castelnuovo di Garfagnana.*"

That caused even more visitors to jam into the monastery. Its guest rooms overflowed, and since there were few places to stay in the village, an enterprising farmer converted an old barn into a guest house. Homeowners put up signs saying "*Stanze in affitto*"—rooms for rent. Two couples got together, knocked down some walls, and established a *ristorante* with homemade meals.

Five months went by and although the visitors brought many crippled and infirm people to the statue, there were no more miracles. The statue did not move. Resentment began to grow. When was this saint going to cure someone else? Did he really have any powers? Perhaps that story about Natalia was made up? Worse, maybe the monks put her up to it so that they would make some money.

The crowds began to dwindle.

Until one day, when another young girl, Anastasia, came to the monastery chapel with her aged grandmother. The girl had been blind since birth, and the grandmother had difficulty guiding her to the statue. Once there, while the girl knelt in prayer, the grandmother prayed in a quivering voice.

"Please, Saint Giacomo, my daughter needs her eyesight. I am getting old and I can't take care of myself anymore. Everyone else in my family is dead. She is the only one left. Everyone! I need my granddaughter to be able to see! Then she can help me, and when I am gone she will be able to take care of herself. Please, Saint Giacomo, help us!"

The crowd fell silent. Then, after a moment, the sound of organ music, the distant choir, the lights. The statue again smiled, and its arms reached out. When things returned to normal, they watched little Anastasia rub her eyes.

"Nonna! Nonna! I can see! I can see! You are beautiful!"

The grandmother pulled the girl into her arms. Everyone was crying, then laughing and applauding.

"*Grazie,* Saint Giacomo! *Grazie,* Saint Giacomo!"

The old woman and the child were almost trampled as everyone crowded around. They wanted to touch her, pat her. Perhaps some of the miracle would rub off on them.

Abbot Nicolo came running, followed by monks from the kitchen, the infirmary, the *scriptorium*, the barns and fields. He wedged his way to the altar and lifted Anastasia so she could see the statue.

"That's him," the abbot said. "That's who cured you."

The girl reached out to touch the figure before her. She had never seen a statue, or an abbot, or anything else before. She began to cry and the abbot returned her to her grandmother.

"We will have to talk about this, but not now," he said.

Others in the crowd began reciting their own petitions, some more consequential than others. "My fields are barren. Please help the beans to grow." "My wife and I would like to have a child." "My back hurts when I get up in the morning." "My neighbor is mean to me."

The abbot sighed. "I hope Giacomo only listens to legitimate requests."

When he looked around, he could see that not another person could fit into the chapel.

"We will have to find a larger place, a very large place for our Saint Giacomo."

TWO DAYS LATER, Abbot Nicolo and five other monks toured the monastery grounds. He had specifically chosen Brother Marco, because he was the eldest and the most respected, and Brother Pietro, because he was the model for the statue. Uninvited, Brother Rocco tagged along.

"We need to find a suitable place for our new saint," the abbot said. "We will need to build a new chapel, a shrine, so that Saint Giacomo can properly greet all our new visitors. There should be almost no limit to the crowds we could accommodate."

The plan, he said, would be to take advantage of the vast grounds south of the monastery. The shrine would contain an altar with the saint's body, the statue, and banks of candles that could be lit as acts of supplication. There would also be a wall where those cured could deposit their crutches, canes, braces and other devices they would no longer need.

The monks walked back and forth looking for a suitable stretch of land and found a perfect place atop a small hill that overlooked the valley and Castelnuovo di Garfagnana in the distance. Abbot Nicolo placed a pole in the center.

"Here is where he will stay."

An even more distant grandson of the original Count Bellini was called upon to design the shrine. It would not, he insisted, be as grandiose as the basilica dedicated to another monk, St. Francis, in the town of Assisi southeast of Florence. "I don't know what Jacobo Tedesco was thinking when he designed that monstrosity," he said. "Francis was a humble man. So was Giacomo. His shrine must be simple."

The architect's plan for the shrine was indeed simple, but Abbot Nicolo had other ideas. He wanted a black-and-white tile floor, two side altars with statues of Mary and Joseph, and stained glass windows. There was a bitter fight, and in the end only the stained glass windows remained.

Work began in 1405, and just as they had a century earlier building the monastery, ox and mule carts hauled stones from quarries in the eastern mountains up to the site. Meanwhile, the space in front of the shrine was leveled, and pathways from the main road and to the monastery were created.

The work lasted thirty-four years.

Abbot Nicolo had died early in the project, and was succeeded by Abbot Maurizio, who, elderly when he was elected, lasted only two years. He was replaced by Abbot Lorenzo, who died just last year. Abbot Claudio was now in charge.

The various abbots had investigated three miracles credited to Saint Giacomo while the construction took place. In one, a young father of three little boys was dying of an unknown internal disease that not even leeches had helped. The family carried him to the statue, and his wife tearfully prayed in front of it. Her husband walked away cured.

In another, a woman afflicted with severe paralysis was brought to the statue on a cot and while her sister prayed, the woman rose up, threw her hands in the air in gratitude and knelt in prayer.

In the third, a young mother suffered such terrible headaches that she couldn't see. Her husband cried out in a loud voice, and she never had such a headache again.

The miracles were always accompanied by organ music, a choir, a light from Heaven and a statue who smiled and whose arms moved.

All of these were investigated by the Holy See and all were recognized as miracles. As a result, the monastery was so filled with supplicants that the monks in residence could hardly wait until the new shrine was completed.

It was no wonder that the dedication of the shrine was such a joyous affair. The Mass led by Abbot Claudio was followed by a procession of clergy from the area, monks from the monastery, villagers from Castelnuovo di Garfagnana and hundreds of pilgrims. The statue was lifted from its altar in the monastery, placed on a sturdy wooden cart and carried by two white oxen to the new chapel. Once hoisted into place with strong ropes and a pulley, Saint Giacomo looked even more beatific. When the sun shone through the stained glass, the statue glowed with rich red and gold hues.

Watching all this through watery eyes was the model for the statue himself, Brother Pietro. Now eighty-four years old, he was the last of the monks who had seen the saint as a ghost. Weak and mostly bedridden, he had been carried to the site by two other monks and placed in a padded chair near the foot of the statue. Alone in the crowd, he thought about how he saw Giacomo as a ghost when he first entered the monastery, how he pretended to imitate him to scare Brother Ludovico, and how he modeled for the statue. He never told anyone, but he was convinced that the saint visited him quite often lately, standing over his bed and smiling.

"What are you thinking now?" another monk asked him.

"I'm thinking that I will be seeing Saint Giacomo very soon."

In fact, only hours after the brothers carried him back to his cell, Brother Pietro passed peacefully away with a slight smile on his face.

WITH SPACE TO SPREAD OUT in the shrine, more supplicants arrived every day. Generally, they were orderly and, rosaries in hand, filed quietly to the statue where they knelt, said more prayers, and returned to their places. Monks from the kitchen set up tables in front of the shrine and brought out long loaves of bread and slices of beef and pork. Collection baskets were nearby.

Although never boisterous, the crowds were happy, convinced that even if their particular prayers weren't answered, Saint Giacomo had heard them and would present them to God. One of them apparently was.

Irma, a teenage mother who had not married, had come all the way from Barga with her infant son, Luigi. Doctors couldn't figure out why the baby slept all the time, why he wouldn't move and why he wouldn't nurse. They threatened to use leeches.

Some in the crowd expressed shock that an unmarried mother would dare to bring her child to this holy place. They grumbled and snickered, but she was determined. Saint Giacomo apparently didn't care. He transmitted his miracle quietly, smiling, stretching out his arms. When Irma looked down, Luigi was snuggling at her breast, nursing contentedly. Those who had snickered now wanted to touch Irma's shoulder.

Other miracles followed, and word of the *"Miraculi di San Giacomo"* spread through Europe. People walked miles—some barefoot—to the site. Churches sent delegations. Songs and poems were written about the saint. Street performers made up plays, largely fictitious, about his life. As the years went by, more miracles, small and large, were reported and investigated. The Vatican kept separate files on each of them, and soon they filled half of a room.

Excitement over the miracles turned into panic, however, after one of them. Matilda Genovisi from a village near Montepulciano in southern Tuscany had suffered from severe headaches that had left her incapacitated for days at a time. Finally, after watching his wife in agony for seven years, her husband, Alberto, brought her to the shrine.

With Matilda stretched out on a cot before him, Alberto tearfully prayed to the saint and, after only a few minutes, the familiar sights and sounds occurred. Matilda got up, raised her arms to the statue and collapsed in her husband's arms.

Matilda and Alberto returned home, and then the unthinkable happened. Three days later, she died. She simply didn't wake up one night. Alberto, distraught, began to scream and yell. "This Giacomo killed my wife! Damn him!"

Vatican officials came to investigate. They concluded that Matilda was indeed dead, but could not offer any explanation and certainly did not want to connect the death to Giacomo. They wondered, though, about the health of others who had experienced miracles. The records went back for decades, and many of those supposedly cured could not be found. Or were themselves dead. The officials decided to let it go.

From the village near Montepulciano to Florence to Lucca to Castelnuovo di Garfagnana, word spread faster than the frequent forest fires in the Maremma region of Tuscany. Giacomo was a fraud. Worse, he couldn't be trusted. Don't go there. You'll take your life in your hands.

Almost immediately, the flood of supplicants at the shrine dwindled to a small stream. People from distant areas of Europe heard the news and declined to make the trip. The songs and poems and plays stopped abruptly.

A few unfortunates still came to the shrine. They were the neediest cases, whose faith in Giacomo belied any doubts about his powers. Then one was rewarded. Augustina, a widow with five young children, had fallen off the tile roof she was repairing and literally broke her back. She was unable to move and the children were becoming destitute.

Augustina's neighbors, a young couple with nothing to share but their prayers, loaded Augustina onto a donkey cart and traveled thirty-six miles to the shrine. Her children walked behind, hand in hand.

At the shrine, the couple prayed the rosary three times, then other prayers, then the rosary again. Perhaps Giacomo was getting tired of the repetition, but after his usual dazzling gestures, Augustina rose easily from her cot and embraced her children.

Soon, the message spread again from house to house, village to village. *"Miraculi di San Giacomo!"*

A few weeks later, there was another. A little boy whose heart was so weak he could barely walk was instantly cured after only a few prayers by his parents.

Again: *"Miraculi di San Giacomo!"*

IN 1760, ALMOST FOUR HUNDRED YEARS after Abbot Nicolo declared Giacomo a saint and miracles began to occur, the Vatican was shaken by reports of what developed after a miracle. This was during the reign of Pope Clement XIII, who was otherwise best known for placing fig leaves on all the classical male statues in the Vatican.

Franco Pilotti, a forty-one-year-old farmer from a village north of Lucca, had brought his eight-year-old daughter to the shrine on a cloudy morning in May. He was accompanied by his wife, Flora, and their two young sons.

Little Florina had been born severely retarded. She could not control her body or her mind. Her mother and father had to do everything for her, including feeding and taking care of her bodily needs. The burden was especially hard on her mother because Franco had become so discouraged by everything that he spent his time in the local tavern when he was not in the farm fields. As a result, they were nearly penniless.

On that day, Franco pushed his way to the front of the crowd and stood, his feet wide apart, before the statue almost in defiance.

"Saint Giacomo, look at me!" he shouted. "Look at my daughter! We need your help. Make her better! I dare you!"

The crowd looked on in horror. No one had ever confronted the saint like this before. They wouldn't have been surprised if Franco Pilotti was struck dead on the spot.

Apparently, Saint Giacomo ignored Franco Pilotti and instead looked at little Florina, lying helpless in his arms. Again, bright lights, organ music and a heavenly hymn. The saint stretched out his arms.

Florina grew so heavy that Franco had to put her down. She stood on her own, walked to her mother and held her hands. "I love you, Mama," she whispered.

Franco fell to his knees, then hugged his daughter, his wife and his sons. His voice could hardly be heard through his guttural sobs. "*Grazie, Grazie, Grazie.*"

When Pope Clement XIII read the report of the investigation of this miracle, he invited the Pilotti family to the Vatican. Since they had no other means of transportation, Franco hitched two horses to a farm cart, his family jumped in the back, and they traveled to Rome. It took almost three months.

The pope greeted the family in his private chambers, blessing each of them and letting Florina sit on his lap. He gave them each a blessed rosary. Franco boldly asked if he could have a few more. Surprised, the pope complied.

Back at home, Franco never tired of telling the story of his encounter with Saint Giacomo and then of the pope, and proudly showed his daughter off. He encouraged her to tell the story, too. Neighbors and even complete strangers visited his rustic cottage to be inspired. Thus occupied, Franco left his fields untended and his crops died. Flora had to find work caring for a neighbor's children.

In the middle of the night a few months later, Franco woke with an idea and poked his wife.

"Flora, wake up. Listen to me."

Flora stirred.

"I just thought of this. If all these people are so interested in Florina's story, why can't we ask them to pay a little to listen to it? I mean, after all, they're learning about this saint and they see little Florina and they aren't even giving me anything for it."

"Franco! How could you even think of such a thing? We were blessed by a miracle! Every time I see little Florina playing or helping in the kitchen or taking care of her brothers, I have to thank God. And Saint Giacomo, too, of course. We should be happy to tell the story of his miracle. We can't charge people to hear it. No, Franco, no!"

"But Flora…"

"No, Franco, no!"

Seething, Flora turned over and didn't go back to sleep for another hour. Franco lay awake, thinking.

He didn't bring the subject up until three days later when they were having a quiet evening after the children were asleep. He received the same reception. "No, Franco, no!"

Franco did not like being overruled. Occasionally, in the past, Flora had suffered physically when he demanded intimate favors. "I'm your husband," he'd say. "I have rights. Now come here!"

When Flora was at the neighbor's one night, Franco tried out his plan. After showing off Florina and talking at length about the visit to the Vatican, embellishing many details—"I told the pope that I liked all the paintings on the wall but that maybe there were a few too many"—he showed off a rosary the pope had given him.

"This is a blessed rosary," he said. "I'm sure the pope said that anyone who held it would be blessed, too."

The visitors, two middle-aged men and the wife of one of them, asked if they could touch it.

"You know," Franco said, "since we've been back, we've been hurting a lot because the crops have failed. Poor Flora even has to take care of the neighbors' children to pick up a few coins. It's very sad."

He took out his handkerchief and wiped his eyes.

His visitors looked at each other and then dug out their leather pouches.

"Here," one said, "thank you for telling us the story of Saint Giacomo's miracle. We are blessed."

He placed three coins in the empty plate at Franco's side.

"Gracie," Franco said. He let the visitors pass the rosary around. After they left, he pocketed the coins without telling his wife.

The scheme worked well. Word got around that Franco had a blessed rosary—some even called it miraculous—and there were so many people who wanted to see it that he had trouble scheduling them when Flora was not around. He kept all the coins in a box in the tool shed.

Unfortunately, Flora, in one of her frequent bursts of energy, decided to clean the tool shed and discovered the box. She couldn't believe the pile of florins inside and confronted Franco. He mumbled and stumbled and made up excuses—he was saving up to buy her a present—but finally confessed.

She feigned horror and disgust, but then looked at the pile again.

"Just don't tell me you're doing this."

She made it a point to be out of the house on many evenings.

Encouraged by the reactions, Franco decided to, as it were, take his show on the road. He enlisted the help of a friend in a nearby hamlet and asked if he could tell his story there. The friend told a tavern keeper who thought it would be good for business, and on a warm night in early July Franco got on his horse. Little Florina sat clutching him from behind.

Word had spread, and people spilled out from the tavern into the piazza. Franco stood on a table, with Florina at his side. She held a large golden plate.

Franco's story was enhanced by many exaggerations. The family had crawled on their knees from their village to the shrine of Saint Giacomo. They were weeping and crying out as they pushed their way to the front. Because he revered the saint so much, he pleaded softly and gently.

"Now I want to show you what Florina was like before we went to the shrine," he said, pulling his daughter up beside him. He instructed her to moan, and, as a dutiful daughter, she did. He told her to flap her arms, and she did. He told her to lie down and thrash about.

The crowd shuddered.

"And now," Franco continued, "you can see what a healthy, beautiful little girl we have now. We owe it all to Saint Giacomo. God be praised! And Saint Giacomo!"

"Saint Giacomo!"

"Now of course we have had many expenses since the miracle, so if you would like to help us out a little, we would appreciate it."

Florina went through the crowd with her plate, and the clink of many florins could be heard throughout the tavern and into the piazza.

Franco was not finished. He had taken the opportunity to stock up on cheap rosaries from a sidewalk vendor near the shrine, and now he held them up.

"When we went to Rome, we visited with the pope. Yes, Pope Clement XIII! We must have talked for more than an hour, and we told him about the wonderful saintly people who are our neighbors. He was kind enough to give us rosaries."

The crowd gasped.

"Of course, an offering should be made for these miraculous rosaries. Little Florina will walk among you again."

He gave the girl two more large plates, and they were soon filled.

Many in the crowd reached out to touch Florina, but Franco whisked her away and was soon home. He and Flora spent more than an hour counting the coins.

As Franco made more appearances, Florina was given two large baskets to carry though the crowds. They always came back filled.

Inevitably, people wondered about the money that had been collected. Franco and Flora didn't seem to be spending it on themselves, so they must have hidden it away.

"The money must be in the house," one villager said.

"Or in the barn," another said.

"Or in the tool shed," a third said.

The couple should not have been surprised to find the wooden box missing from their tool shed one day. Gone!

"We should not have done that," Flora said.

Franco could only agree.

Saint Giacomo may have taken notice. There were no miracles for more than one hundred years.

A FRIENDSHIP SHAWL

1860

AT FIRST, after he boarded the rickety train in Florence, Michele wondered why the other passengers were staring, and smiling, at him. He knew that his scarred face was lined with dirt and that his shoes were so torn they barely covered his muddy feet.

It was not until he was seated that he realized the others were pointing at his shirt.

Yes, it was torn, with stains on the front and back, and the right sleeve had been cut off above the elbow to accommodate his cast.

But it was also red!

Then the porter came to take his ticket. He was at least eighty years old, with a grizzly beard and strands of white hair flowing from his cap. His hands shook as he took Michele's ticket.

"Garibaldi *Spedizione dei Mille?*"

Michele hesitated. *"Sì!"*

Of course! He was being recognized as a member of Giuseppe Garibaldi's Expedition of the Thousand, the Redshirts, who, only three months earlier, in May 1860, conquered Palermo in Sicily as one of the first steps toward the unification of Italy.

With tears in his eyes, the porter touched Michele's cheek, the part where the scar had not yet healed.

"Grazie," he said. *"Grazie mille."*

Not knowing what else to do or say, Michele adjusted the sling over his right arm, grabbed the porter's hand with his one good hand and kept repeating, *"Sì! Sì! Sì!"*

Then the middle-aged man in the seat across the aisle began to clap. The couple behind him did the same, and soon the entire car was filled with the sounds of clapping and cheering and *"Grazie! Grazie!"*

When the passengers all stood, Michele leaned forward, waved his left arm, smiled, and crunched back into his seat. His face was almost as red as his shirt.

Just as the train was leaving the station, an elderly woman who looked remarkably like his grandmother settled into the seat next to him.

"Let me add my gratitude, young man," she said. "We, all of Italy, are so grateful for what Garibaldi and all you soldiers did. Italy has been divided in so many directions for centuries and centuries, and now at last it's going to be unified. *Grazie!*"

Michele squirmed deeper into his seat. No! No! No! If she only knew what really happened, he thought.

"My grandson wanted to volunteer, but his father said that he couldn't," the woman said. "Antonio was very disappointed."

Michele thought he'd better make conversation.

"My name is Michele," he said. "I'm from Camporgiano. That's in the Garfagnana."

"And I'm Elizabetta and I live in Florence. So very pleased to meet you."

She held his hand tightly before letting it go. "Do you want to tell me how a young man from the Garfagnana went off to a war like this?"

Michele clutched his right arm with his left hand. He knew he was going to be asked about this many times and so he had prepared a response. He told Elizabetta that his friend Francesco from outside of Florence had heard that the great general Giuseppe Garibaldi wanted to form an army of a thousand men to go to Sicily and conquer the island. Garibaldi actually got 1,089—teachers, writers, lawyers, physicians, painters, sculptors, even priests.

He said that he and Francesco had gone over to Genoa where the volunteers were organized and given their uniforms.

"The red shirts?"

"And gray pants. I guess the general liked the idea. He used red shirts for his volunteers in Uruguay years ago."

"And he equipped you well?"

"No, our muskets were so outdated we didn't know if they'd even fire."

The train was out of Florence now and heading north into the hills. Michele thought that Francesco's home must be somewhere out there. He thought he should visit Francesco's parents someday. Right now, he couldn't think about Francesco.

Elizabetta touched his arm again. "You were injured in the fighting?"

"Yes."

"And you're healing now?"

"Yes."

Michele turned away and looked out the window. He didn't want to—he couldn't!—tell this woman the whole story.

"I'm so sorry," Elizabetta said. "I won't ask any more questions."

The train had passed Prato and was approaching Pistoria. Michele remembered taking the train to Florence to meet Francesco five months ago. They were both twenty years old, the oldest of their families and second-year students at the University of Pisa. Since Francesco was from Florence, he knew a lot more about life than Michele, who grew up in the tiny village of Camporgiano north of Barga.

Francesco taught Michele so many things—about how to deal with various situations, what to eat, what not to eat, but mostly about girls. Michele had never had a girlfriend.

When they reached Barga, the porter helped Michele pull his knapsack onto his back and he awkwardly descended the steps of the train and emerged into the warm August sunlight. It was thirteen miles to Camporgiano and there was no public transportation. He began to walk.

Drivers of horse-driven carriages shouted as they saw the young man in a red shirt. *"Saluto! Grazie!"* Two girls playing in a farm field threw daises and giggled. A shopkeeper offered a glass of water, which he gratefully accepted.

An ox-driven cart with ropes tying its cargo in the back slowed down and waited for Michele to catch up.

"Spedizione dei Mille?" the driver asked.

"Sì!

"Where are you going? Do you want a ride?"

"Thank you!"

With one arm useless, Michele needed help climbing onto the seat, but once settled he thanked the driver. A man about fifty years old, he wore a woolen shirt and dark pants, heavy boots and a cowboy hat. A chain with a cross hung around his neck.

"We are all grateful for what you did. *Grazie!*" the driver said.

Michele was getting tired of this and, more important, embarrassed. He knew he didn't deserve it, and he didn't want to talk about it.

"Thanks for the ride. My name is Michele. I'm going to Camporgiano."

"Not far at all. I'm going back to the Abbey of Saint Gaudentius, so it's not out of my way at all. I'm Father Eugenio."

"You're a priest?"

"Yes, Benedictine."

"My parents took me to that abbey once. Some sort of big Mass. And we've been at that shrine of Saint Giacomo a couple times."

Father Eugenio stopped the cart as a line of sheep slowly crossed the road in front of them and then had trouble getting the ox to start moving again.

"Ah yes, the shrine. No major miracles lately that I've heard, just some minor ones that we don't even report to the Vatican. Still, the crowds keep coming, and of course we don't turn them away. Prayer is always good."

They drove along in silence, watching the Serchio River bubble along on their right.

"You were injured in the fighting?" the priest asked.

"Broken arm, but the doctor said the cast could come off soon."

"Do you have somebody to do that?"

"I dunno. I guess my dad could take me to Barga or someplace. There aren't any doctors in Camporgiano."

"Don't go to Barga. Don't spend money like that. Come to the abbey. Father Nico in the infirmary can easily do that. Just let me know when you're ready and I'll come pick you up."

"Wow. Really? Thanks."

They could see the fourteenth century fortress now as they neared Camporgiano. Michele was getting excited. He hadn't seen his family in eight months.

"Michele," Father Eugenio said, "I know that fighting in a war can leave many scars, not just on your arm and face. If you ever want to sit down and talk about anything that happened, please come to see me, all right?"

"Um, sure. Thanks."

Michele squirmed in his seat. Did the priest know something about what happened? How would he know? Maybe priests knew something that other people didn't.

"Well," Father Eugenio said, "it looks like the people here are glad to see you. Look at that sign."

On via Alberto Bertolini near the Church of Saint James the Apostle, a large cardboard sign had been erected.

"Benvenuto Eroe Michele!"

"Hero?" Michele thought. "If they only knew."

EVERYONE HAD GATHERED at the Pistilli home to greet the returning war hero: Michele's father, mother, three brothers, two sisters, and various aunts and uncles and cousins. Plus some neighbors.

They all poured out of the house as soon as they saw Father Eugenio's cart pull up and Michele step gingerly out onto the street. Tears, hugs, kisses, slaps on the back. Much of the rest of Camporgiano came out of their houses to watch, and Father Eugenio was invited to stay and meet the whole family.

Michele's mother, Luisa, began to cry when she saw the cast on his arm and she wouldn't let her son go. His father, Fredi, kept his hand on Michele's back as they entered the house.

"I didn't know when you were coming, but we'll have a little something to eat in just a while," Luisa said. "Sit, sit. You must be so tired."

"I'm fine," Michele said. "Really. Now don't fuss. Let me change first."

In his old room, Michele found a work shirt and pants in the closet and brought his red shirt and gray pants to his mother.

"Mama, please throw these out. I don't want to see them again. Ever."

His mother nodded, but she knew she could never throw out the clothes her heroic son had worn into battle. She would wash and iron them and put them away.

Asking Luisa Pistilli not to fuss was like telling the Serchio to flow upstream. Soon, the tables—three were needed to accommodate all the relatives—were laden with fried chicken, sliced beef, ravioli, spaghetti, green beans, beets, three salads, breads and, eventually, fruit, tortes and ice cream.

"Look," Luisa said, "I knew you'd want your favorite cherry pie."

Three hours later, the tables were cleared and everyone settled down around the living room and adjacent spaces. Because Michele's father was a solicitor at the courthouse in Barga, the only professional person in the village, they had the biggest house in town. Michele was the only young person of his generation to go away to university.

It was after 10 at night, but they wanted to hear Michele's story firsthand. Start from the beginning, someone said. Tell us about Genoa.

He had the narrative planned but he had to edit it.

For Michele, Genoa was a blur. Once he and Francesco had completed the paperwork for Garibaldi, he said, they mainly waited around for more volunteers to sign up. This took days, weeks. What he didn't say was that they were billeted in a cheap hotel, and that they spent their nights in various bars and brothels, using up the small stipend they were given. Michele lost his virginity the second week.

He certainly didn't want to talk about that with his family, so he tried to remember the sights he had seen.

"First, we went to the Palazzi dei Rolli, which is a beautiful palace, and the Palazzo Reale, it's also beautiful. And we saw the Palazzo Rosso, it's beautiful, too. And the San Lorenzo cathedral is beautiful, too. And this lighthouse, the Lanterna, is beautiful."

Michele was studying engineering at the university, not literature.

"OK," one of his brothers said, "everything in Genoa is beautiful. How was the ship that you took to Sicily?"

"There were two ships," Michele said, "*Il Piemonte* and *Il Lombardo*, and we were on the *Piemonte*. It was a pleasant ride, some high seas."

Actually, the ocean was turbulent and Michele hung over the railing throwing up all the way.

"After we landed we marched to this town called Calatafimi, which isn't far from the coast. We were so jived up we sang all the way. Garibaldi had this song written."

In a squeaky voice, Michele started to sing:

"All'ármi! All'ármi!
"Si sco pron le tombre, si levano i morti,
"I martiri mostri so tutti risorti!..."

"Alarms! Alarms!
"The tombs are pronounced, the dead are raised,
"The martyrs' monsters I know all risen!..."

"OK, OK, that's enough," another brother said. "We don't care about the singing. Tell us about the fighting."

Michele was about to talk about that adventure when he noticed a young woman, perhaps seventeen years old, at the far end of the couch. Her blond hair hung loosely down to her shoulders and her lemony yellow dress was cut low. When she smiled, her eyes crinkled. Michele had never seen her before.

"Michele? Michele? Are you going to tell us more?" the third brother asked.

"Um, yes. Well, we got to the outskirts of Calatafimi. We were outnumbered but they didn't seem to want to fight. We fired a few shots and they all gave up. Some of them even joined us because Garibaldi promised them land."

Michele did not note that even though the fighting was sparse, he had remained in the background, joining the rest of the volunteers when they disassembled their rifles and got organized again.

"It was pretty late by then," he said, "so we had to wait until the next day to march to Palermo."

"Was it a nice hotel?" his mother asked.

"No, Mama. It wasn't a hotel at all. We slept on the ground."

"On the ground? Oh, Michele! Wasn't it hard? Weren't you cold?"

"Mama, we were tired. We slept fine."

"Well, I can't believe Garibaldi would bring you all the way to Sicily and not make hotel reservations in advance. I should write to him."

"No, Mama, you shouldn't. We were fighting a war, remember?"

Luisa Pistilli wiped her eyes on the edge of her apron.

"So tell us about what happened at Palermo," one of Michele's sisters said.

"Palermo?"

"Yes, Palermo. You wrote that your arm was broken in the fighting at Palermo. Tell us about it."

"Palermo…" Michele's voice was hardly above a whisper.

"Yes, Palermo. Tell us what happened."

"What happened?"

"Yes, what happened. Michele, why don't you want to tell us?"

Michele looked at the grandfather's clock in the corner. "Um, why don't we wait until tomorrow. It's late."

The relatives who wouldn't be around the next day grumbled, but agreed that it had been a long day and that Michele should go to bed. He, however, wanted to meet the young woman on the couch, but then became so busy saying goodbyes to the others that she disappeared.

"Who was that girl on the couch?" he asked his brother Rocco. "The one with the yellow dress."

"Oh, that's Cristina. They moved here a couple of months ago."

"She's pretty."

Rocco slapped Michele on the back. "Oh, oh, my brother's smitten. Too bad, Michele. I heard she has a boyfriend."

Father Eugenio shook Michele's hand before leaving. "Remember, if you ever want to sit down and talk, come see me."

"Yes, Father."

So that Michele could be alone, his brother was evicted from his room to the living room couch.

"He's fought in the war," Luisa said. "He slept on the hard cold ground. He should be alone now."

When he looked around his old room, Michele thought all the signs and souvenirs scattered around now seemed a part of his distant past. So much had happened in the last eight months. Grateful as well as exhausted, he crawled into bed and fell asleep minutes after his head rested on the pillow.

And in the middle of the night everyone in house was awakened by his screams.

"Francesco! Francesco!"

WHEN MICHELE'S FATHER, HIS MOTHER, one brother and both sisters rushed into his room, they found him curled up on the floor, moaning.

"Oh, my God!" Luisa cried as she cradled his head in her arms. "Oh, my baby, my baby."

His father helped Michele up to the bed, where he hunched over with his arms tightly wound around his chest. His eyes were vacant.

When they tried to ask him questions, he didn't reply. When a sister offered him a glass of water, he took only one sip. When his brother tried to make a joke, he didn't respond.

"What a terrible nightmare you had," his mother said.

"I think it was more than a nightmare," his father said. "He was terrified by something."

"I've heard of this," the brother Franco said. "When somebody comes back from the war they go into shock when they suddenly remember what happened."

"I don't think so," Luisa said. "I think he's hungry. Did you notice that he hardly ate anything last night? I'll go fix a little something."

Fredi stopped her. "No, Luisa, he's not hungry. Don't make this any more complicated. I think he needs a drink of something. I'll go downstairs."

Michele might have been in another room. He paid no attention to what everyone was saying but sat immobile on his bed. The others were helpless.

When his father returned with a glass of brandy, Michele took a couple of swallows and settled back on the bed.

"OK," Fredi said. "That was a bad experience. It's 2 o'clock in the morning. Get some sleep now. We'll let you alone."

As Michele pulled a blanket over his head, the others went out into the hall to return to their rooms.

"I wonder why was he so calm last night and then had this terrible dream or whatever it was," his sister Anna said. "He seemed perfectly normal. He talked about everything."

"Not everything," Franco said. "When he got to the part about Palermo he didn't seem to want to talk anymore. Something must have happened there. Something bad."

"It must be about breaking his arm," Anna said.

"But why did he wake up in the middle of the night yelling Francesco's name?"

"I've often wondered what happened to his friend. He mentioned him for a while in his letters but then he didn't anymore."

They all went to their rooms and tried to sleep.

Michele slept until after noon. His mother checked on him about every half hour, tiptoeing into the room and laying her hand on his damp but cool forehead. He never opened his eyes.

"He's exhausted," she told her husband. "Well, of course he would be. He was in that terrible battle. I imagine he even killed some people. He needs his sleep."

While his brothers and sisters steered clear of the kitchen, Luisa prepared scrambled eggs, slices of ham, milk and warm bread with jelly for Michele the next morning. He looked at the food and then away.

"I guess I'm not hungry, Mama. I'm sorry."

Luisa burst into tears and went to her room.

Franco had an idea. "Want to go fishing at the Serchio? My buddy caught three trout last week. Big ones."

"Not right now, Franco. Thanks for suggesting it."

"I mean they were really big! Ten pounders!"

"Not today."

"You used to love to go fishing, Michele, before you joined the Redshirts."

"Yes, that was before. Now is now."

Michele wandered out to the back yard and settled in a wooden chair under a pine tree. His sister Bianca found him there an hour later. She was ten years old and carried a cloth bag that rattled.

"Michele! Want to play marbles? I can make a circle on the grass here. Want to?"

"Thanks, Bianca. Not right now. You can play and I'll watch."

"That's no fun."

"Well, OK, just one game."

Michele got down on his knees and watched while Bianca drew a circle in the grass with chalk and dropped all but two of the marbles in the middle. She gave Michele a blue one and kept a red one.

"I know you like blue," she said. "I'll go first."

She flicked her marble toward the others in the middle and was able to knock six out of the circle. Michele tried his and got four. Bianca got the next five, Michele two, and Bianca three.

"Only two left," Bianca cried. "My turn!" The space was soon empty.

"I won, I won," she shouted.

"I think you cheated," Michele said. For a few minutes he had somehow forgotten what happened last night. But now it all came back and he slouched in the chair again.

He closed his eyes and tried not to think about anything. But there was nothing. Nothing. Nothing.

"Hey, Michele! Look who I found out on the street!"

Rocco was leading a young blond woman by the hand. She wore a light blue dress with a low neckline.

"Remember Cristina from last night? You didn't have a chance to meet her, so I thought I'd go find her now."

"Rocco! You went and got her? She may not have wanted to come, you know."

"Of course, she wanted to come, didn't you, Cristina?"

Cristina let go of Rocco's hand and took Michele's left hand in hers. "I'm sorry I had to leave last night. I did want to meet you. Rocco has told me so much about you."

"He has?"

Rocco thought it was time for him to go into the house. "See you later!"

"Look, I'm sorry," Michele said. "Sometimes Rocco takes things into his own hands. You were probably busy."

"No, not at all. May I sit in this other chair?"

"Yes, yes. I'm sorry I didn't meet you last night."

"Michele," Cristina said, "I wish you'd stop saying you're sorry. Look, I know you've been through a lot and if you want to talk about it, fine. But if you don't want to talk about it, that's fine, too."

"Thanks. I'm sorry I..."

"Michele?"

"OK, OK, I'll stop saying that. It's just that..."

Cristina put her hand on his cast. "Michele, Rocco has told me about how you've been studying in Pisa. Oh, how I'd love to go there someday. Does the tower really lean like that? Aren't people afraid it's going to fall over? And is that cathedral really that white? I've read that it is. Oh, tell me all about Pisa, Michele."

From her kitchen window, Luisa looked out at the scene of a young man and a young woman with their heads close together and deep in conversation.

"Thank you, God!" she whispered.

CRISTINA WAS INVITED to stay for supper—"just a bite, just leftovers," Luisa said—and after checking with her home, she agreed. Michele was on one side, Rocco on the other, and the other two brothers directly opposite. They were so absorbed in their guest that they hardly ate anything.

Although Michele remained silent, the rest of the family bombarded Cristina with questions. Her mother died last year, she said, and her father had sent her from Castelnuovo di Garfagnana to Camporgiano to live with her aunt Valentina.

"Oh, Cristina," Luisa said, "we're so sorry. Was your mother sick for a long time?"

"More than two years." She didn't seem to want to talk about this and Luisa didn't ask any more questions.

They talked about life in Castelnuovo di Garfagnana, where the family loved to visit because it was bigger than Camporgiano. Luisa said she liked to go to the Duomo and admire the terracotta of the Madonna and the Saints. Fredi said he had gone to Ariosto's Castle five times and liked to imagine he was back in the Middle Ages. Little Bianca said she wanted to go to the Shrine of Saint Giacomo again.

"Nobody believes me, but I swear I saw the statue move once."

"Oh, Bianca," Rocco said, "nobody believes that the statue moves."

"It's true! He stretches out his arms and then there's a miracle. There have been about a million miracles. It's true. Everybody says so."

"I'm afraid," Luisa said, "the miracles don't happen very often anymore so it's strange that people keep coming."

Bianca still argued. "Well, what about that boy who lost his sight and then he could see? And what about that old lady who couldn't move? They were miracles, right?"

"Not everyone believes that," Rocco said.

"I don't care," Bianca said. "I believe they happened. Saint Giacomo made them happen."

Cristina looked up from her apple pie. "My aunt believes in the miracles. But then, she's strange."

Everyone hoped that she would clarify this thought, but she continued eating and no one asked.

After the meal was finally finished and Cristina had helped with the dishes over Luisa's objections, Michele walked her home and they stood in front of her house talking about, oh, anything. Michele talked about life at the university and how he had met students from all over Italy. Cristina said she would love to study at a university but her father didn't have any money to send her. She said she thought that someday she would meet someone and marry "and have a lot of children."

"Is that what you want?" Michele asked.

"I don't know. I haven't even met any boy I'd want to marry."

"But I heard you had a boyfriend. My brother said so."

Cristina laughed. "Boyfriend? No, not at all. Just a guy I talked to once in a while in Castelnuovo di Garfagnana."

There was an awkward silence after that, and Cristina said she'd better go in or her aunt would worry, "though Aunt Valentina is so odd she probably doesn't realize I'm still not home."

"What do you mean 'odd'?"

"I'll tell you sometime. I'd better go in. This was such a nice day. Thank you."

"Well, thank you for staying, and thank you for not laughing at my crazy family."

"They're not crazy. I think they're very sweet."

Michele surprised himself by saying, "And I think you are, too."

Cristina took Michele's good hand. "We need to talk more, all right?"

"I'd like that. I was having such a rough day and you made it better."

"I'm glad."

At Cristina's doorstep, Michele took a chance and kissed Cristina lightly on the cheek. She turned her head and kissed him gently on the mouth, then ran into the house.

If there had been ground underneath his feet, Michele didn't feel it, and he floated all the way home.

Thinking of little besides Cristina that night, Michele fell into a deep sleep. That is, until he began having nightmares. He was back in Palermo, not in the thick of the fighting but not in the back either. There were thousands and thousands of men defending the city—Michele learned that they were called Bourbons—and Garibaldi had little more than a thousand.

He and Francesco were the only Redshirts in the area and were surrounded by dozens of the enemy. The noises were deafening. Michele found himself on the ground with a half dozen of the enemy about to shoot him. Francesco was running toward him.

Then Michele woke up.

Shaking, he sat up in bed and tried to cover his face as best he could with his broken arm. His mouth was dry and, unlike the previous night when he had a similar dream, he could not cry out.

When he finally opened his eyes, he saw the curtains on the lone window fluttering and then blowing wildly. Something—someone!—was entering. A shadowy figure dressed in a red shirt and gray pants stood by his bed.

"Francesco?" Michele whispered. "Francesco?"

The figure raised his arm and reached out to touch the terrified occupant of the bed.

Then the figure disappeared. The curtains on the window stopped fluttering. Exhausted, Michele lay on his stomach, stuffed his face into the pillow and sobbed.

In the morning, Michele gulped down his eggs and toast and told his mother that he was going to the Abbey of Saint Gaudentius. There was, he said, a priest there who could remove his cast. He ignored Luisa's questions about the need for such a hurry, and began the long walk to Castelnuovo di Garfagnana and then up the steep hill to the monastery.

What he really wanted to do was talk to Father Eugenio. He wandered around the vast abbey and finally found the priest sitting in a rear pew in the chapel. Stopping every few minutes, he told the priest how he was visited during the night by the ghost of a friend who was killed in Sicily.

"Father, I'm sure it was him, Francesco. He even wore the red shirt. I don't know why he did this or if he wants something, and I'm so scared and nervous. I think something terrible is going to happen."

"Michele, I know this must have been terrifying for you, but let me ask some questions. First, did the figure seem at all threatening?"

"No, he just stood there."

"Did you see his face?"

"No. It must have been in the shadows."

"Did the figure move?"

"He gestured to me, but not otherwise."

"When the figure was with you, were you frightened?"

"No. In fact, it was nice to have him near me again."

Father Eugenio could have referred Michele to the resident exorcist, but it was obvious that the boy was not possessed by the devil. He could have dismissed the whole story and told him that he had a bad dream and that he should drink some warm milk before going to bed.

But Father Eugenio felt the need to console the boy, even if he wasn't sure what to say.

"Michele, I can't give you a good answer, but I do know that God works in mysterious ways. For some reason, I think He wants Francesco and you to resolve something between you two, and he's given Francesco a chance to do that. The fact that Francesco didn't frighten you is important."

For a moment, Michele thought he should tell the priest more about what happened in Sicily, but decided against it.

Father Eugenio stood up. "I would say let's wait and see what happens. See if Francesco returns. Can you come back next week and we'll talk again?"

Michele was now more confused, but agreed to return. Father Eugenio took Michele to Father Nico in the infirmary, who swiftly and easily removed the cast and recommended some gentle stretching. Michele began the long walk home.

"Wait? How can I wait?"

NIGHT AFTER NIGHT, it was always the same. Michele waited until long after the others had gone to bed to finally go to his room. He tried not to sleep, but inevitably he dozed off. Then the same nightmare, always ending at Palermo, followed by the fluttering curtains, the figure reaching out at his bedside, and the awakening in a cold sweat.

During the day he walked around as if in a daze, not knowing what to do, not eating his mother's extravagant meals (and causing her to rush from the table in tears).

He couldn't talk about what was happening to his family. He knew his mother would become hysterical and everyone else would yell and argue. Michele now knew there was only one person to whom he could confide.

Cristina.

He had been seeing her every day, sometimes for hours. If she grew frustrated or impatient by the way he was behaving, she didn't show it.

"I'm sorry for acting like this," he said one day. "You're a saint."

"Will you please, please, please stop saying you're sorry. There's nothing to be sorry about. And as for being a saint, well, you should ask my aunt about that. Now how about a walk along the river?"

After weeks of rain, the Serchio had risen almost to its banks and Michele and Cristina walked gingerly on the muddy bank. They found a bench that overlooked the river, took off their shoes and enjoyed the panini that Cristina's aunt had made for them.

"This is good," Michele said. "Thank your aunt. What is she doing today?"

"Um. She's having some people over and they play some sort of game."

"What kind of game?"

"Oh, we can talk about it later, OK?"

Again, Cristina was mysterious about her aunt, which caused Michele to be only more curious. But Cristina changed the subject and, being young and in love, they found many things to talk about.

Michele knew that this was the day he would finally tell Cristina the whole story.

"Cristina, you said if I didn't want to talk about what happened in Sicily I didn't have to. But now I think I have to. In fact, I know I do."

"Only if you want to. Go slow, Michele, go slow."

"Well, first of all, Francesco had become my best friend. I never had many friends, but somehow we bonded and we had a lot of fun together and talked a lot. We really cared about each other. When we were in Genoa, we made a promise. If we were in a battle and one of us was hurt, or if one of us needed help, the other one would come to the rescue."

"That's so brave!" Cristina said.

"When we were at Calatafimi, the first battle in Sicily, Francesco went right up to the front and fought with the Bourbons. Me? I hung back. I don't know why, I just did. Cristina, this was the first time I was in a battle like that. All these soldiers with their rifles. We were really outnumbered. I was scared, Cristina, I was scared."

Cristina put her hand on his arm, now free of the cast. "Of course you were. Who wouldn't be?"

"Well, the fighting ended. Francesco came back to where I was. He was all dirty but he hadn't been hurt and he said he wounded a guy but didn't kill anybody. But this is what happened. He didn't ask where I had been in all this. He knew, but he didn't ask. He just acted like I had been in the battle with everyone else. I knew the truth, of course. I started to confess, but he began talking about something else and wouldn't let me."

"Oh, Michele. How hard that must have been for you."

"We got to Palermo on the 27th of May. I remember the date because it's Rocco's birthday. General Garibaldi told us that the city would be defended by about sixteen thousand men. Can you believe it? Sixteen thousand! And we were little more than a thousand."

"Oh, my God."

"Well, fortunately for us, they were badly organized and their general, a man named Ferdinando Lanza, was timid and confused. We formed two columns on the outskirts of Palermo. Francesco and I were together. We were going up a side street when we ran into about two dozen of the Bourbons. They started shooting. Francesco shot back. I tried to, but I was having trouble loading my rifle and suddenly I tripped and fell on the cobblestones. I broke my arm and hurt my face. I stupidly broke my arm!"

"Oh, Michele."

"Francesco rushed back to help me because the Bourbons were advancing toward us. He lifted me up and I was almost on my feet. And then they…and then they…"

"Michele, what happened?"

"They shot Francesco in the back. In the back! Four times! I grabbed onto him and he died in my arms. I could feel his breathing and I could see the blood all over. And he died! As I was holding him! Cristina, I will never forget the look he had on his face. It was pure terror."

"Oh, Michele, Michele."

"He was trying to protect me and he was killed, Cristina! He was killed! He died because I was such a fool that I tripped and fell and broke my arm! I should have been shooting! I should have been standing with him!"

Michele's sobs could be heard in the farm fields near the river. Cristina took him into her arms and let him cry on her bosom. She stroked his back and kept murmuring, "It's all right, it's all right, it's over now."

"It's not all right! It's never going to be all right! People treat me like I'm a hero and I'm the furthest thing from a hero. I was injured in the war because I fell down and broke my arm. That's all! And Francesco, the real hero, is dead. My friend is dead!"

Cristina watched as two farmers led their cattle on the road along the river. Four or five boys played with a ball in a field. A woman carried a load of laundry to wash in the river.

"And it's not over, Cristina!"

Michele told Cristina how he'd been having nightmares about Sicily and how the dreams became real when the curtains fluttered and Francesco appeared at his side in the middle of the night.

"Francesco comes to you?"

"Yes! I know you don't believe it, but he does."

"Michele, if you say Francesco comes to you in the middle of the night I believe that Francesco comes to you in the middle of the night."

"I don't know what he wants. Maybe revenge. Maybe just to scare me. Well, I'm scared, and I don't know what to do. And there's nobody who can help me. No one. I talked to a priest at the abbey and he said to wait and see if Francesco returns. Well, Francesco has returned every night! What am I going to do, Cristina? What am I going to do?"

Holding Michele tightly in her arms, Cristina thought for a long time. She looked at the woman washing her clothes in the Serchio, and then she had an idea.

"Michele, perhaps my aunt Valentina can help you."

MICHELE HAD NOT MET Cristina's aunt before. Valentina Zorella was a small woman, dressed entirely in black, but with bright red slippers peeking from the bottom of her dress. She wore six or eight long necklaces, some with expensive jewels, some with cheap beads, but all in bright colors. Two dangling gold earrings hung on each side of her face. Her cheeks were painted bright orange-red. Multiple rings dazzled from her fingers.

Her most fascinating feature was her hair, the brightest red imaginable and arranged in dozens of tiny curls. Her age was undeterminable. She could have been sixty—or eighty.

"Michele, Michele, Michele. We meet at last." Her voice was so low Michele wondered how it could come from such a tiny body. "Cristina has told me so much about you. Come in. Coffee? Tea? Something a little stronger? I have…"

"No, Auntie," Cristina said, "I don't think Michele would like anything strong at 11 o'clock in the morning."

"Then a little something to eat? A snack? Biscotti? Panettone? Cannoli? Let me look at what we have."

"No, Auntie. I just want you to meet Michele, and perhaps you can help him."

"Well, well. Of course I would be happy to help him. What do you need, young man?"

They sat at the kitchen table and Michele, with prompting from Cristina, told the whole story of what happened in Palermo—and what had been happening each night since he returned home to Camporgiano. At the end of it, Michele was shaking and Cristina stood behind him, holding his shoulders.

"Oh, poor boy," Valentina said. She had tears in her eyes. "I'm so sorry, so sorry."

"Do you think you can help him, Auntie?"

"I don't know. This is serious. I will have to think about it. Anyway, we can't do anything now. It's too bright. Come back tonight, about 11 o'clock, and we'll see. There's a full moon then, and that's always good. All right?"

"Thank you, Auntie. We will."

Valentina hugged her niece and then, impulsively, hugged Michele, too. Her perfume, a mix of gardenias and jasmine, was so strong he began to cough.

"Overwhelmed?" Cristina asked Michele as they left the house.

"Um. Yes. And not just by the perfume."

"I guess I should have explained Aunt Valentina before bringing you to her."

They sat on the bench behind the house and Cristina told the story.

Valentina, she said, had supernatural powers.

"She's a witch?"

"No, no, no. She was just born with the ability to do things that cannot be explained naturally."

Cristina said she was certain that her aunt could read the lines in one's palms to predict the future, could know what someone was thinking, and could levitate, "but that's just a trick that she doesn't use often."

What is important now, she said, is that Valentina could call up people from the other side and converse with them.

"You mean like Francesco?"

"Well, it's worth a try, isn't it?"

Since he was not satisfied with the response from Father Eugenio, Michele had to agree, but of course he had many questions. For example, how did she get these strange powers?

"She was born with them," Cristina said. "Her mother and grandmother also had these talents. And the talents have flowed through Auntie to her daughter, granddaughter and on and on, always the female member of the family. They live in Gallicano now."

"Gallicano?"

"It's a small town near Molazzana, just south of Castelnuovo di Garfagnana."

Michele wondered where Valentina's husband was, and Cristina looked away.

"He got tired of everything that was happening in the house and just packed up and left. Valentina has never heard from him again."

Michele thought it was time for him to go home, and he spent the rest of the day lying on the bed in his room. Shortly before 11 o'clock, when everyone except Rocco had gone to bed, he told Rocco he was going to Cristina's "to watch the full moon."

He then left his brother rolling on the floor with laughter.

Bathed in moonlight, Cristina greeted him at her door. "Auntie is glad you waited until now. The spirits seem to be more free just before midnight."

She led him through the kitchen and dining room, which were sparsely furnished, and pulled a colorful beaded curtain aside to enter a third room. Unlike the others, its walls were painted in soft blues and grays, and a patterned rug covered the floor. Heavy curtains prevented moonlight from entering the room. A large painting of an angel in an ornate frame hung on one wall. In the middle, a small table, covered by a green damask cloth, held four candles.

Valentina now wore a flowered cloth over her shoulders. "This, my dears, is what I call my friendship shawl. Sometimes, visitors from the other side like to use it to show their affection for someone on this side. Isn't it beautiful? Oh, I know we are going to have a lovely time."

She instructed them to sit at the table and to light the candles. Then they joined hands on top of the table.

"Now," Valentina said, "we will go slow. Francesco has never done this before, so we must be patient. We will give him time to respond, all right?"

Michele's hands were shaking in Cristina's.

"Now," Valentina continued, "I will use this glass of water to let Francesco communicate with us. I'm sure he will know what to do."

She placed a glass, three-quarters filled with water, next to her. She sat as if in a trance, and Michele could smell gardenias and jasmine. He looked at Cristina, who also had her eyes closed.

"Now, Michele," Valentina asked, "what would you like me to ask Francesco?"

Michele didn't know this was going to be a question-and-answer session, and hesitated.

"Well, I would like to know if he's angry for getting killed when he was trying to protect me. And if he will ever forgive me for being so clumsy and tripping and breaking my arm. Oh, and is he going to continue visiting me every night?"

"Those are good questions, simple to answer. Now, let's be very quiet."

With eyes closed, the three sat silently. Michele tried his best, but felt sweat gathering on his forehead, as it always did when he was nervous. He tried to mop it and Cristina gripped his hand tighter.

"All right," Valentina said at last, "I think it's time."

She placed her hands on the table.

"Francesco, if you are present, please give us an indication."

Valentina and Cristina closed their eyes again, but Michele looked frantically around the room. He was startled when the glass of water suddenly began to shake.

"Ah, Francesco," Valentina said, "we are so pleased you are here. Thank you for joining us. Now, may we ask a few questions?"

Michele tried to find signs of his friend and thought for a second that a shadow passed over the painting of the angel. The water in the glass shook again.

"Thank you, dear. Now I must tell you that your friend Michele misses you very much. Did you know that?"

The water shook violently.

"Well, Michele will be glad to know that. You were such good friends. Now he has a question for you. If your answer is 'yes,' please knock on the table once. If it is 'no,' knock twice. Here is the question. Are you angry with Michele that you were killed when you were trying to protect him?"

They didn't have to wait long before there was a loud knock on the table, and then another. From nowhere! Michele's hands were so sweaty he momentarily lost Cristina's.

"Thank you. I know Michele will be pleased to know you are not angry with him. Let's pause a bit before I ask another question."

Valentina took ten deep breaths.

"Now, another question. Will you forgive Michele for tripping and breaking his arm and thus causing you to get killed?"

Again, another loud knock. Just one. Sweat poured down Michele's face and he desperately wanted to look under the table to see if Valentina was doing the knocking.

"Thank you again," Valentina said.

She paused again, breathing heavily, then continued.

"We don't want to keep you, Francesco, but we have one more question. Will you continue to visit Michele every night? While he likes your visits, they have become, well, a little distracting."

This time, two more loud knocks.

"Thank you. I know Michele will miss your nightly visits. Now, Francesco, is there anything you'd like to tell us before you leave?"

Valentina explained to the others that since this wasn't a "yes" or "no" answer, it might be difficult for Francesco to respond.

They waited. And waited. Just as Valentina was about to conclude that Francesco had returned to the other side, her scarf suddenly lifted from her shoulders, hung momentarily above her head, then crossed the table and wrapped itself around Michele's shoulders. All three began to sob and Cristina gripped Michele's hand even tighter.

"Oh, Michele," Valentina said, "I've never seen anything like this before. Francesco says he likes you very much. He says you will always be his friend. Thank you, Francesco. Now Michele knows that you will always be his friend."

When Michele wore the shawl the next morning at breakfast, he deflected all the questions and just smiled.

THE CRYSTAL BALL

1944

EVERY DAY NOW, it was clear that the war was getting closer. On the ground, Axis armies were edging nearer as they fled from the Allies. In the air, Allied warplanes were in pursuit. The secluded village of Molazzana in the central part of the Garfagnana was trapped in a vice, and as 1944 drew to a close, the Neri family could only wait.

There was nowhere to go.

Stefano looked out the window at the barren landscape. After the worst growing season in years, rain continued to pelt the muddy earth, creating rivulets that flowed into massive puddles all over the farmland. If Pasquale and Luciana weren't talking in the barn, there would be no sign of life. Stefano closed the curtains, afraid to look anymore.

Distraught, Carolina pleaded, as she had for days, "What are we going to do? What are we going to do? We have to find the children a safe place to live. Where, Stefano, where?"

She leaned over the kitchen table and let her tears fall on the plates for lunch. Her husband wrapped his arms around her, but he had no answers, and there was nothing he could say. Both knew, however, what the other was thinking.

Forced to remain inside because of the chronic rain, they did what they had been doing for days. Stefano put up a shelf, took it down and put it on another wall. Carolina cleaned the stove. Again. They hardly said a word.

When Pasquale and Luciana came in, they dried themselves at the stove and then wandered around the house looking for something to do. As usual, Pasquale, who was twelve years old, glared at Carolina and Stefano and settled into a corner to whittle some sticks. His sister Luciana, who was ten, went to another corner and picked up two books, *The Story of Pinocchio* and *The Legend of* La Befana. They were the only books she had and she'd read them countless times.

While Pasquale let his feelings be known, and they were always strong and hostile, Luciana was withdrawn and silent. During the day she mostly lay on her bed reading the two books or making up stories for her doll, Francesca, which she'd had since she was a year old.

Carolina tried to hug the girl. "I love you," she said.

Luciana's body tightened.

At night, the girl had terrible dreams and nightmares, filled with creepy people and horrifying happenings. She often screamed, and Carolina had to go in and hold her.

Looking away from the children, Carolina glanced at her husband. "I think it's time," she whispered.

"Not yet," he mouthed.

So the decision was put off again. Carolina put bowls of spelt soup, two slices of hard bread and two boiled eggs before the children. The chickens weren't laying many eggs. With the terrible weather the Garfagnana had been experiencing, the potato bin was virtually empty, the supplies of beans and even lettuce were dwindling. With the pigs sold, there was no meat.

"I'm sorry, children," she said. "That's all we have."

Carolina and Stefano looked on as the children tried to make their meager meal last. They themselves would wait to see what they could scrounge up later. They had aged so much so fast. Stefano's head was almost bald and his plaid shirt hung loosely on his shoulders. Carolina no longer braided her hair, which had turned prematurely gray, and let it fall loosely down her back. She didn't care how she looked anymore.

By the end of the week, with more Allied bombers overhead and ground fighting nearer, they knew they had to make a decision. Stefano said they should ask help from the parish priest. The church was just down the muddy street.

His eyes glazed over, Padre Giovanni Lucci was shuffling through papers on his desk in the parish rectory. There were too many bills and almost nothing in the collection baskets. He wouldn't have been able to celebrate Mass if the Benedictine monks at the Abbey of Saint Gaudentius hadn't sent him bottles of wine they would otherwise have discarded, or if the good sisters at the Convent of Our Lady of Sorrows in Gallicano hadn't supplied him with hosts for Communion and never asked for payment.

He had let his housekeeper go and tried to take care of all the maintenance problems in the church. Hundreds of years old, the building was rapidly falling apart, and he often felt the same. Tall and gaunt, he looked like a wisp of a wind could have blown him away. He didn't know how he could cope with the cracks in the bell tower, which no longer contained a bell, with the swallows and pigeons that flew into the church through shattered windows, or with the floor that buckled because of leaks in the roof.

Nevertheless, he greeted Stefano and Carolina with a thin smile.

They knew the priest was exhausted so they got right to the point.

"Padre," Stefano said, "you know that we have been caring for Pasquale and Luciana for four years…"

"Ever since Mia and Nicolo were killed in that accident," Carolina added. "We couldn't believe it. That cement truck came around that corner like…"

"Anyway, the kids had nowhere else to go. Their grandparents were dead, their aunts and uncles didn't want to take them…"

"Fine relatives they are…"

"And so we took them in," Stefano said. "We had always been their best friends. Always. We grew up together. We did everything together."

"After all," Carolina said, "we didn't have any children of our own, though God knows we tried."

"We thought it would be temporary," Stefano said, "but here it is four years later. Pasquale was eight then and Luciana was six. It's so hard to believe."

They talked about how the children were so traumatized after the accident that they didn't want to stay. Pasquale kicked and screamed and thrashed and often struck them both. He broke a window when he threw a rock. He was still belligerent and sullen and hardly talked to his adoptive parents.

"We've never been able to overcome Pasquale's anger," Stefano said. "He's so angry at his parents for getting killed, and he's angry at God for letting this happen. You notice that at Mass he doesn't go to Communion but rather just sits there."

"I've noticed," the priest said. "I'm so sorry."

Luciana, they said, remained a mystery. She was so withdrawn that they had even taken her to a doctor, "but all he said was that she had suffered a great loss and that she would get over it eventually," Stefano said.

"But she hasn't," Carolina said. "We can't get through to her."

They didn't mention the nightmares.

"The poor children," Padre Lucci said. "I can understand. They've been through such a terrible tragedy."

"We're going to miss them so much," Carolina said.

But the imminent danger of a full-scale war in the Garfagnana and the loss of their crops had left them with no alternative, Stefano said.

"We don't want to do this," he said. "It's the last thing we want. We love these children. This is breaking our hearts. But we know this will be the best for them. We need to send them to somewhere safe, someplace where people can care for them and be able to feed them, maybe even love them."

Carolina was in tears now. "We can't do it, Father. We just can't anymore. We know Mia and Nicolo would want us to keep them, but we also know they would want the children to be safe."

Padre Lucci shuffled the papers again. "I am trying to think of people who could help. Certainly, in the past, there might have been couples who could take them in, but everyone seems to be in the same situation now. Everyone is destitute, and everyone is afraid of what might happen in six months, a year."

In the silence of the late afternoon, with the sun beaming on the tattered rug, they could hear two swallows swooping in the church next door.

"Look," the priest said. "Let me make some phone calls. I can't promise anything, and I can't promise that the children will remain together, but I will try."

WHEN PADRE LUCCI called the Abbey of Saint Gaudentius near Castelnuovo di Garfagnana, one monk after another tried to understand his request until finally the abbot, out of breath, picked up the phone. He said he would have to think about it.

When Father Lucci called the Convent of Our Lady of Sorrows in Gallicano, an elderly nun, hard of hearing, hung up and he had to call back. When he got through to the mother superior, she said she would have to think about it and would get back to him.

Neither responded for a week and Carolina and Stefano became more anxious and depressed. They asked Father Lucci to call again. After three days, the monastery and the convent responded. The Abbey of Saint Gaudentius would take Pasquale but not Luciana. The Convent of Our Lady of Sorrows would take Luciana but not Pasquale.

"Oh, my God," Carolina cried. "They're going to be separated. This is terrible."

"It's the best we can do," Father Lucci said.

"It will be better than staying with us," Stefano said.

Before bedtime, they took the children aside and explained that with the Germans' advance, Molazzana would no longer be safe, and they would have to move to places that would not be attacked, like an abbey and a convent.

"Couldn't we stay here until the Germans come?" Pasquale asked.

"And be at their mercy?" Stefano said. "No! Anyway, we don't know when that will be. It could be next week, it could be next month. We just want you to be safe."

Pasquale declared that he didn't want to stay with "some old monks."

"Pasquale," Stefano said, "this is what we have to do. Perhaps someday things will get better and you can come back here."

"I don't want to come back here! And I don't want to go there! I wish…I wish…I wish my mom and my dad were here."

For the first time since his parents' funeral, he began to sob and fled to the bedroom.

Breaking her silence, Luciana was also crying. "I don't want to go away! I want to stay here! Why can't I stay here?"

It was best, Stefano and Carolina thought, that they deliver the children right away. The next morning, Pasquale carried a cardboard suitcase and Luciana clutched her doll and a paper bag that contained her few clothes and her books. They climbed into the rusty old farm truck and drove slowly in the rain south to Gallicano.

They could hear muffled artillery sounds in the distance, along with occasional explosions. Carolina pulled Luciana onto her lap so she could hug her better.

The Convent of Our Lady of Sorrows was housed in a fifteenth-century villa facing the main piazza of the village. The twenty-eight nuns spent their days praying, making hosts for churches in the area and taking food and other supplies to the poor.

Luciana remained placid but held Carolina's hand tightly when Mother Elena opened the thick oak door.

"Oh, what have we here? What a sweet little girl! And is that your little friend?"

Since Luciana stared straight ahead, Carolina answered. "She loves that doll. She's had it forever. Its name is Francesca."

"Francesca! Well, we have a special devotion to Saint Francis, so I'm sure Francesca's going to be at home here. And what is your name, little girl?"

Luciana now stood behind Carolina, who told the nun her name.

"A lovely name," the aged nun said. "You know that Luciana means light. Heaven knows we need some light in this dreary world. Well, come in. Let me show you around."

The girl squeezed Carolina's hand as they began the tour. Built more than two hundred years ago as a palazzo, the convent had been carefully restored, with tiles on the floors and frescoes on the ceilings. The vast library had been divided to create cells for the nuns. Mother Elena's office, where they signed some papers, had also once been used as a guest room.

Stefano noticed a machine covered with a black cloth in the nun's office. He knew what it was and avoided answering Pasquale's questions about it.

Mother Elena led the way to Luciana's cell, at the end of a long corridor. It contained a bed, a desk, a chair and a simple kneeler for prayer.

"I'm sorry," Mother Elena said. "You must have had a nicer room at home."

"No, no," Stefano said. "We had one bedroom, with two beds. Luciana shared a bed with her brother."

Mother Elena seemed surprised at this, but continued. "Well, at least you will have your own bed here. And you will like your neighbor, Sister Rosetta. She is our youngest sister."

Sister Rosetta arrived then and it turned out "young" was a relative term. At least forty-five, she was tall and thin, and the white wimple that encircled her pink face could not detract from the twinkle in her blue eyes. Reluctantly, Luciana allowed the nun to hold her hand.

"Why don't you come with me, dear," she said.

Luciana didn't move.

Sister Rosetta bent down and whispered. "I know where there's a piece of chocolate cake in the kitchen."

Luciana looked at the nun and then at Carolina, who nodded that it was all right for her to go.

"We love you, Luciana," Carolina said.

"We love you," Stefano said.

Pasquale waved a little, but didn't say anything.

Without even saying goodbye, Luciana took Sister Rosetta's hand and vanished down the hall.

Stefano and Carolina took Mother Elena aside.

"Mother," Stefano said, "you should know that Luciana sometimes has terrible nightmares. She's likely to scream."

"I know this is a lot to ask, but if someone could go in and hold her for a while?" Carolina said. "She'll settle down."

"Eventually," Stefano said.

"Of course, of course," Mother Elena said. "Don't worry about it. Sister Rosetta will be happy to do it. She'll be fine. Such a sweet girl."

Relieved, Stefano and Carolina and Pasquale now drove north, and soon the Abbey of Saint Gaudentius loomed in the distance, rising high at the top of the hill. Even in the rain it looked both majestic and forbidding.

"Look, Pasquale," Carolina said, "it looks like a castle!"

"Not quite, but I'm sure you're going to like it here," Stefano said.

For his part, Pasquale stared at the imposing structure and clenched his fists. "They'd better be nice to me or I'm not staying."

Abbot Tadeo, in his twelfth year heading the congregation, greeted them at the door.

"Welcome! Welcome to our little monastery. And is this our new little guest?"

"I'm not little!" Pasquale shouted.

"We are so pleased to have you join us. I'm sure the other monks will appreciate having a young person among us."

"I'm not a young person! I'm twelve years old!"

"Of course. Anyway, we hope you like it here. Perhaps you'd like to see what's inside your new home?"

With Pasquale commenting along the way, Abbot Tadeo led the tour through the refectory ("I don't eat breakfast"), the dormitory ("I want my own room and I don't want anyone near it"), the chapel ("I don't pray and I'm not going to Mass"), and the infirmary ("These old people look like they're going to die").

Pasquale did seem interested in the wine making in the cellar and asked to taste it. Abbot Tadeo politely changed the subject.

On the way back, Stefano asked about the muffled voices behind a thick wall.

"Are people behind that?" he asked.

"That? That?" the abbot quickly replied. "That's nothing, nothing at all. Let's go back."

In a sitting room, Abbot Tadeo explained that fifty-eight monks lived in the monastery now, fewer than the seventy who were there when the abbey was completed in 1378.

"We manage, but with the war going on we're not getting any new men," he said. "Perhaps when the war is over things will get better. If the war is ever over. It's a terrible thing, this war. So many people displaced. So many refugees. But now the partisans are becoming more active, thank God. We have been safe so far because we're so high, but who knows how long that will last?"

As if on cue, another round of artillery, accompanied by the drone of planes, shook the windows of the room.

Abbot Tadeo leaned back. "We live with this now. And I'm afraid it's going to get worse."

It was time to go. Stefano shook his Pasquale's hand, and when Carolina reached out, the boy hesitated and then plunged into her embrace.

"It's going to be OK, Pasquale," she said, wiping away his tears. "Be good. Do what the monks tell you. Maybe we'll see you soon."

His shoulders bent, the boy followed the abbot into the abbey, and Stefano and Carolina, both sobbing, found their truck.

The rain had dwindled to a drizzle and gun battles seemed farther away as Stefano and Carolina drove back to Molazzana, but, lost in their thoughts, they hardly noticed. It was not until they were near their home that Carolina asked, "Did we do the right thing, Stefano? Did we?"

"We had no choice. We had to give them up."

"Poor Pasquale, I hope he settles down and isn't so angry."

"Poor Luciana, I hope she doesn't have any more nightmares. She needs to have a friend."

"I think they're going to grow up very fast."

PASQUALE DIDN'T SLEEP WELL on his first night in the Abbey of Saint Gaudentius. Outside, cold winds whistled through the trees and his dank cell reeked of something he didn't want to think about. The bed was hard and lumpy, and the window so high he couldn't see out.

Incessant bells awakened him at 2 o'clock in the morning, and just as he was dozing off the bells rang again at 7 o'clock.

"What the…?"

Pulling on his clothes, he ventured out the door to see monks scurrying down the halls.

"Time for Mass," one said over his shoulder as he rushed past.

He had never gotten up before 10 o'clock, and it was usually noon, when he lived with Stefano and Carolina.

One of the monks tugged him along and he found himself in the chapel where, instead of being awed by its beauty, he could only think that it was "old."

Dozing off, he paid little attention to the Mass and remained in his pew when everyone else went to the altar for Communion.

"Don't you want to receive the Body of Christ?" one elderly monk asked as he passed by.

"No."

After the Mass, he followed everyone to the refectory and through the line. Although he had claimed that he didn't eat breakfast, he loaded his tray with eggs, sausages, oatmeal, bread, cheese and milk. He hadn't had so much to eat in years.

He noticed an empty place at a long table and joined a dozen monks.

Until this point, the boy had been the object of long glances and whispers, and now the questions were asked: Who was he? Where did he come from? Why was he here? Was he going to enter the order? How long was he going to stay? Why did his parents abandon him? And also: Why didn't he go to Communion?

Except for the last, Pasquale answered the questions quickly and briefly. He wondered himself why he was sent off to live with old monks in an old monastery.

As they were putting their trays away, another monk, younger than all the others, tapped him on the arm.

"Look, I don't know why you're here and I'm not going to ask, but I know this is all very strange to you, so if you have questions, please ask. I'm Brother Antonio, but just call me Tonio. I'm three cells away from you toward the chapel."

He shook Pasquale's hand, smiled and walked away. The tears in Pasquale's eyes prevented him from seeing a chair in the way and he tripped and fell.

"Sorry," he said to the empty refectory.

After getting lost wandering down one hallway and then another, he found his way to Abbot Tadeo's office. The door was partly closed, but through an opening he could see the abbot bent over some machine. He knew it wasn't a typewriter but couldn't figure out what it was.

Hearing Pasquale's knock, the abbot quickly covered the machine with a black cloth and opened the door. He looked flustered.

"Pasquale! I'm glad you stopped by. We should talk."

The boy told his story. How his parents were killed in an automobile accident four years ago and how some friends took him and his sister in. How they tried to be good parents but that they were afraid the Germans would be attacking their village and they wanted him and his sister to be in a safer place.

"How devastating for you," the abbot said. "I can't imagine all that you've been through. First your parents, and now this. Well, you should know that we will indeed take care of you, and so far at least we have the food. How long that will last, we don't know."

The abbot told of the monastery's history beginning in the fourteenth century and through the ages. He skipped over some parts, like the monk who beat himself for his sins. And the ghost.

"The abbey has even produced a saint," he said. "Saint Giacomo? You've heard of him, I'm sure."

"No."

"Well, he's famous. We even have a chapel a little way down the hill and there's a statue of him there that people say works miracles. Before all this fighting, people came from all over to pray there, but now they're afraid, so no one comes."

"Really? Can I see it?"

"Of course. I'll have someone take you there someday."

The abbot warned, however, that it was not safe anymore to be wandering the hills alone. The war had become too close.

"Don't ever, ever, go out by yourself. Promise? For one thing, there are forests all over and you could easily get lost. And now, of course, there are other dangers."

"Like what?"

"Many dangers."

"I guess I promise."

"There is more and more fighting every day, Pasquale," the abbot said. "There was a firefight between the Germans and the partisans on the way to Corfino two weeks ago and two Germans were killed. The partisans were pretty aggressive. None of them even got hurt."

Pasquale didn't even know what partisans were, and the abbot explained that they were bands of civilians who were resisting the German army through such tactics as blowing up railroad lines and dynamiting roads and fields.

"In our own small way, we try to help them as much as we can," he said.

"How?" Pasquale asked.

"That's all I can say."

Pasquale wondered if the machine in the abbot's office had something to do with that.

"You should also know that we are trying to help some people who have been fleeing the Nazis, but I won't say any more about that at this time either. Now, if you have any problems here, please come to see me. We want you to feel welcome."

If nothing else, Pasquale had always been curious, sometimes getting into trouble because of it. He was glad to run into Brother Antonio an hour later.

"Um, Brother Antonio…"

"Tonio, please."

"Yes, Tonio. Well, I was talking to the abbot a little while ago and I have some questions."

"Let's go to the courtyard. It's such a nice day after the rain."

Seated on a bench, Pasquale asked about the partisans.

"Yes, there's a group in the forest about five kilometers from here. They've become more active because a lot of people around here don't like the Germans. They have a leader, a young guy who deserted the Italian army, and he's rounded up a couple of dozen people, mostly young men but there are some women, too. His code name is Leopardo and all the others have taken on animal names."

Pasquale wanted to know how the abbey was involved. Tonio looked around to see if anyone was listening.

"I shouldn't be telling you this, but you're not going anywhere, right?"

"No. This is where I have to stay."

"Well, this may be useful to you sometime. There is a large network of abbeys and convents that have radio transmitters and supply the abbot with information about German troop movements when they hear about them. The Convent of Our Lady of Sorrows in Gallicano is one of them. The abbot is sort of Operation Central and when he gets any little piece of information he lets the partisans know about it. Just two weeks ago the abbot heard from a convent that the Germans were planning to attack Corfino and the abbot told Leopardo. Leopardo rounded up his troops and they attacked the Germans. Two Germans were killed and the others fled. The partisans weren't hurt."

"Wow. That's what the abbot said! That's amazing."

He suddenly felt far away from the quiet life in Molazzana.

"But," Pasquale said, "the abbot started talking about something else, about helping people who are fleeing the Nazis, and then he didn't want to talk anymore. What's that about?"

"Well, you must know about the racial laws that were passed in 1938."

Pasquale said he couldn't remember if his Catholic school taught that.

Tonio sighed. "Well, the first laws restricted the civil rights of Jews. Their books were banned and they were excluded from holding public office or teaching in higher education. Then more laws stripped Jews of their assets, restricted their travel and even said they could be sent to concentration camps."

"Really? I didn't know that."

"Then when Italy entered the war in 1939 some Jews were actually sent to two separate concentration camps in Italy. And that's why so many are fleeing. The next thing will probably be sending them to Germany, where they'll surely be killed."

This was too much for anyone to absorb, much less a twelve-year-old.

"I never knew any of this. But I know of one family in Molazzana, the Rosens. I was friends with the son, David. All of a sudden they weren't there anymore. We never found out why."

"It's terrible to think how inhuman human beings can be. But now there are many monasteries and convents and parish houses that are hiding Jewish people. Yes, the Abbey of Saint Gaudentius is one of them."

He looked around again and whispered in Pasquale's ear. "There's actually a family in the cellar now. Parents and four kids. I think one of the boys is about your age."

Pasquale did not sleep well again that night, but it was not because of the smell or chapel bells.

IN THE MIDDLE of her first night, Luciana began to scream. Sister Rosetta ran in to hold her, but Luciana didn't want to say anything other than "bad people." The nun told her stories and hummed simple hymns, and eventually the girl settled down and went back to sleep. Sister Rosetta didn't sleep after that.

In the morning, Luciana held the nun's hand as they went to the chapel for Mass.

"You know, Luciana," Sister Rosetta said, "this is the convent of Our Lady of Sorrows, so there is a statue of her in the chapel."

Luciana said she'd never heard of Our Lady of Sorrows.

"Then I'd better tell you so you won't be shocked by the statue," Sister Rosetta said. "Our Lady of Sorrows is one of many names that have been given to the Blessed Mother. This devotion started many centuries ago, way back in the 1200s. Now there are prayers said to her in countries all over the world."

"Why is she called Our Lady of Sorrows?"

"Someone long ago counted seven great sorrows in her life. I don't think I can remember them all, but I know there was the time that Jesus was lost in the temple and Mary and Joseph were so worried. And the crucifixion of Our Lord, of course. And the soldier who pierced His side with a sword. That's three, I can't remember the others."

Luciana made a face. "It all sounds very sad to me."

The chapel, converted from a ballroom in the old villa, was filled with statues, big and small, and where there was space between them, vigil lights glowed. Luciana had never seen so many saints and didn't know the name of a single one. The statue above the altar was indeed sad. Mary had seven swords piercing her heart and she looked heavenward in great agony.

"I don't like her," Luciana said. "She's scary."

"Yes, well, she's our patron. Mass is about to begin."

The convent didn't have its own priest but was served by those from the Abbey of Saint Gaudentius. Today the priest was Father Luca Pelllegrini, a man with broad shoulders and a long beard who rushed through the Mass as though he wanted to get back for breakfast. The Mass lasted less than a half hour.

"Do you like to go to Mass?" Sister Rosetta asked as they left.

"We didn't go much at home."

"Oh, that's a shame. Do you know why?"

"Stefano, he's the man who took us in, told my brother and me once that we didn't have to go. He said he was mad at God for letting our parents be killed, so he didn't go. And we could be mad at God, too."

"Are you mad at God, Luciana?"

"No. Well, sometimes. I don't know."

With that, she began to sob, and Sister Rosetta put her arms around her. "Well, I'm sure God isn't mad at you."

They moved on to the refectory and Luciana allowed the sister to fill her tray.

"Look," Sister Rosetta said, "we have scrambled eggs today. Wouldn't you like some?"

Luciana chose bread that she dipped in milk instead.

The other nuns gushed, patted her hair and tweaked her cheeks when they finished and returned their trays. Luciana hated it.

"Try to like all this," Sister Rosetta said. "We nuns aren't used to having a precious little girl around. Come. Let's help the other sisters make Communion hosts."

They went into the room off the kitchen, which was jammed with a half dozen nuns working with hot griddles and cutting machines. Luciana's first task was to measure pitchers of water that to be mixed with flour, and then to use a large wooden spoon to take all the lumps out.

She was too young to get near the griddles that turned out large, round, paper-thin wafers. These would be chilled overnight and then put into another machine to be cut into the smaller hosts the next day.

"We can get seventy hosts from one of these large ones," a cheerfully plump Sister Filomena said as she took a rack out of the refrigerator. "That means, if we're going to supply all the parishes around here, we need to make at least forty-two hundred hosts every day."

Luciana was given the task of counting out batches of fifty hosts and putting them in plastic bags. She soon found this boring, and instead of fifty, she was putting forty-eight, forty-nine, fifty-two into the bags. She began to cry.

"There, there, I know," the sister said. "I know this isn't much fun, but the churches need the hosts for Mass. Some of them can't even afford them so we give them away."

Sister Rosetta didn't know what to do next with the little girl, who seemed to tag along wherever she went. Convents didn't have many fun things for a ten-year-old.

"I know. Why don't you sit on the front steps and watch the people in the piazza?"

"Do I have to?"

"It would be nice."

After placing Luciana on the front steps, Sister Rosetta told Mother Elena, "I think we may have a problem here."

BECAUSE EVERYONE ELSE in the monastery worked on other tasks, Pasquale was free to roam throughout the cavernous building on his own. Whenever he was asked where he was going, he found an excuse: looking for the lavatory, going to his cell for a rest, just taking a walk. No one believed him, and he was grateful for their smiles.

He avoided the infirmary and didn't spend much time in the chapel, except to count the number of tiny votive candles in the place. Two hundred and eight-two.

Pasquale found a friendly monk in the kitchen who easily snuck leftover pastries to the boy and, meeting Brother Antonio, he found something to do.

"Come," Tonio said, "I want to show you something I'm certain you've never seen before."

They climbed to the *scriptorium*, where beautiful handmade jewel-encrusted books still stacked the shelves.

"In the Middle Ages," Tonio said, "teams of monks copied these books letter by letter, word by word."

He took down a thick volume covered with dust and opened the pages. "See what I mean? They are truly works of art, aren't they?"

Pasquale was usually not easily impressed, but even he stood in awe. Speechless, in fact.

"We had," Tonio said, "many many many years ago a member of the congregation called Brother Marco. He made the most beautiful of all the books here. Here, this is one of them."

He took down another book and opened a page to a brilliantly colored painting of the Annunciation to the Blessed Mother.

"Look at that," he said. "This could belong in a museum."

Even Pasquale had to agree.

"We can't let these books remain here," Tonio said. "We need to put them in boxes and store them in a hidden room in the cellar. We've heard the Germans are raiding monasteries and other places for artworks and they will certainly want these. Do you want to help?"

"Sure."

He soon found out that the books were heavier than he imagined. He could carry only three at a time, down the circular steps and then down a back stairway to the lowest regions of the abbey. Tonio unlocked a dusty, windowless room that had once been used to store empty wine casks. The moldy smell lingered.

"The books may not smell as well if they stay here long, but at least they'll be safe," he said. "And let's hope they won't stay long."

They arranged pallets to keep the books off the damp and broken floor, and then found boxes. It was past the evening meal before they completed the work. Although the cellar was cold and damp, they were both sweating.

"Wait," Tonio said. "Before we go up I want to check on something."

He led Pasquale through a long corridor, into and out of two other musty rooms and against a concrete wall.

"We're here," he said.

"Where?"

Tonio reached around a stone that jutted out of the wall, pulled out a key, pounded on the wall hard three times and softly four times, and unlocked what had appeared to be just a part of the wall. A door opened.

"Neat!" Pasquale shouted.

Pasquale's eyes gradually adjusted to a large room lit only by a few lanterns. Next to it he could see a small room with a toilet and sink.

"We used to store empty wine bottle crates here," Tonio said, "but now we're putting it to better use."

A middle-aged man and woman sat on a wooden bench, and four children, two boys and two girls, sprawled on the floor. The monks had furnished the room as best they could with four cots, benches, a couple of chairs, a table, old rugs, a Bible and children's books.

"Hello!" Tonio said. "How are you all doing? I brought a new young friend who is going to stay with us for a while. This is Pasquale."

The boy shook hands with the father, Baruch, the mother, Esther, daughters Leah and Miriam, and sons Menachem and Levi, and then stood awkwardly in a corner.

Tonio explained that the Bilderman family had been the only Jews in Castelnuovo di Garfagnana, where the father worked as a carpenter and the family was accepted like any other. Since the fighting began, however, residents had conflicting opinions. Some expected the Germans to invade the town and take the family away, and if that happened, others might be arrested for complicity. They feared for their own lives.

Others were more sympathetic and looked for a place where the family could hide and be safe until the fighting had ceased. They found the Abbey of Saint Gaudentius four months ago.

Tonio and Baruch discussed the family's needs, which weren't many. The kitchen had been attempting to make their meals as kosher as possible, although the rules were often bent. Fortunately, chickens, eggs and vegetables were in good supply.

Each evening, before dusk, they were permitted to spend an hour in the courtyard before *Arvit,* the evening prayer, providing that no artillery could be heard in the hills.

"We thank God every minute that we are here," Baruch said. "What more can we ask for?"

"I will try to get you more books, perhaps even something in Hebrew," Tonio said.

Levi, the oldest boy at twelve, went up to Pasquale and, like boys everywhere meeting for the first time, didn't say anything, just stood there.

"Hi!" Pasquale finally said.

"Hi!"

That broke the ice and they tried to find something of mutual interest. Since professional soccer teams had been abandoned during the war, they couldn't talk about the Italian teams. Since Levi wasn't allowed to go to movies, he didn't know any stars. They finally discovered that both liked to play guitars.

"I had a guitar when I was a kid," Pasquale said. "But I didn't take it with me."

"Where did you go?"

Pasquale declined to talk about his history with this new friend. "I just went someplace else."

"I had to leave my guitar at home when they took us away," Levi said. "But look what I have."

He pulled a harmonica out of his pocket. "My father says I have to play this real soft. He doesn't want anyone to hear it. Anyway, I only know a few songs."

After dusting the mouthpiece, he began to play a shaky version of "Mary Had a Little Lamb."

"Hey!" Pasquale said. "That's neat."

Levi obliged by trying "Home on the Range," stopping every few seconds for air.

"I'm just learning that one, but, hey, I know this one really well." "Auld Lang Syne" was nearly faultless.

"Think you could teach me?" Pasquale asked.

"Sure. Wait. I have to ask my father something."

Returning with the question answered, Levi said he actually had another harmonica. He dug into another pocket.

"Want this one?"

"Really?"

"I don't need two."

He said Pasquale could come to visit anytime and they could practice.

"I'm not going anywhere," he said.

"Neither am I," Pasquale said.

SISTER ROSETTA was grateful that the nuns' weekly visit to poor families in Gallicano was the following day. She would take Luciana along.

"This village may be small," Sister Rosetta explained, "but there are many poor people. Some of the men have been drafted, so there's no one to take care of the fields or the animals. And of course the weather has been bad this year and the crops have been horrible."

She handed Luciana a basket containing loaves of bread and bunches of beans, lettuce and corn. She herself carried two baskets with more food, three men's shirts and two pair of pants.

"These are from old Luigi Pini. He died a few weeks ago and his widow thought someone else might be able to use these."

The first stop was at the home of Rosella, a woman in her seventies who had never married. With too much makeup and with her gray hair flowing past her shoulders, she greeted the visitors with hugs and kisses.

"You don't know how much I've waited for you to come. Nobody comes to see me anymore. They say I talk too much. Well, I don't think so. It's just because I'm lonely and I want to see people. But nobody comes to see me anymore. You were the last people, and that was a week ago, and I used up all the eggs by the third day, but I don't mind. As long as you're here, that's what matters because no one ever comes to see me anymore."

Sister Rosetta gave her a hug. "We're happy to see you again, Rosella, and glad that you're looking so well."

"Well, I try. It's hard living alone and having such awful neighbors. They yell and scream and I yell right back. I see them staring at me through the window. I know what they're thinking. They wish I would go away. But how can I go away with all the fighting going on? It's terrible, this fighting."

Sister Rosetta moved in front of Luciana so that Rosella couldn't see that the girl was terrified. She handed over bread, beans, eggs and three ears of corn, and hugged the old woman again. She promised she'd see her again in a week.

"Don't be afraid of Rosella," Sister Rosetta said. "She's really a very nice person, just so lonely and afraid to live alone in a time like this."

At the next home, the nun gave the shirts and pants to an elderly woman who whispered that her husband was having many "accidents" and that she couldn't keep up with the laundry. Sister Rosetta also found a chocolate bar in her basket.

"Why don't you split this?"

Their next stop was at the Marconi home. Withered grass surrounded what was little more than the old shed it once was.

"We won't stay long here," Sister Rosetta said. "Adolfo left home a year ago and his wife is still angry."

"Whaddya want?" Monica Marconi screamed from inside the house.

"We brought you a little food," the nun called back.

"Leave it outside!"

"Do you think we could see little Pietro? We didn't see him last time."

The door opened and a scrawny boy about five ventured out. He wore nothing but a pair of underpants.

"Pietro! How are you?" Sister Rosetta bent down but, having learned from past experiences with the boy's temper, did not touch him.

"Gimme the stuff," he said.

She put a loaf of bread, four eggs and some vegetables in a paper bag. He grabbed it out of her hands and ran back into the house.

Pietro reminded Luciana of her brother, only much younger. She wondered what Pasquale was doing now.

"Come along now, Luciana. We have one more stop to make."

Viola Zorella's cottage was surrounded by tall elms at the edge of the village. Sister Rosetta and Luciana walked up the cobblestone path, and although the day was bright and sunny, the house was hidden in a forest of pines. Luciana thought that it looked like the house of the legendary old woman *La Befana* like in her book.

Small and tidy, it was painted bright blue with a red door and shutters. A half-moon was painted under the eaves, and a weathervane with a rooster stood in the peak where the four sides of the tiled roof met.

"Now don't be nervous," the sister said. "Once you get to know her, Viola is quite nice. It's just that some people say she has some unusual talents."

"Like what?"

"Well, they say she can see into the future. Some people believe it, and they come here to have their fortune told. The Catholic Church doesn't believe any of this, of course, but Viola is a sweet woman and we need to love her."

"Is she a witch? Like *La Befana*?"

"No, no. She's a very nice person."

The door opened and a woman of uncertain age, with a mass of frizzy red hair arranged in dozens of curls, and with freckles on her face and arms, appeared. She wore a long black dress that barely concealed bright red slippers. A dozen necklaces covered her bosom and multiple rings sparkled from her fingers. Her cheeks were painted orange-red.

"Sister, Sister! I knew you'd come today! I love it when you come here! Come, give me a hug!"

Sister Rosetta obliged, and Luciana stayed far behind.

"And who is this lovely child?"

Introductions were made.

"Oh, you must meet Gemma!" Viola said. "Gemma! Come out here. Now!"

With even brighter red hair and freckles, Gemma appeared in the doorway. She was about a foot taller than Luciana, with husky arms and big hands. She wore a plaid shirt and brown pants.

"What do you want?" she asked her mother.

"I want you to meet little Luciana. You two can be friends. You can play together."

Luciana hid behind Sister Rosetta's black habit.

AFTER TWO WEEKS, Pasquale was clearly bored with life at the Abbey of Saint Gaudentius. When he was at Molazzana he could at least go outside and wander through the farm fields and into the hills. He could swim in the pond and lie on the banks looking at the sky. He had a secret cave where he stored his treasures: a piece of plaster that he was certain had come from Roman times, a wooden box with old coins, a dead butterfly, the bell from his bicycle, the collar of his dog Luna from the time when he was home. He missed old Luna.

That made him think about his parents. Sometimes now he had trouble remembering what they looked like, but he knew that their home was always a warm and comforting place. Then he thought about Stefano and Carolina. Once in a while he felt bad about the way he had treated them. When he saw them again, he would tell them he was sorry. If he ever saw them again.

In Molazzana he could play games with Luciana even though she always cheated. He wondered what Luciana was doing. Probably having more fun than he was. It was the first time he had thought of his sister since he arrived at the abbey.

Since the monastery was so big, he spent his first days discovering various hidden places, including what apparently was a stash of hard liquor in the laundry room.

If he stood on the chair in his cell he could look out the window onto the green hills in the distance and miniature villages in the valleys. He desperately wanted to go out and run and run and run, but artillery fire often blasted the silence and he felt more and more confined.

Life for a twelve-year-old boy in an old monastery with old monks was stupid.

Brother Antonio knew this and tried to amuse the boy with stories. "Didn't the abbot mention our saint? Saint Giacomo?"

"Yes. He said there's a shrine and it has a statue that works miracles."

"Some people believe that. But Giacomo was a holy young man and he was probably murdered, so we like to pray to him."

"Why was he murdered?"

"Who knows? They think another monk was jealous."

"Well, I don't think a statue can work miracles," Pasquale said.

"Have I told you about the ghost?" Tonio asked.

"Ghost? What ghost? No!"

"Well, in the fourteenth century a ghost was supposedly seen around the monastery many times. He wasn't scary. In fact, he was rather gentle and the monks were even glad to see him."

"Why was there a ghost in the first place? Was some dead monk seeking revenge?"

"No, I don't think so. The story is—and remember this was centuries ago and the story has probably changed over the years—the story is that the ghost was trying to scare a monk who was beating himself for his sins."

"Wait! Whoa! Beating himself for his sins. You're making this up."

"I am not! Oh my, do I have to go into all this?"

"Yes! Tell me!"

So Brother Antonio gave a brief history of the Flagellant movement in the fourteenth century and how people marched around beating themselves, but then the pope condemned the whole thing and it died out.

"But there was still this monk who did it?"

"The pope said that people could do it on their own, so the monk thought that was OK."

"Didn't people try to stop him?"

"The abbot tried but the monk wouldn't listen."

"And the ghost? Did this ghost really scare the monk?"

"Yes, as a matter of fact. The monk turned his life around and started to help the poor, sort of like Saint Francis."

Pasquale thought for a while. "I don't think I believe any of this."

"It's up to you. But you know that cell next to yours? That's where the monk lived. You can still see blood stains on the floor."

"Really? Can I see?"

"Some other day. Let's go to the kitchen and see what desserts we're having for dinner."

The best part of the day was the evening when he could join Brother Antonio or other monks in visiting the Bilderman family in the cellar and he and Levi could go outside for an hour. The same age, they had become best friends, well, each other's only friend.

They didn't do much, just lay on the grass and looked up at the stars that were emerging from the heavens.

"Look, there's the Big Dipper," Levi said one night. "And there's the Great Bear."

"Where?"

"The dipper's handle is the bear's tail, see?"

"Oh."

"My father," Levi said, "told us all about the stars and constellations. Aquarius, Aries, Cancer, the Centaur, Corona Borealis. When I was little I could recite all of them."

"Oh." Pasquale didn't tell his friend he didn't have a father to tell him about the stars.

They looked at stars some more.

"I wish I could fly," Levi said.

"Me, too."

"I'd fly all the way to...all the way to...all the way to Barga."

"I don't even know where that is."

"My father told me about it once. He studied at the temple there."

They thought about that for a while.

"I never liked school," Pasquale said.

"Me neither."

They stared at the stars some more.

"Pasquale," Levi said, "did you bring your harmonica along?"

"It's in my pocket."

"Want to play?"

"Sure."

Levi began:

"Oh give me a home…

Pasquale responded:

Where the buffalo roam…

And alternately:

"And the deer and the antelope play.
"Where seldom is heard
"A discouraging word
"And the skies are not cloudy all day."

Levi and Pasquale were laughing so hard Levi's father came over to tell them to quiet down.

"Your mother and I are trying to have a conversation."

Pasquale and Levi moved farther away, but were still in sight of the rest of the family. They tried another song.

"Mary had a little lamb
"Little lamb, little lamb
"Mary had a little lamb
"Its fleece was white as snow…"

The boys were so thrilled they shook hands.
"Hey," Levi said, "I just learned another one."

"Row, row, row your boat
"Gently down the stream
"Merrily, merrily, merrily, merrily
"Life is but a dream…"

Levi's father came over again.
"Boys, I'm sorry, but you're still too loud. Move a little farther away. Maybe just over that little hill. But not too far, remember!"

Putting their harmonicas in their pockets, the boys crawled through some ruts and wet grass until they were suddenly in a darkening forest.

"Pasquale," Levi said, "we can't see my family anymore."
"Are you afraid?"

"No. Why should I be afraid?"

They walked a little farther and found a path.

"Want to see what it leads to?" Pasquale asked.

"Yes!"

SISTER ROSETTA said she had good news for Luciana. Because the convent was having its semiannual mini-retreat that afternoon, all the nuns would be in the chapel from 1 o'clock to 5 o'clock praying, meditating and reading spiritual books.

"I won't be around to be with you," she said, "but I've arranged that you can go play with Gemma."

"Gemma? That big girl in that funny house?"

"Yes! Remember you met her two weeks ago? I'm sure Gemma is very nice and you'll have fun playing together."

"But she's so old!"

"I know she's big for her age, but she's only eleven, and you're ten, so you're practically the same age."

"Do I have to?"

"Luciana, I really don't want to leave you alone here. There's nothing to do in the afternoons when we don't go on our visits."

"I could read my books. I could play with Francesca."

"Luciana, it would be good to make new friends, OK? Otherwise you're stuck with all these old women all the time."

The girl tried not to cry.

"OK," she said.

When they arrived at the Zorella home they found that Gemma had had the same reaction when her mother told her of the plan for the afternoon.

"That kid?" Gemma had said. "I'm supposed to play with that little kid?"

"Look, I don't know anything about her, where she's from, why she's with Sister Rosetta, but the sister has been so good to us so when she telephoned, I couldn't say no. And the girl seems nice. A little shy, but she's only ten, and you're eleven."

Gemma was standing glumly at the doorway when the visitors arrived.

"There you are," Viola said, hugging Sister Rosetta again and pushing Gemma toward Luciana. "I'm really glad Luciana could come over to play. Gemma was getting bored, weren't you, Gemma? Well, you two girls have fun. I'll be downstairs if you need me."

With that, and with Sister Rosetta on her way back to the convent, the girls found themselves alone.

"Why did you bring that stupid doll?" Gemma asked.

"This is Francesca. She's been with me forever."

Luciana felt tears building up again.

"Dolls are for little kids. Let's go to my room."

When Luciana was young, before the accident that killed her parents, she had her own room, decorated in pink and white and with frilly curtains and a chenille bedspread. A painting of the Virgin Mary was on one wall and one of Jesus with a bleeding heart on another. After the accident, and the move to the new home, she shared a bedroom with Stefano and Carolina and Pasquale. There were no pictures on the walls.

Gemma's room was painted bright orange, but most of that was hidden by posters: Alberto Rabagliati, Trio Lescano, Nunzio Filogamo, Chiaretta Gelli.

"These are my favorite Italian singers," Gemma said. "My grandfather, he lives in Barga and has a phonograph, and I play his records when I go there."

Luciana had never heard of the singers and wasn't quite sure what a phonograph was.

Gemma sat in the only chair in the room and Luciana sat on the floor. She hid Francesca behind her back.

"OK," Gemma said, "want to play some games?"

Luciana nodded, not sure what was in store.

"I have this book of riddles. Let me try you."

She took a book off a shelf and opened it.

"Here's one. Why did the orange stop in the middle of the road?"

"Um. I don't know," Luciana said.

"Because it ran out of juice. Well, OK, that's not so great. Let me look for another one. Here. What kind of fish chases a mouse? That's easy."

"I don't know."

"A catfish! Get it, a catfish!"

Luciana tried to smile.

"Want me to do a magic trick?" Gemma asked.

"OK."

Gemma took a calendar off the wall and gave Luciana a pencil and a piece of paper.

"OK, choose three dates in December, but they have to be in succession, one after the other, and write them down. I'm not looking."

Luciana wrote down December 24, 25 and 26, but didn't show Gemma her paper.

"OK, now add those up and what do you get?"

"75."

"OK, you chose the 24th, 25th and 26th of December."

"How did you know that?"

"Well, I'm not supposed to tell you, but I divided 75 by 3 and got 25 as the middle date, so then the other dates are December 24 and 26. You can do it with any three numbers as long as they're in succession."

Luciana tried to remember this.

Gemma pulled a deck of cards from the shelf. "Want to see a card trick?"

Luciana's father used to play cards with friends, but he never showed her any tricks.

Gemma shuffled the deck over and over, then fanned the cards and asked Luciana to pick one and put it at the bottom of the deck.

She then made a big show of cutting the cards four times. Then she started flipping the cards until she saw one and asked Luciana, "Is this the one?"

"Yes! How did you do that?"

"I'm just smart. That's kid's stuff. I can do a lot more things. My mother taught me."

"Like what?"

"I can tell you something that's going to happen."

"Can't!"

"Can!"

"Show me."

"I will. What do you want me to tell you?"

Luciana stumbled, and the only thing she could think of was whether it would rain tomorrow.

"All right," Gemma said. "Now don't say a word. Be real quiet."

Gemma lay down on the bed and closed her eyes. Her arms at her sides, she didn't move. Soon her breathing slowed until it got to the point where Luciana feared she had died.

Then her breathing resumed and she sat up.

"It's not going to rain tomorrow. It's going to be sunny."

"Really? How did you know that?"

"I know things."

"How?"

"My mother showed me. My mother's amazing!"

When Sister Rosetta arrived to take her back to the convent, Luciana was excited.

"Sister, Gemma knows things that are going to happen. She said it's going to be sunny tomorrow."

"Luciana, it's been raining for the last twelve days and the forecast is for rain from now until Christmas. I think Gemma is pulling your leg."

Luciana wasn't surprised the next day when the sun came out early in the morning and shone the entire day. The rain only resumed the following day.

That night, Luciana slept until dawn and didn't have a nightmare.

WITH THE SUDDEN NIGHTFALL, the towering trees in the forest blotted out the sky and seemed even more menacing. Two hawks broke the eerie silence screeching at each other. Only a sliver of a moon gave occasional light through the wavering pines.

"Levi," Pasquale whispered, "I think we should go back. Your parents are going to worry."

"I know I'm going to be late for *Arvit*," Levi mouthed.

"What's that?"

"The evening prayer."

"Why are we whispering?" Pasquale asked.

"I don't know. There's nobody here. Let's turn around."

But where? They were confronted by a path going in one direction, and another going the other way.

"Didn't we come from that way? We passed that big rock. I remember."

"No, we came from that way, where the tree lost its bark. I remember that."

They stood still.

"I'm sure it was that way," Levi said.

"No, that way."

"Are we lost?"

"No! We just need to find the way back."

Lacking any sense of direction, the boys stood still. Pasquale put his arm around Levi. Levi put his arm around Pasquale. They could feel each other's heart racing.

"If only…" they said together.

"Maybe if we played our harmonicas, my father could hear us," Levi said.

"Good idea."

Levi played a few bars of "Mary Had a Little Lamb" and Pasquale played a few more and they waited. And waited.

Silence.

Pasquale tried "Home on the Range" and Levi joined in.

Silence.

They tried "Row, Row, Row Your Boat." Nothing.

"Let's go," Pasquale said. "We have to try one way."

Before they could decide which way to go, a large hand gripped Pasquale's shoulder and another hand grabbed Levi's. They couldn't move.

"Who are you?" a voice said. "What are you doing here?"

In the darkness, they could hardly make out the face of the man. It was smeared with black paint. His clothes were also dark and he wore a crimson bandana around his head. A rifle hung on his back. He was out of breath, as if he'd been running. Four other figures stood in the darkness behind him.

"We…we…we were just walking in the woods," Pasquale said.

"Just walking?"

"Yes," Levi said, "but we sort of can't find our way back."

The man let go of Pasquale's shoulder. "What's your name? Where do you live?"

"My name is Pasquale. I used to live in Molazzana but now I live in that big monastery over the hill," he said.

"And you?"

"I'm Levi. I used to live in Castelnuovo di Garfagnana but now I live in that monastery, too."

"The monastery over the hill? You mean the Abbey of Saint Gaudentius?"

"Yes, that one."

"How odd. I happen to know someone there. We, uh, we keep in touch."

"Who are you?" Pasquale dared to ask.

"You can call me Leopardo."

"Leopardo!" Pasquale said. "Brother Antonio told me about you. You're the partisan that the abbot talks to. He told you about the Germans coming and you fought them and two of them were killed but not any partisans."

"The abbot is a wonderful man, taking chances like that. If the Germans ever found out they'd kill every monk in the monastery."

"Really?" Levi said.

"And you, Levi, what are you doing there?"

"My family lives in a room in the cellar."

Leopardo knew all too well why the family was there. Jewish families were hiding in at least four churches and convents in the area.

"We're just getting back from a skirmish at Camporgiano," Leopardo said. "We heard about it from, um, a source. No big deal. They lost four. We didn't lose any."

"Wow," Pasquale said.

Leopardo introduced the others. There was Cane, who had dropped out of the University of Pisa after his brother was killed in the battle of Stalingrad. Tigre said his wife left him, taking two kids, when he joined Leopardo. Gatto was one of six women in the band. She was only seventeen, the youngest daughter of a construction worker in Barga. Leone had been studying to be a priest and didn't know now whether he would go back to the seminary. There were others, Leopardo explained, but they were on patrol.

"Maybe we'd better go back to the abbey before the Germans get closer," Levi said. "Can you point the way?"

THE DAY AFTER Luciana's visit with Gemma, Sister Rosetta was surprised—and delighted—when Luciana not only asked, but actually begged, to go back to Gemma's house.

"I thought you didn't like her, that she was too old for you."

"No, actually she's nice. She knows so much stuff. She said she has some more things she wants to show me."

Since the convent was way behind in making hosts and needed her help, Sister Rosetta agreed. When she took Luciana to the Zorella home right after lunch, Gemma was waiting.

"You know what?" Gemma said. "My mother says you can watch her do something this afternoon. There will be other people there."

"What is she going to do?"

"You'll find out. My mother is amazing. She can do all these things. She can tell your fortune. She can see into the future."

"How does she know all that?"

"I dunno. She said she inherited it. Her mother could do it, too. And her grandmother. And her grandmother's mother. I don't know how far back it goes. Come on."

Gemma led Luciana inside to what appeared to be the living room. The dark curtains were closed and the only light came from two blue candles on a buffet against the wall. There was an odd smell.

"What's that?"

"Incense," Gemma whispered.

"Like in church?"

"Yes. Be quiet. And sit on this bench with me."

A round table in the middle of the room was covered with a black cloth. In the center was a large white globe made of some kind of glass. Gemma's mother again wore a long black dress and bright red slippers. She had a rhinestone tiara in her red curls. Even in the darkness her assorted necklaces and rings sparkled. She sat on one side in front of the candles.

An older woman with gray hair in a bun at the top of her head was on her left, a younger woman with blond hair and glasses was on her right, and another older woman was across the table.

"Welcome, Luciana," Viola Zorella said softly. "Now we can begin."

Gemma nudged Luciana. "Now don't say a word."

Viola Zorella put her hands on the table and, staring at the ball, began to breathe deeply, just as Gemma had done in her room.

Now Viola closed her eyes. She was barely breathing. The other women, also with their eyes closed, sat quietly, their hands in their laps.

Luciana was getting nervous and looked at Gemma. But Gemma was also in some sort of trance. Luciana tried not to jiggle her feet and tried closing her eyes, but she was so curious about what was going on that she kept opening them and staring at the women, especially Gemma's mother.

The clock on the wall seemed to have stopped, but the big hand had actually moved fifteen minutes when Viola suddenly leaned closer to the ball.

"I can see something now."

The other women moved forward.

"There are black clouds. They are filling the space. They are moving. Now there is an opening."

Luciana held her breath.

"I see a village," Viola said. "There is a name on it."

"What is it?" the woman with her hair in a bun whispered.

"Castelnuovo di Garfagnana."

Viola waited, then shook her head. She put her hands on the crystal ball and opened her eyes. She began to breathe normally.

"I don't like that message," she sighed.

"What does it mean?" the younger woman asked.

"Well, we know," Viola said, "that the Germans are advancing north, killing everything in their path. They must be on their way to Castelnuovo di Garfagnana."

As one, the women gasped. "They're moving faster than we thought." "What are we going to do?" "We need to get word to someone."

"Wait," Viola said. "I see clouds. They're black again. Very black. Very very black."

They waited some more.

"There is a bridge. That's all I see. The clouds have disappeared."

All of this remained a mystery to Luciana, but when she returned to the convent she told Sister Rosetta what happened and then she said that the people thought that the Germans were approaching Castelnuovo di Garfagnana, "wherever that is," and that somehow there was a bridge.

"Castelnuovo di Garfagnana? Yes, there is a bridge there. I must tell Mother Elena."

Hearing the news, Mother Elena dropped her prayer book, rushed to her office and took the black cloth off her machine.

"What am I doing?" she thought to herself. "Sending a message to the abbot from a ten-year-old girl who says a woman saw a message in a crystal ball? This is ridiculous. Still, I can't take chances."

IN A CAVE LIT BY A SINGLE LANTERN, Leopardo and the others prepared for another skirmish. All they needed was word from a source on where it would be.

"Waiting, waiting," Cane said. "This is the worst part."

Wide-eyed, Pasquale and Levi sat on rocks in a corner.

"Are you scared?" Levi asked.

"No," Pasquale said.

"Me neither."

"What do you think is going to happen?"

"I dunno. I hope they'll take us with them when they go," Levi said.

"Really?"

"Sure."

"Don't you want to?"

"Sure."

Tigre took out a paperback novel with a lurid cover and tried to read by the dim light. Leone sketched an owl on a notepad. Gatto pulled out a scarf she'd been knitting for weeks.

Then Leopardo heard a signal.

"This may be it," he said.

He went into the darkest corner of the cave. When he returned, he called everyone around a large boulder and spread out a long piece of brown paper that now served as a map.

Standing behind them, Pasquale and Levi peered over the partisans' shoulders. They could make out their hometowns, Castelnuovo di Garfagnana and, just south, Molazzana.

"That's where I used to live!" Levi whispered.

"And me!" Pasquale said.

"I just got word from my source," Leopardo began. "He told me that the Nazis were here and were moving north to Castelnuovo di Garfagnana. They should be there tomorrow. We have to get there before dawn."

"We'll have to hurry," Leone said.

"Look," Tigre said, "there's a bridge over the Serchio at Castelnuovo di Garfagnana. They'll have to cross it to go farther north."

Levi held his breath and nervously shifted from foot to foot.

"Can we dynamite the bridge?" Leone asked.

"It's going to be hard," Leopardo said. "It's big, it's high, it's long. But it's the only way the Germans can go north. If we can blow up the bridge when they're crossing, it will be a big victory."

Levi raised his hand. "I know that bridge! I used to live in Castelnuovo di Garfagnana. I swam under that bridge all the time. Really!"

"So?" Leopardo said.

"So can we come?"

"No, of course not. It's too dangerous. You're just kids."

"We're not kids!" Pasquale said. "We're twelve years old!"

"No," Leopardo said.

"Please," Levi said. "We won't be a bother. We won't say a word."

"No," Leopard said. "No."

"And maybe I can tell you things about the bridge," Levi said. "I know every inch of it, almost."

"No."

Cane whispered in Leopardo's ear. "What are we going to do? We can't leave them here alone, can we?"

"I don't know..."

"It's really not safe here," Cane said. "All the stuff that happens around here. Wild boars..."

Pasquale overheard that. "Wild boars?" he squeaked.

Leopardo looked at the other members of his band, then at Pasquale and Levi.

"Let me think," Leopardo said. "OK, let's load up."

The boys watched as the partisans packed a crate with sticks of dynamite and then armed themselves with a motley array of stolen rifles, pistols, guns they had used for hunting, daggers and knives. They slung bandoliers over their shoulders. They covered their faces with pitch and pulled on caps and heavy gloves.

"OK, let's go," Leopardo said.

"Us too?" Pasquale asked.

Leopardo frowned. "All right. You can't stay here. But stick with us. Like glue! Do what we tell you to do. And don't say a word. Understand?"

"Yes!" the boys said together.

Gatto covered the boys' faces with pitch and gave them dark hats to wear. Pasquale and Levi had never been so proud.

The group crawled out of the cave into a densely wooded area, and, ten feet apart, inched their way down a narrow path. Leopardo was followed by Gatto, then Pasquale, then Leone, then Levi, and, last, Tigre and Cane carrying the heavy crate of dynamite and equipment between them.

It was now 3 o'clock in the morning.

No one spoke. Moonlight, occasionally breaking through the pines, guided the invaders through the forest. Pasquale and Levi tried to keep pace with the others, and both boys stumbled and fell three times. Once, Pasquale nearly panicked when he lost sight of Gatto until he saw her slight frame far ahead. He hurried to catch up. They had to stop every twenty minutes to allow Tigre and Cane to put the crate down and rest.

It was now 4 o'clock.

Even though it was December 21 and chilly, all of them were sweating. And getting exhausted. Pasquale's feet hurt because he was wearing only sandals. Levi had boots, but they were old and torn. The backpacks they'd been given felt as if they were loaded with rocks and getting heavier with every stumbling footstep. They struggled to keep from crying.

It was now 6:30.

The skyline of Castelnuovo di Garfagnana was vaguely visible far in the distance. Levi recognized the bulky Ariosto's Castle and the tower of the Duomo. If he could have talked, he would have told Pasquale their history.

Farm fields replaced the woods as they got closer to the village. They could hear cows and horses rousing from their sleep. Without the cover of tall trees, they crouched lower to the ground.

It was now 7:15.

They reached the embankment to the Serchio and tripped, slid and tumbled down to the water's edge. They were at the south end of the bridge and it loomed above them. Leopardo gathered everyone in a clump of trees.

"OK, we have to hurry," he said. "The sun is already coming up. We don't have time to drill holes for the dynamite sticks. We'll just have to place them in good positions."

"Where?"

They walked under the bridge as far as they could and discovered that there were ledges high on both sides under the roadway.

"We'll have to put the dynamite up there," Leopardo said. "But we need someone small to climb there."

"I'm pretty small!" Gatto said. "I can go up there."

"I don't think small enough," Leopardo said.

The partisans looked at each other. Except for Gatto, who was not that small, all were husky men.

"I'm small!" Pasquale said.

"I'm small!" Levi echoed.

The partisans looked at the boys and at each other.

"No," Leopardo said. "We can't let you take the chance. What if you fell? What if you dropped the dynamite? No."

Everyone looked at the boys again.

"Leopardo," Tigre said. "We don't have a choice. Can't you see that?"

Leopardo walked around the others, stopped and put his hands on the boys' heads. "All right," he said.

Tigre and Cane put the detonator on the ground and the others loaded the boys' knapsacks with dynamite.

"OK," Leopardo said. "Be careful! Be very careful!"

He shook their hands. Gatto ran up and kissed the boys on both cheeks. "Please," she said, "don't take chances. Mother of God!"

They started to go when Leone whispered, "How will we know you got there and did the job?"

Levi looked at Pasquale. "We have a signal. Don't worry!"

With Pasquale on the east side and Levi on the west, they scrambled up the girders like little monkeys. In minutes they were out of sight.

"I hope we did the right thing," Leopardo said. "Oh, God!"

Minutes went by. Ten, fifteen, twenty, thirty. The partisans began to pace. They all lit cigarettes.

"Something's happened," Tigre said. "I know it."

Thirty-five minutes. Forty.

"I don't want to think about it," Leone said.

They paced some more. Cane began to tie twigs together. Leone kept checking his watch, the only one in the group. Gatto prayed aloud. *"Santa Maria, Madre di Dio…"*

Then far above them, they heard a faint sound. Music. It was on the east side of the bridge.

"Row, row, row your boat."

And from the other side: *"Gently down the stream."*

"What the…?" Leone said.

"Sounds like a harmonica," Tigre said. "Those kids!"

Faster than they had climbed up, the boys shimmied down the girders and ran to the group. Handshakes, hugs, kisses. Tigre produced a flask and passed it around, even to the boys, who were allowed to take very small sips.

When they had settled down, Leopardo told them to stay under the trees with the detonator.

"Now we wait. This may take all day."

THE NUNS at the Convent of Our Lady of Sorrows were distraught. Word had spread that because the Germans were so near, people should stay in their houses and should not gather in large groups.

"What are we going to do?" Sister Clara asked. "We can't call it off, can we? We've had the *Celebrazione della Natività* every year. For many many years."

"What's the *Celebrazione della Natività?*" Luciana asked.

Sister Rosetta sat the girl down in the study and explained.

For as long as anyone could remember, the Convent of Our Lady of Sorrows in Gallicano had been sponsoring live performances of the nativity story, the *Celebrazione della Natività*, on the three nights before Christmas each year. Under the nuns' supervision, a young mother would play Mary and an older man would be Joseph. Other villagers would play shepherds, kings and angels. A newborn baby would be found to play Jesus.

The performances were played out in front of the convent in the piazza before the eleventh-century church of San Jacopo Apostolo. People came from all over, some from as far away as Barga, and gathered around the square. Not a few brought along beer or bottles of wine. By the time the performance was to start, the place was lively with songs, jokes and jostling. Some people carried chairs and sat around the piazza or crouched on the eight long steps in front of the Romanesque-style church.

At 9 o'clock things quieted down, and all eyes turned toward via Domenico Bertini. Soon, a small horse, substituting for a donkey, carried Mary down the street to the crowd. She was followed by Joseph and the others. When they reached the piazza, the spectators cleared the way to the center, where the participants took their places. Medieval songs were sung, the scripture passage from Luke about the birth of Jesus was read ("In those days Caesar Augustus issued a decree that a census should be taken of the entire Roman world..."), and the priest blessed everyone with incense.

At that point, four little children carried a large basket containing a baby to Mary. She lifted it up, the crowd cheered, more incense was scattered, another hymn was sung, and the performance was over. It was followed by more colloquial songs, more drinking and more jokes and fun. Before the war started, the evenings concluded with fireworks, bright, noisy spectacles that lit the sky behind the church.

"This is such a shame," Sister Clara said. "Everybody has been rehearsing for weeks. The choir has been singing those old songs and the costumes have come out of the attic."

"And they've found a month-old baby boy for Jesus," Sister Matilda said.

Luciana, who had been ignored during all this, asked, "Why should it be canceled now? I don't understand."

Mother Elena explained that because of the Germans nearby, people should not be gathered in groups.

"Why not?"

"What if the Germans invaded us during the performance?" Mother

Elena said. "There would be all those people there. They wouldn't even have to round them up. And they'd shoot everyone dead in minutes."

Sister Rosetta covered Luciana's ears.

All of the nuns were well aware of the reports of the Germans doing just that across Italy. Only last August 12, in the village of Sant'Anna di Stazzema near the western coast, SS troops of the Panzergrenadier Regiment 35 had gone house to house executing villagers and then rounded up more than a hundred and forced them to the piazza in front of the sixteenth-century church. Despite the pleas of the parish priest, machine guns were turned on him and everyone else. After that, their bodies were burned. The SS men then sat down and ate lunch. In all, five hundred and sixty villagers were killed in three hours.

The horrific story spread across Tuscany and terrorized everyone who heard it. The nuns recited special prayers for the victims every night.

The nuns looked out at the empty piazza.

"Well, I guess we won't have the *Celebrazione della Natività* this year," Mother Elena said. "We'd be starting tonight."

"The first time since…since I don't know when," Sister Rosetta said.

The only thing they could do now was pray, and everyone went to the chapel to recite the rosary.

"*Santa Maria, Madre di Dio…*"

Luciana fingered the rosary that Sister had given her. She wondered if all this had something to do with Gemma's mother and the crystal ball. She wished she could go back and see what else Gemma's mother could predict.

Then the housekeeper burst into the chapel.

"The abbey just called!" she cried breathlessly. "The partisans…the partisans…have blown up the bridge at Castelnuovo di Garfagnana! The Germans were crossing and they were all killed!"

She had to catch her breath.

Mother Elena raised her arms.

"Thank you, God, and Blessed Mother," she cried. "Now we can have the *Celebrazione della Natività!*"

BACK IN THE ABBEY, Pasquale and Brother Antonio rushed down to the cellar where Levi had just begun to tell his family about the adventure.

"Wait!" Pasquale said, "let me tell!"

"I can do it!" Levi said.

"But I can tell it better!"

Brother Tonio interceded and told the boys to start at the beginning and then alternate in describing what had happened in the last days.

"Well," Levi said, "we had gone in the woods over there for just a minute and this huge guy—I mean he was gigantic—grabbed us and we knew he was a partisan..."

"His name was Leopardo and he had black paint on his face and..." Pasquale interrupted.

"Let me tell!" Levi said. "Anyway, he told us we couldn't come back here and we had to go with him and the others—there were others, too, maybe ten or twelve of them—into this secret place in the forest."

They continued the story, adding many dubious details, about how the partisans begged them to accompany them because they knew about the bridge and how dangerous it was in the forest. When they got to the part about the bridge they recounted in detail every step they took to get to the top, how they placed the dynamite sticks on the ledges and how they climbed down.

"The partisans were so happy for us," Pasquale said. "They hugged us and threw us up in the air and they said we were heroes."

"I bet we get a medal after this is over," Levi said.

"Who would give you a medal?" Tonio asked.

"I dunno. Somebody," Levi said.

"And then," Pasquale said, "we waited around until the Germans came and at the exact minute—the exact minute!—that they crossed the bridge, Leopardo gave the signal and the bridge blew up. And all the Germans fell into the river!"

"That's amazing!" Levi's father said. Everyone hugged and kissed and Tonio ran and got a couple of bottles of wine.

When all the shouting was over, Pasquale went to a corner and sat with his head in his hands. Tonio found him there.

"Tired?" he asked.

"Yes, but there's something else."

"Want to tell me what that is?"

"Levi has a family so they can be proud of him," Pasquale began. "I wish, I wish I had a family to tell this to. My papa and mama are dead. I don't know where Stefano and Carolina are. I don't even know where Luciana is."

Tonio put his arms around the boy. "I know, I know. I'm sorry."

Pasquale's tears stained Brother Tonio's black robes.

"When this is all over," Tonio said, "we'll find Luciana. When, dear God, this is all over."

TWELVE YEARS LATER, in 1956, Sister Mary Luciana received a letter from her brother. Pasquale was now studying history at the University of Bologna.

Dear Luciana,

I want to thank you again for inviting me to the celebration of your final vows, and I'm glad you scheduled it in conjunction with the *Celebrazione della Natività*. It was a beautiful ceremony, even if Baby Jesus cried all the while, and I still smile when I think of you wearing that black habit with the white wimple. I hope you are used to it by now.

It was also such a pleasure to see Stefano and Carolina again. They looked good, considering all that they've been through. I'm glad the farm is doing well again. I know I wasn't a very good son to them, and I realize now how much they did for us, taking us in like that. I'll always be grateful. I'm going to visit them on my next break.

And I was pleased that my friend from the monastery, Brother Antonio, or Tonio, was able to come down for the ceremony. I'm afraid he didn't look too well, but they still have so much work to do. Everyone thinks it was terrible that the Allies bombed Saint Gaudentius so late in the war, and there are only a couple of dozen monks now in what's left of the abbey. They don't even plan to rebuild Saint Giacomo's chapel, which was demolished.

I thought you'd be interested knowing that I've started the research for my dissertation. It's going to be on the role of the partisans in the battles in the Garfagnana around Christmas of 1944. I'll include my big role for those three days!

I've discovered that there were many battles that the Germans won during that time. I guess our little victory at Castelnuovo di Garfagnana was one of the few for the partisans and even the Allies. I still can't figure out how the abbot knew about the bridge there. I know he told the partisans, but how did he know? Amazing.

Well, anyway, thank goodness the war finally ended. We must always be grateful for the role of the partisans.

Now I have to write two more letters. First, to my friend Levi Bilderman, who is studying painting at the Accademia D'Arte in Florence. Then to the leader of the partisan band who went by the name Leopardo but who is really a lawyer, Nicolo Franco, in Genoa.

I will write again soon. Looking forward to hearing all about life in the convent.

With love,

Pasquale

Sister Mary Luciana folded the letter and put it in her prayer book. She would write back, telling him about convent life, about how they were still making hosts, and how she and Sister Rosetta were still delivering food to the poor. She was sorry that Mother Elena wasn't around anymore, and she missed Gemma and her mother, who had moved back to Camporgiano, where the family was originally from. Sometimes she stood in front of that funny house and wondered if Viola really could see things in that crystal ball.

THE VILLAGE THAT WENT TO SLEEP

2016

THE VISITORS

HEADPHONES FIRMLY IN PLACE, Andrew closed his eyes tight and mouthed the words to the song. *"Raise a glass to freedom/Something they can never take away/No matter what they tell you/Let's have another round tonight…"* His left foot kept time to the music, his fingers reverberated with the sounds. It was—his parents would swear—the four-thousand-six-hundred-twenty-eighth time that their son had listened to the score of the hit Broadway musical *Hamilton*.

Next to him, his sister Grace was sound asleep but smiling sweetly. The book she'd been reading seemed perilously close to falling to the floor.

One seat over, their mother, Nancy, was reading the latest gossipy book about Broadway. That is, until she slapped the book on her lap and nudged her husband, seated next to the window on her right.

"Carlo, there are so many mistakes in this book. Don't they have editors? Don't they have proofreaders?"

"What's this one?" Carlo asked.

"It says here…look, right here…it says 'Younger Than Springtime' is in the second act of *South Pacific*. Everyone knows it's in the first act. How they could be so stupid?"

"Well, maybe the author has never seen the show."

"Who in the world has not seen *South Pacific*? How could he write a book about musicals and not see *South Pacific*?"

"Not everyone has directed *South Pacific* like you have, Nancy."

"Four times! I'm getting sick of it, actually."

"I'm getting tired doing the sets for it, too. Really, I think those palm trees are getting moldy."

"The last Emile was so young. I think he was about twenty years old."

Nancy picked up the book again, daring the author to make another mistake or she wouldn't finish it. Carlo resumed reading today's *La Repubblica,* which he'd found at the airport in Frankfurt. After taking lessons four times he was now able to read Italian slowly and speak it if the other person was extremely patient. Nancy was even more adept. Languages came easily to her and she was fluent in French and Spanish as well. Even Andrew and Grace could get by now that the family had already visited Italy three times, and their father tried to have at least brief conversations in Italian at home.

Looking up, Carlo said, "I think we'll be landing in Florence in about an hour."

"Oh my God," Nancy said. "We're over the Alps. Grace, wake up! Andrew! Andrew!"

"He can't hear you with those headphones on," Carlo said. "Tell Grace to poke him."

Stretching from her nap, Grace poked her brother, who with a great display took the headphones off. "What? What?"

"We're going over the Alps," his mother said. "Look! They're so magnificent. My heart skips a beat every time we do this."

Andrew dutifully looked out the plane's window, shrugged and put his headphones back on.

"What can you expect from a fifteen-year-old kid," Carlo said.

"A lot more than this," Nancy said as she leaned over her husband to get a better view.

The plane soon banked and a short time later they were over Pisa.

"We're almost there," Carlo said. "Get organized."

Nancy and Grace put their books in their bags under their seats. Andrew remained lost in in the world of Alexander Hamilton and Aaron Burr.

"My heart starts racing every time I get this close," Carlo confessed. "I don't know why. It's strange."

"Well," Nancy said, "you're going back to your roots. I know that's important to you. I wish I had one country to claim."

"You've got more German than anything else."

"And French. And Danish. And Spanish. I'd do one of those Ancestry things but I don't think I want to know. What's the difference anyway? But you. You know exactly where you're from."

"Not only country, not only region, but the same village. There seems to be a Mantucci family in Sant'Antonio going back hundreds of years. If my grandfather and grandmother had stayed there after they got married, I wouldn't be here."

Nancy took out her lipstick and turned to her husband.

"It's going to be different this time, isn't it?"

"Yes," Carlo said.

"Without Lucia and Paolo."

"Yes."

"You're going to miss them. Well, we all will."

"Yes."

"It's too bad we couldn't get to their funeral. There just wasn't enough time, what with final exams to correct and the kids in school."

"Yes," Carlo said. "But now at least we can go to the anniversary Mass."

Zipping her purse, Nancy wondered, "Carlo, sometimes I forget how exactly you and Lucia were related."

"Her father and my grandfather were brothers. I guess that makes me…what…her second, third cousin? I don't know."

Carlo became engrossed in the big puffy clouds that floated underneath the plane. Momentarily, the earth was invisible and they were suspended in the universe.

"So now," Nancy said, "there's no one left."

"Well, Dino, of course. They're coming from Florence for the Mass."

"It'll be good to see him and Sophia and Tarik again. And Ezio and Donna."

"It's nice," Carlo said, "that Ezio and Donna were able to buy Lucia and Paolo's house and move down from the Cielo. I don't know how they could drive up that mountain all these years."

"Especially in winter. And they're in their nineties now."

They were going through the clouds now as the small plane began its descent. In Italian and English, the announcer told the passengers to fasten their seatbelts.

"Grace," Nancy said, "poke your brother again and tell him to take those headphones off and get organized."

She adjusted her seatbelt and turned to Carlo. "Have you decided what we're going to do after being in Sant'Antonio a couple of days? We've been to Rome and Venice…"

"…and Florence and Pisa and Siena. Three times. I don't know. I wish we could find a new place, an exciting place to visit. Well, we'll just see what happens."

They were all exhausted. The trip had begun yesterday afternoon with a one-hour drive from their home in Pennsylvania to the Philadelphia airport. Then a two-hour wait to board the eight-hour flight to Frankfurt. Then a five-hour wait before boarding another flight to Florence and another hour and a half in the air.

"There has to be an easier way, isn't there, Carlo?" Nancy asked as she pushed her empty cardboard coffee cup into the pocket on the seat in front of her.

"Nothing that we could afford. I'm pooped. We all are. But, you know, every time we land in Italy I am suddenly rejuvenated. I wait for this trip all year, and it's finally happening."

As always, they were surprised how small, how crowded, Florence's airport was. But it was efficient, and they went through customs and collected their bags in no time. Carlo led the group to the car rental area and made the transaction. Soon, they were headed on A11 past Prato, past Pistola.

In the back seat, Andrew, of course, wore his headphones and was oblivious. Grace closed her eyes and tried to sleep. Nancy commented on the green hills, the occasional hamlet, the lack of highway signs. In the warm June sun, Carlo just enjoyed being in the place where he felt so much at home.

AFTER THEY'D MADE the turn around Lucca, they knew they were close to their destination. It would be the first time they'd stayed at the Cielo since Ezio and Donna had moved out and down to the village. Happily, the new owners, Antonio and Francesca, continued to welcome visitors in what Italians called *agriturismo* and what Americans knew as a bed-and-breakfast with a little manual work involved.

"There seems to be more ruts in this road than usual," Carlo said, maneuvering the Fiat around one treacherous turn after another as they climbed up the mountain to the old farmhouse. "I didn't think there could be any more."

Nancy and Grace shut their eyes and hugged themselves. Andrew kept his eyes closed and his arms folded but was still in *Hamilton*'s grasp.

Finally, they pulled into the gravel parking space, and Antonio and Francesca rushed out to greet them. With the couple's vague understanding of English and a lot of gestures and hand maneuvers, the American family of four was soon settled in rooms on the second floor.

Carlo and Nancy had the big bedroom with a crimson bedspread and drapes. Andrew and Grace, despite their protests, were together in the smaller room across the hall. They had to share the bathroom.

"Good night," Nancy told the children.

"*Buona notte,*" Carlo said.

Andrew and Grace, although used to breakfasts with eggs and bacon and pancakes and cereal and toast at home, knew what to expect the following morning when Francesca invited them to *mangiare* with a basket of hard rolls and jam.

"Eat," Carlo whispered. "This is breakfast in Italy. We'll have lunch soon."

Led by Antonio, they toured the Cielo grounds, treasuring the views that stretched all around them. Rolling green hills with a church or a farmhouse here and there. Rows of cypresses. Acres of vineyards. Patches of olive trees. Down below, Sant'Antonio looked like a toy village.

"Let's go, kids," Carlo said. "It's time for the Mass."

The drive down to the village was even more heart-stopping than the ride up. Carlo had to shift gears frequently and at one point went off the road to let an approaching cement truck pass. When they finally reached a reasonably level road they let out a collective sigh.

Dino and his wife and their son were waiting at the door of the village church, an odd combination of Romanesque and Gothic architecture.

"Good to see you again," Dino said. "How was your trip?"

"Someday I want to go to America," Sofia said.

Tarik blushed when the visitors remarked how tall and handsome he was.

Since this was a weekday, only a few people, mostly elderly women in black, were on hand for the Mass. Carlo and his family sat with Dino and his family in front and nodded to Ezio and Donna in the back. The Mass, by the elderly pastor, was over in a half hour and afterward they all walked through the cemetery next to the church. More than a dozen graves had white headstones marked Mantucci with photographs of the deceased encased in glass.

"I wish I knew who all these people were," Carlo said. "I should have asked Lucia."

As they were in life, Lucia and Paolo lay side by side in a new portion of the century-old burial ground.

"Lucia and Paolo were our best friends," Ezio said. "We miss them every day."

"Paolo should have stopped driving years ago," Dino said.

"His hearing had gotten so bad, even with the hearing aids," Donna said. "I'm sure he never heard that truck coming around the curve. And it was over in an instant."

"Well," Ezio said, "at least they went together. They were hardly ever apart."

"If only we'd had a chance to say goodbye," Sofia said.

"I regret now," Carlo said, "that I didn't get to know Lucia better, didn't ask her more questions. It wasn't until the fourth or fifth visit that she told me about her family being holed up in that farmhouse during the German occupation. Or how she met the young partisan named Dino."

"Who was my father," Dino said. "And how she married Paolo after he was killed."

"This all seems like something out of a novel," Nancy said. "Maybe somebody should write it."

In happier news, Tarik reported that he was now working as an engineer for Rolls-Royce in Modena.

"He's come a long way from being an orphan from Albania," Dino said.

Sofia hugged her son. "Adopting him was the best thing we've ever done."

DINO HAD TO GET BACK TO WORK in Florence, so after farewells, Carlo drove the half mile to Ezio and Donna's house. Getting out of the car, Carlo pulled his children aside.

"Andrew, you are not, repeat not, going to take those headphones inside. Grace, leave your book in the car. You will listen quietly to what we're saying. OK?"

"OK," Grace said.

"OK," Andrew grumbled.

"If you want to join in the conversation, fine."

Inside, hugs and kisses and "how was your trip" and "you're looking so great" and "oh my, how you've grown" and "what a great job you've done on this kitchen."

Donna was still tall and erect and moved as easily as ever. Her blond hair had more gray streaks now, and her hands were a little more wrinkled. Ezio seemed slightly more stooped, and a cane rested on the floor near his chair. His curly hair was now completely white, but his blue eyes still twinkled brightly.

"I've just made a little lunch," Donna said, and proceeded to lay out ravioli, then baked chicken, fried zucchini, a salad of greens and tomatoes, and finally oranges. As always, Ezio's firm hand cut off big pieces of Donna's salt-free bread.

All the while there was a lot of catching up to do.

"Sant'Antonio looks the same," Carlo said. "Any changes?"

"The biggest change is that a developer plans a luxury hotel in that mansion on the top of the hill where Signor Bernadetto Magnimassimo lived," Donna said.

"Good luck," Ezio said. "It will take years before he gets all the approvals and the financing. We'll never see it."

Also, they reported that Marianna, the daughter of Mario and Anita, had just gotten married, and that two refugee families from Syria had moved into the village.

"What's the reaction?" Carlo asked.

"At first," Ezio said, "a lot of distrust. People didn't know what to make of them. It's taken a while, but I think now they're pretty much accepted. I don't know if they're exactly welcomed with open arms, but I think people just want to live their own lives and let them lead theirs. Agree, Donna?"

"Yes. Everyone knows how terrible their lives were before, and how they had to get here. There's so much hatred toward migrants in Italy now. We saw the boats on TV and how so many people drowned. So the least we can do is accept these new people. Maybe someday we'll all be friends."

"Let's hope," Ezio said.

"How's your old restaurant doing, Donna?" Nancy asked.

"Just fine. The new owners have kept the same menu. We eat there every couple of weeks."

"It's not the same," Ezio said. "The pasta is tough, the veal is undone."

"Oh, Ezio, it's fine."

They had now finished eating. Donna and Nancy piled the dishes in the sink and they settled down in the living room for coffee. Carlo and Nancy sat on the sofa covered with an afghan, and Andrew and Grace crouched on the floor looking at old photo albums.

"So, Carlo, your work is going well?"

"Yes. Yes, it is. I'm teaching two courses at Central State now, History of Musical Theater and a jazz ensemble. The jazz students are great, really interested, and there's a lot of talent there. The musicals class…well, this is a course on a list. Everyone on campus has to take one of them, so it's a struggle at first but by the end I think they've learned something."

"And you're still designing the sets for plays?" Ezio asked.

"Yes," Carlo said, "we do a straight play in the fall and a musical in the spring and another one in the summer."

"Which as I remember," Donna said, "you direct, Nancy."

"Yes, besides teaching costume design and a Shakespeare course."

"Mom," Andrew said, "tell them about *Hamilton*."

"You tell them. You know more about it than I do."

Andrew started pacing. "Signora! Signore! There's this great show called *Hamilton* that has hip-hop music and it's a huge success. Huge!

Imagine! Hip-hop music! On Broadway! Who would have thought it? We've been trying to get tickets for months!"

"Hamilton?" Ezio said. "Wasn't he a president of the United States?"

"No," Andrew said, pumping his arm, "but he was the first secretary of the treasury and he was behind the economic policies of George Washington's administration and he founded the Federalist Party and the United States Coast Guard and…oh, so many things. Look, he's on the ten-dollar bill! I'll show you. See!"

Andrew pulled out his shabby wallet and extracted a bill to show around. Carlo and Nancy had never seen their son so excited about anything in months. They had never heard him talk so much.

"Wait," Ezio said. "Hip and hop music? What's that? I'm ninety-two years old and I've never heard that word before."

"Some people call it rap, Signore," Andrew said. "Instead of singing, people sort of chant. Really fast. I mean really really fast. It's so cool! And one song leads to another. They hardly talk at all, just sing! It's so cool!"

Carlo looked at Nancy. Nancy looked at Carlo. "Who is this kid?" they mouthed together.

"Well, Andrew," Ezio said, "it all sounds very interesting. Maybe there will be a production in Italy someday. I can't wait."

Donna refilled the coffee cups.

"Grace," she said, "do you have an interest in musical theater, too?"

"No. It's all so silly, so pretentious. People get up on that stage and show off. Some of them are really bad. It's so boring."

"Thank you for your comments, Grace," Nancy said. "Well, why don't you tell them about the book you're reading."

"Oh, Mom, they wouldn't be interested."

"Yes, we would," Donna said. "Of course we would. Ezio and I love to read. We've just read the last book by Elena Ferrante."

"I don't read fiction."

"Oh. What are you reading?"

"Our Bodies, Ourselves."

"Oh, really. How old are you, Grace?"

"I'm almost fourteen," Grace said.

"In eight months," Andrew interjected.

"I find this book so very powerful," Grace continued. "It was called the gold standard of women's health issues when it was published. All my friends are reading it. Lots of people read it. Even old people. Maybe you'd like to look at it, Signora?"

"Grace, I read it forty years ago when it came out. I think it's on the shelf over there."

"Oh. My friends and me have read *The Feminine Mystique,* too. That was real good."

"Yes, real good," Donna said. "It's on the shelf, too."

EZIO ATTEMPTED TO CHANGE the subject. "Say, speaking of powerful women, did you hear about Clara Marincola?"

"Clara...I don't think I remember," Carlo said.

"She was the girl from here who became the first girl to be in a flag throwing demonstration," Donna said. "You know, the flag throwers are these guys who dress up in medieval costumes and throw these huge flags in the air and to each other."

"We saw a group last time in Florence," Andrew said. "Didn't we, Dad? They were amazing!"

"Well," Ezio continued, "a few years ago Clara's brother was in a group in Lucca and she dressed up in his clothes and took his part..."

"...right in the big piazza of Lucca..." Donna interrupted.

"...and she fooled everybody. At the end she took off her cap and let her hair down and everybody cheered."

"'*Brava,* Clara!' they cried," Donna said. "She wanted to prove that a girl could throw flags as well as men."

Now Carlo and Nancy remembered.

"Of course," Carlo said. "It was even shown in the States. On CNN, remember, Nancy?"

"I think there was even something in the *Times.*"

"What happened to her?"

"Well," Donna said, "that's the sad part. Everybody loved her in the piazza. "*Brava! Brava!* But then gradually she started getting grief. Worse than grief. Men would make really crude remarks, right to her face."

"She couldn't go down the street without somebody saying something,"

Ezio continued. "Even women were against her. They said she was a traitor to women."

"What?" Grace cried. "Why was she a traitor to women? That's terrible. I would have spit in their faces."

"And the thing is," Donna said, "it didn't change anything. There are dozens and dozens of flag throwing groups in Italy and there's not a woman or girl in one of them."

"Oh, that's terrible!" Grace said. "How can that be?"

"Clara said it was the worst thing that ever happened to her and she'd never do it again," Donna said. "She finished school and got a job at a bank in Lucca but everyone recognized her. So she quit that and got a job at another bank in Florence. But even there people started to know who she was and what she had done."

"So," Ezio said, "she wanted to go to a place where nobody would know her. She went to the Garfagnana."

Only Carlo had heard about the Garfagnana, so Ezio gave an explanation. He told them that it was a rugged and mountainous area north of Lucca between the Apennines to the east/northeast and the Apuan Alps to the west. There was one fairly large town, Barga, but mostly there were scattered villages and hamlets. There were a lot of forests.

"It's not known for tourists," Donna said.

"Lately, though, hiking has become very popular," Ezio said. "And horseback riding."

Nancy wondered why Clara Marincola had chosen to move to the Garfagnana.

"Precisely because it's so off the beaten track," Donna said. "Certainly no one from Lucca or Florence would go there. It's mostly Germans and other foreigners, I think."

How could she make a living there? Carlo asked.

"Not very well," Donna said. "She set up a tourist information office in Barga, where she lives, for the hikers and horseback riders. And sometimes she gives tours herself. But I guess she's managing. Anyway, her mother says she's happy there and wouldn't move back to Florence or Lucca for all the money in the world. And certainly not to Sant'Antonio."

"Well," Grace said, "I think it's just horrible that she was banished to this terrible lonely place all because she dared to prove that women can do anything. It makes me very mad."

"What," Carlo said, "would you think of driving up there when we leave here? We don't have anything else planned and it would be fun."

"I'm not going hiking!" Andrew declared.

"I'm not going horseback riding," Grace said, "but I guess we could go up there. I'd like to meet her. And thank her."

"Well," Donna said, "if you do decide to go to the Garfagnana, Clara's office is somewhere near the bank in Barga."

With that, the Mantucci family decided that it was time to return to the Cielo for one more day in Sant'Antonio. They were all still jet-lagged.

"Come back soon!" Ezio said.

"We will!" they all cried.

"Wait!" Donna said as she rushed up to the car. "Grace, I just want to tell you that I wouldn't be surprised if someday you were going to be the first female president of the United States."

"Oh, Signora," Grace said. "I won't be the first. There will be at least two or three by the time I'm old enough. You have to be thirty-five. I looked it up."

"Well, good luck."

Back at the Cielo, they wondered what they should do during their last days in Italy.

"How about the beach at Versila?" Andrew suggested.

"Too far," Carlo said. "We wouldn't have enough time to really enjoy it."

"I wish we had time to go to Bologna," Nancy said. "They've got a school of musical theater there, the only one in Italy."

"Next time, I'm afraid," Carlo said.

"Why can't we just stay in our rooms and read?" Grace asked.

"Oh, poo," Nancy said. "We can do that at home. We have to do something Italian, something we can't do anywhere else."

"Well," Carlo said, "I know a place not far from here."

"What?"

"The Garfagnana, of course."

UNTIL NOW, the weather had been idyllic, warm but not hot during the day and cool at night. A few clouds, but not a drop of rain. The next morning, they knew it was going to be hot, and so they dressed accordingly. T-shirts and shorts for each of them. Nancy's shirt had a scowling cat saying "This *Is* My Happy Face." Carlo's said "Old Enough to Know Better." Andrew's had the logo of the *Hamilton* musical, and Grace's declared "Feminist With a Long To-Do List."

Somehow, they all happened to wear white shorts, too. Carlo and Nancy wore sandals, but Andrew and Grace opted for flip-flops.

"OK, let's do it," Carlo said as they all crunched into the Fiat, Andrew with his headphones on, Grace reading her book, Nancy holding a map on her lap and eager to see the countryside, and Carlo gripping the steering wheel. He was not used to driving a stick shift.

Since the air conditioning didn't work, all the windows were open, making conversation impossible. Encountering light traffic, they sped east toward Lucca and then north. A little later, the village of Borgo a Mozzano seemed ordinary enough until they looked to the left.

"Oh my God," Nancy said. "Look at that!"

"That's incredible," Carlo said.

Even Andrew and Grace looked out the window. "Let's stop! Let's stop!"

So, digging out their phones, they took each other's picture as they walked across the magnificent humpback stone bridge across the Serchio River.

"This is very old," Andrew said, stating the obvious.

"Medieval, I'm sure," Nancy said.

Having exhausted every angle for their photos, they climbed back into the car and wound their way through the hills to Barga, only to find that parking was forbidden in what was called the old city up above. They parked below and trudged up the steep cobblestone streets and pathways until they reached the top of the hill and the cathedral. They noticed a bank.

"Donna said Clara Marincola's office was near here," Carlo said.

They walked up and down the street, looking at the window signs until they saw one with small lettering: "Tours."

"Must be it."

Clara was seated at a desk in front of a wall plastered with travel posters, most of them from the Garfagnana. She was smaller than they had expected, with her hair cut short, and she wore a blue plaid shirt over tan pants. Startled to find four visitors at her door, she leaped up to greet them.

"*Buongiorno, buongiorno!* Welcome!"

"We're glad we found you in," Carlo said. "We thought you might be out on a tour."

"Ha! I haven't led a tour in three weeks. You're American, right?"

"Amazing," Carlo said. "How could you tell?"

"Maybe because of the T-shirts?"

"OK, OK, I guess we're pretty obvious. But we started our trip in your hometown, Sant'Antonio, and…"

"Sant'Antonio? Really? My parents still live there."

"We know," Carlo said. "Lucia Sporenza was a cousin of mine, so we've visited there before. There was an anniversary Mass a couple of days ago."

"I heard about the accident," Clara said. "I'm sorry."

Carlo explained that their friends Ezio and Donna, who had lived in the Cielo on the mountain, had bought Lucia and Paolo's house and had moved to the village.

"So when we visited them the other day they told us you had moved here."

"Yes, I moved here because of, well, some unpleasantness."

Grace interjected. "Signorina, I just want to say that we heard about what you did with the flag throwers and I think you should be given the biggest medal there is."

"Well," Clara said, "thanks, but that's all in the past now. I'm here. Nobody knows me, and it's a very quiet life. There are a few people who want to go on tours. Not many, but enough to keep me in cappuccino and pastry."

"Signorina! Signorina!" Andrew interrupted. "When we were coming up here we passed this fantastic bridge. It's all stone and it's curved real high and it looks like something out of a fairy tale. It's so cool!"

"At Borgo a Mozzano?"

"Yes, that's the place," Carlo said.

"Oh, that's the Devil's Bridge," Clara said.

"What?" Andrew and Grace said together.

"Well, its real name is the *Ponte della Maddalena*," Clara said. "But nobody calls it that. It's *Ponte del Diavolo*."

Clara went on to tell the story.

Sometime in the Middle Ages, she said, a master builder was contracted to construct a new bridge across the Serchio, which winds its way through the Garfagnana.

The builder's work went slowly until he realized he couldn't make the deadline the villagers had given him. He was desperate.

Suddenly, Clara continued, a tall, well-dressed merchant stood next to him. The man told the builder that he could finish the bridge that night, but there was one condition. The builder must give him the soul of the first living thing that crossed the bridge when it was completed. The builder agreed, and the next day the villagers had their beautiful bridge.

When they congratulated the builder, he told them that no one should cross the bridge until sunset. The builder then rode his horse to Lucca to seek the bishop's advice.

Fool the devil, the wise bishop said. Send a pig across first.

The builder found a pig and let it cross. The devil, Clara said, was so furious that he had been tricked that he threw himself into the Serchio.

"Well," she said, "that's the story, but I read that there are nine devil's bridges in Italy alone and maybe up to two dozen in Europe. The devil must have been very busy."

"That's a wonderful story," Nancy said.

"Well," Andrew declared, "I don't believe it. Come on! A devil building a bridge?"

"You don't believe it?" Carlo asked.

"No!"

"You have no imagination."

"There are lots of odd supernatural stories in the Garfagnana," Clara said. "I mean, look at the terrain. Mountains and valleys, lots of mist and fog. Very strange and mysterious things are supposed to happen all over."

"Like what?" Andrew wanted to know.

So Clara told them the story of Saint Eduardo. He was, she said, a fourteenth-century French nobleman who renounced his wealth and went on a pilgrimage that ended in the Italian town of Voghera, now part of the Province of Pavia. This was the time of the Black Death, and legend has it that Eduardo worked as an itinerant healer, tending to the dying and their families.

Then, she said, he fell sick and moved to a simple wooden hut in the forest. He lived on, sustained by a natural spring of fresh water that miraculously appeared in a nearby rock, and by a small dog who brought chunks of bread to the hut each morning.

"Look," she said, "over there is the Church of San Eduardo and in front of it is a statue of the saint. His dog is at his side, and Eduardo is lifting the hem of his tunic to show the sores of the bubonic plague."

"Water from a rock and a dog who gave him food?" Andrew said. "Come on."

"Well," Clara said, "then there's the story about the Room of the Voices in the Grotta del Vento near Gallicano. If you get there, go on the underground tour and you'll get to this room in complete darkness. This was once the base camp where many explorations started. Now, you can hear voices in the distance."

"Mom," Grace said, "this is getting creepy. Can we just go back?"

"No," Andrew said, "I want to hear more."

Clara obliged him with the story of the witches' covens on Mount Matanna. She said that witches went up the mountain to carry out supernatural practices "and you can still see a very smooth table where they were supposed to sacrifice their victims and make their spells."

"Come on," Andrew said.

"Well, people don't go there at night because there's supposed to be a scary ghost carrying a scythe to protect hidden treasure."

Grace tugged at Nancy's T-shirt. "Mom, this is really creepy."

"Of course," Clara said, "there's also the story of the ghost town."

CLARA ASSURED THE VISITORS that this story started out rather routinely, and it was not that long ago.

"There was a town called Fabbriche di Careggine near Castelnuovo di Garfagnana. When a hydroelectric dam was built after World War II, a huge man-made lake was formed. In order to create the lake, Fabbriche di Careggine had to be flooded and its residents were moved to the nearby town of Vagli Sotto.

"Every decade or so, the lake is emptied and people can actually walk around in the mud and see what is left of the buildings. They see a church, stone buildings, a cemetery, a bridge. Look, I'll show you."

She took out an iPad from her desk drawer, typed a few letters and soon was on YouTube.

"Here, you can see people walking through the village."

"Yuk," Grace said, "it's all dirty."

"Well, it's been underwater," Carlo said. "What do you expect?"

"Some people call it *Paese Fantasma,* the ghost village," Clara said, "and they say ghosts have been seen and strange events have occurred since the old village was flooded. On cold winter nights, some people say, the bells in the bell tower can be heard, even though the bells were removed long ago."

"Dad," Andrew said, "can we go there?"

"No," Grace said. "Let's not."

"All you'll see now is a lake," Clara said. "You can't see the buildings underneath."

"Maybe if we had a telescope?" Andrew asked.

"No, I'm afraid not," Clara said. "If you're so interested in supernatural things it's too bad that you weren't here before World War II. For centuries there was a shrine near the Abbey of Saint Gaudentius, which is near Castelnuovo di Garfagnana. It was dedicated to Saint Giacomo and there was supposed to be a statue there that worked miracles."

"Come on," Andrew said.

"Well, a lot of people believed it. In fact, there had been so many miracles that's why Giacomo was declared a saint in the first place."

"You know," Carlo told Nancy, "I've been having some pains in my back. Maybe we should go there."

"Too late," Clara said. "Both the abbey and the shrine were bombed by the Allies in World War II. There's hardly anything left of the abbey, and the shrine was destroyed. Nothing left at all."

"Not even the statue?" Grace asked.

"Not even the statue. Well, I guess I should also mention the Legend of Villaggio di Montagna."

"Yes, you should," Andrew said. "What's that?"

"Well, it's such an odd legend I hate to even bring it up. But, oh well.

It seems there was a village named Villaggio di Montagna deep in the valley between Monte Sumbra and Pania della Croce. The mountains are especially high there, and the valleys very deep. So deep that there is mist and fog there all the time. Well, in the late twelfth century the village disappeared. Not a trace."

"Oh, come on," Andrew said.

"Well," Clara said, "I don't believe any of this either. But there were accounts from hunters over the centuries that there was an area between those two mountains that was so thick with fog and mist that no one could see two feet ahead. Then a hunter claimed he had forced his way through the mist and had found a village that looked as if it had been in the Middle Ages. The inhabitants were dressed in medieval clothes and they talked in a kind of dialect. They didn't have any modern tools. They didn't have stoves. They did have a church and the Mass was still almost the same. In Latin, of course."

"Of course," Nancy said.

"Well, this hunter said he stayed until it got dark and then he left."

"I don't blame him," Andrew said.

"But he said he went back the next day and the village wasn't there. He said he looked for miles, in the mountains, in the valleys, but he could not find a single trace of it."

"Of course not," Andrew said, "because he was drunk the first time."

"Nobody believed him, of course, but then years, decades later, another hunter said the same thing. He broke through the mist, went to the village, even talked to people, but the next day he couldn't find it again."

"Like *Brigadoon*!" Carlo and Nancy said together.

Clara had never heard of the term, but Andrew and Grace remembered that Central State had wanted to put on a musical by that name seven years ago, but then discovered that a nearby school had already gotten the rights.

"*What a day this has been/What a rare mood I'm in,*" Carlo began to sing.

"*Why it's almost like being in love,*" Nancy joined in.

"*There's a smile on my face...*" her husband continued.

"OK, OK, Mom and Dad," Andrew said, "that's enough."

Carlo explained to Clara that *Brigadoon* was a musical by Alan Jay

Lerner and Frederick Loewe in which two Americans discover a village in Scotland that comes to life every hundred years.

"Well, that's what this legend says, that Villaggio di Montagna comes to life every hundred years," Clara said.

"Signorina! Signorina!" Andrew said. "That is so cool. So what happens when it comes to life?"

"That's really all I know. I shouldn't have brought it up. The only thing we do know is that there was a lot of fighting among the towns and villages in that area for centuries. People had feuds and vendettas and sometimes it got bloody. Maybe that had something to do with it."

"Really?" Andrew said.

"Look," Clara said, laughing, "sometimes I think all of these stories have been promoted by people in the Garfagnana just to hook tourists. I don't believe a word of any of them myself."

Grace gripped Nancy's hand. "Mom, this is really really ghoulish. Can we go back to Florence now?"

"Wait," Carlo wanted to know, "when was the last time this village is supposed to have come to life?"

Clara thought for a while. "Hmmm. Come to think of it, the last account was about a hundred years ago."

"Really?" Carlo, Nancy, Andrew and Grace shouted together.

"Look," Clara said, "this is all a legend. I don't believe any of it. You don't have to either."

The visitors agreed that these accounts were too fanciful to be believed, but that they'd have some fun stories to tell their friends when they returned to the United States.

"Well," Carlo said, "it's been great talking to you, but I think we'll be on our way. We're just going to drive around and see what there is to see."

Clara supplied them with a map and a guidebook of the Garfagnana and suggested they might start their tour by crossing the Serchio and visiting the lovely medieval town of Castelnuovo di Garfagnana.

"It's about half the size of Barga, and quite quaint."

"If we see any ghosts," Carlo said, "we'll let you know. Here's my card. If you hear of any, send us a note."

"Thanks."

Less than an hour later they hiked up and down a few streets in

Castelnuovo di Garfagnana and found themselves standing in front of the massive twelfth-century Ariosto's Castle.

"OK, I've seen my castles for the day," Andrew said. "Let's find that village under the lake."

Shortly after, they did find Vagli Sotto, not far away, and they saw the lake, but no sign of a church or houses or anything else. Andrew decided he wanted a better view and disappeared down one side of an embankment.

"Where'd Andrew go?" Grace asked. "I don't think we should be separated. There's supposed to be ghosts around here."

"He'll catch up," Carlo said.

"O-o-o-o-o-o-o-o-o-o-o-o."

"What was that?" Nancy wondered.

"O-o-o-o-o-o-o-o-o-o-o-o."

Grace grabbed her mother's arm. "Let's get out of here."

"O-o-o-o-o-o-o-o-o-o-o-o."

"OK, Andrew," Carlo yelled, "you can come out now."

Andrew emerged from a clump of trees. "Ha! Had you fooled, didn't I?"

"We knew it was you all along," Grace said.

"Let's go," Carlo said.

Through the steep craggy mountains and high pasturelands, through dark beechwood forests and along rushing streams, they drove to one village and another: Pieve Fosciana, Camporgiano, Villa Collemandina.

The sun had settled low in the sky and a light fog nestled in the valleys.

"All right," Carlo said, "let's go back. We'll go back to Lucca tonight and get to Florence tomorrow morning. We can spend a few days there before going home. Where are we now, Nancy?"

Nancy had been in charge of the map and tried to pinpoint their exact location.

"Well, we were at Villa Collemandina, and then we turned left."

"I thought we turned right," Carlo said.

"No left. Well, just keep on going. We're bound to hit some village soon and we can ask directions."

Although there was mist, the heat was still oppressive, and Carlo wiped the sweat off his forehead.

They drove. And drove some more.

"Odd," Nancy said. "I would have thought we'd come to a little village by now. How's the gas?"

"The gas is OK, but I wish we knew where we were."

They drove more miles, peering through the mist for any sign of a house or a farm or a church or anything. Suddenly, without warning, a curtain of heavy fog dropped down in front of them. It spread across the road like a thick blanket.

"My God!" Nancy cried. "We're going to hit it!"

"I can't stop! We're going downhill!"

Still not used to the stick shift, Carlo tried to move the clutch from one speed to another, but nothing worked. The Fiat barreled through the fog and Carlo hit the brakes hard.

"Look! We've run out of gas. It was full ten seconds ago."

The engine stalled. He tried to start it again, to no avail.

"We're stuck out in nowhere and we're out of gas and the damn car won't start!"

"Don't get upset, dear. We'll figure this out."

Carlo got out of the car to see if there was a gas leak. No trace. He hurried back inside.

"It's freezing out there! Close the windows! Must be twenty degrees colder than when we started."

"Mom!" Grace cried, "what's happening?"

"Nothing, dear. We'll be fine."

"I'm scared!"

"It's all right, Grace. We'll be fine."

"Damn!" Carlo said under his breath. "Andrew, get on your phone and see if you can find an emergency number."

Andrew already had the phone in his hands and kept punching buttons.

"Nothing works, Dad. I've been trying and trying."

"Great! In the middle of nowhere and we're out of gas and the car doesn't start and the phone doesn't work and it's freezing out there! And it's going to get dark soon! Damn!"

"Don't get upset, dear," Nancy said. "We'll find our way out."

"I'm not upset!"

"Mom!" Grace said. "I'm scared. Can we go back?"

"We'll be fine, honey. We're just a little lost."

"We're not lost!" Carlo shouted. "Just a little…misplaced. Nancy, see if you can find a flashlight in the glove compartment. There must be one."

Nancy found one, but it was old and rusty. Carlo tried to loosen the cap.

"Damn. Now I've cut myself."

"Carlo, you're bleeding all over. Wrap this handkerchief around your hand."

Carlo opened his door. "We gotta get out of here. Lock anything valuable in the trunk. We don't know what kind of crooks are out there."

"Or what kind of animals," Andrew said helpfully.

Wearing only T-shirts and shorts and poor excuses for shoes, they shivered together in the cold. They also realized they were standing precariously close to the edge of a cliff. Slowly, the mist began to disappear.

"Look!" Andrew cried. "There's a village."

In the distance they could see the top of a bell tower and a church. Red tile roofs. A cluster of houses. All enclosed in a high stone wall with towers of various heights at four corners.

Carlo looked at Nancy. "Do you think?"

LORD GIANCARLO

LIKE OTHER VILLAGES in the Garfagnana, Villaggio di Montagna began modestly, with only a scattering of farms trying to survive amid the tortuous mountain ranges, harsh winters and long rainy spells. Chestnuts provided one source of income, lentils another. The farmers discovered that certain kinds of wheat could be made into *farro,* a crunchy grain that could be used in salads and soups. It eventually became so famous that it was called *Farro della Garfagnana.*

Slowly, over many years, one farm developed into another, then another. The need for a central market grew. An ironsmith was needed to make shoes for the horses, a mill to make chestnut flour, another to grind the wheat. A small church was built, replaced much later by a larger one.

Authorities took notice. They gave a name to what was now a small community, Villaggio di Montagna, which simply meant mountain village. It was no more than that.

Naturally, some farmers succeeded more than others, and some became quite wealthy. Gradually, they took leadership roles among their neighbors, making decisions for building and expanding, deciding where to put roads, planning for the future. Inevitably, a sort of army for protection was established because it was at this point that various factions were fighting over much of the Garfagnana.

First came the Visigoths, one of the nomadic tribes that roamed Europe during the late Roman Empire. They marauded through much of the region but didn't bother with tiny Villaggio di Montagna. The Lombards, another Germanic tribe, fought the Visigoths and took over much of Italy. Villaggio di Montagna took little notice of the change in ownership. Still another Germanic tribe, the Franks, fought the Lombards and took control over their lands.

Then in the tenth century, an imperial family, the House of Canossa, gained dominance over the Garfagnana along with much of the adjoining territory. The founder of the dynasty was a man called Adalberto Atto, who was the father of a man called Tedald, who was the father of a man called Boniface, who was the father of one of the most interesting women in all of Italian history, Matilda of Canossa, in the eleventh century. One of the few medieval women to be remembered for her military accomplishments, Matilda sometimes donned armor and rode into battle herself.

She also led a fascinating personal life, one that has sometimes amused historians. Her first marriage was to her stepbrother, Godfrey the Hunchback, but he was assassinated during what was euphemistically called "answering the call of nature." Since Matilda had been accused of adultery with the pope the previous month, she was suspected of ordering her estranged husband's death. Ignoring those rumors, Matilda, then in her early forties, married the heir to the Duchy of Bavaria, Welf V, who was probably fifteen to seventeen years old at the time.

During all this time, she oversaw dozens of battles to secure her land holdings, and also found time to build some one hundred churches, monasteries and bridges between the Alps and Rome. Among the bridges was one dedicated to Mary Maddalene called the *Ponte della Maddalena* at Borgo a Mozzano near Lucca. It became known, however, as the Devil's Bridge because of a legend that the devil himself actually built it.

The residents of Villaggio di Montagna were unaware of all the intrigue involving their nominal ruler, but they certainly were aware of the battles over their territory that only became worse during the feuds between a faction called the Guelphs, which supported the pope, and the Ghibellines, a faction supporting the Holy Roman Emperor. The struggle between the spiritual and temporal powers played out across central and northern Italy for decades, and even involved Villaggio di Montagna.

The village, like all of the Garfagnana, was under the control of Lucca during this time and was governed by the Guelphs. When the Ghibellines invaded, the people had to defend themselves.

In Villaggio di Montagna, the most powerful family to emerge was called the Sachetto. Francesco, who had built a small fortune from his wheat production, was the first. He was followed by his son Benedetto, who expanded the family enterprise. When he died, his only son, Giancarlo, was expected to take over.

But Giancarlo was having too much fun. He gambled with his friends, got into fights in taverns and went off into the hills whenever he felt like it. He often rode into battle with the Guelphs, winning praise for his fearless abilities.

In Assisi one day he met a monk dressed in a tattered brown robe who was leading a group of other monks. They talked for a while and Giancarlo told the monk, whose name was Francis, that he was tired of the life he was leading and wanted to do something more. Francis invited him to join his small band of followers. Giancarlo became one of Francis' most devoted monks, finding food and clothing for the poor and faithfully praying three times a day.

One day, Francis took Giancarlo aside. "You don't belong here," he said. "You belong in Villaggio di Montagna. Those are your people. They need your help. Go."

Reluctantly, Giancarlo returned to his village. In time, he became the most respected, the most loved, of any of the Sachetto dynasty. He established an organization to help poor families. He gave generously to the church and found a famous painter from Florence to create a fresco of Saint Agnese behind the altar. He created the Piazza del Popolo in the center of the village, and shops and booths grew around it. He installed a system of pipes from the nearby River Forno so that the villagers could have fresh water.

It seemed as though he knew everyone in the village by name—and there were about eight hundred of them by then—as well as their nicknames and hobbies and favorite foods. When he walked to a shop for a pair of boots or some fresh tomatoes he stopped and talked to everyone.

He was also a fearless warrior. Leading his small army into battle, he fought off the Ghibellines time and again. He was rewarded with the title of "lord."

In order to protect the village, Giancarlo built a castle, small by the standards of others in the Garfagnana, but big enough to house his family, which included a son and daughter, and a few servants. The place featured a Great Hall and guest chambers, a large kitchen and a tiny chapel. A moat and ramparts kept out intruders.

Every year he hosted a large celebration that included a sumptuous meal in the dining hall: ravioli, boiled veal, roebuck, venison, hare, roast capon, partridge, pheasant, tench and other fish, roast eel, white broad beans, stuffed olives, pears, cakes and pies. One course followed another and another, and the meal lasted for hours.

Then all the guests moved to the great lawn behind the castle for jousts. Since the village was so small, it had only two *contrade,* or neighborhoods. One was called the *Drago,* the dragon, and the other the *Oca,* the goose. Each *contrada* had its own meeting place, a tavern, its own flag and its own motto. For the jousts, one warrior was chosen from each and, dressed in armor, they had a mock battle with rusty swords. Everyone cheered, no matter which side won.

With a high wall around the village and with four towers to guard it, life in Villaggio di Montagna was isolated from the rest of the Garfagnana. Villagers didn't have to go anywhere because all their needs were met right there.

There was, however, a mysterious side to Lord Giancarlo, one known only by his wife. At least twice a month, Severo the Soothsayer from somewhere near Lucca set up a booth in Piazza del Popolo to tell the futures of the residents of Villaggio di Montagna. He was an elderly man and, knowing that he had a reputation to uphold, dressed the part with a long black gown, long white beard and pointy hat.

Most people scoffed at his predictions, saying they were too obvious.

Yes, the harvest would be good. No, it wouldn't snow before Christmas. Yes, your son will mend his ways and lead a good life.

Giancarlo had found solace in the predictable predictions, and it was only recently, when forecasts became more ominous, that he became worried.

"You will meet a man dressed in black," Severo the Soothsayer said.

"I see men dressed in black all the time," Giancarlo answered.

"He will have a crooked nose."

"Should I be afraid of him?"

"Do what he tells you." Severo the Soothsayer would say no more.

When Giancarlo told this story to his wife, she of course said the obvious: "He's Severo the Faker. Ignore him."

The conflicts between the Guelphs and the Ghibellines reached a climax in the Battle of Villetta, a small village west of Villaggio di Montagna. The Ghibellines had conquered more and more territory, destroying villages and pillaging farms along the way. The Guelphs retreated again and again. Now the two sides were to meet in a decisive battle. Whoever won would control Villaggio di Montagna.

With Giancarlo's frightened wife and two children watching from a nearby hill, the battle began at daybreak, and the village's meager Guelph troops did not seem a match for the mighty Ghibellines. Three times they were forced to retreat, and throughout the day it became more obvious that the Villaggio di Montagna would be turned over to the hated enemy. In one encounter Giancarlo suffered a deep cut on his right hand.

In late afternoon both sides called a halt to the fighting. Everyone was worn out. They retreated to opposite hillsides. When the battle resumed, the tide turned for no apparent reason. The Guelphs took command and easily won. The troops returned home to Villaggio di Montagna without a single casualty.

But Giancarlo was not to be found. Or his wife and children. Disappeared. Without a trace.

In Villaggio di Montagna, the people couldn't understand how this had happened. Where was he? And if Giancarlo was not here, what would become of them? They cried and yelled and screamed and mourned. Then, exhausted, they went to bed.

And slept and slept.

THE VILLAGERS COULD NOT HAVE KNOWN what happened during that lull in the fighting. Certainly Giancarlo was not around to tell them.

It seems that after the truce was called he was resting on the side of a hill alone. His troops were on a nearby hill enjoying the brief respite by telling bawdy jokes and munching on the bread and cheese their wives had packed.

Giancarlo tried to think of maneuvers that would bring the Guelphs a victory, but no plan seemed feasible. He would lose too many men. He couldn't let that happen. And he wondered about his own abilities. He was in his late forties now and the battles had taken their toll. His arms and legs ached, and he knew he wasn't as alert. His son was only fifteen, so he couldn't go into battle yet. He fingered the white bandage that was always around his right hand, a reminder of the battle in which he was injured. Maybe he should just go back and concede defeat.

Sapped of all energy, he drifted into a drowsy dream until he was awakened by a sharp kick in his leg.

"What the…?" he yelled.

"No time to sleep, Giancarlo." The man wore a dark robe with a heavy chain around his neck. The fingers on his small hands glittered with jewels. His long hair was jet black, his face milky white, his long nose like a hook. Giancarlo had seen so many dead bodies on battlefields that he wasn't afraid.

"Who…who are you?"

"A friend."

"A friend? I don't know you. Who sent you?"

"All right, one of your friends sent me. Severo the Soothsayer. He told me you might need some help."

"Help with what?"

"It seems pretty obvious. The battle, you fool. What do you think?"

"What? Are you going to fight with us?"

"Nothing that pedestrian."

"Then why are you here?"

"As I said, I'm here to help."

Giancarlo was getting tired of this. "OK, who the hell are you anyway?"

"I am known far and wide. I'm famous!"

"I've never heard of you."

"I think you have."

"When? How?"

"You've heard of my deeds, I'm sure."

"Name one."

The man sighed and sat down on a big rock next to Giancarlo.

"This is so tiresome. Well, all right. Here's an obvious one. You know about that bridge at Borgo a Mozzano?"

Giancarlo did know. Villaggio di Montagna was isolated, but he had traveled when he was younger, and he had even seen the beautiful arched bridge over the Serchio River near Lucca.

"Of course, the one built by Matilda of Canossa."

"Ha! Matilda of Canossa? Don't make me laugh. Matilda couldn't make a pie without my help. Build a bridge? Ha!"

"She is supposed to have built a hundred bridges in Italy," Giancarlo insisted. "And churches. And monasteries."

"Oh, really? That's what her stupid followers want you to believe. Well, let me tell you about some of the bridges I've built in Italy. Besides the one at Borgo a Mozzano, there's one at Cividale del Friuli in the province of Udine. There's one at Bobbio in Emilia Romagna. One in Blera in the northern part of Lazio. Two, in fact, in the Piedmont, one in Dronero and the other in Lanzo Torinese. My name is on bridges all over Italy, all over Europe."

"But everyone says the one at Borgo a Mozzano was built by Matilda of Canossa."

The man sighed and twisted the rings on his fingers.

"Everyone! Ha! Let me tell you what happened. There was a man, they called him a master builder, but he really wasn't, who was supposed to build that bridge. But he was so lazy and incompetent that he couldn't finish it. So I stepped in and told him I'd build it overnight. And I did. And all I asked for was the soul of the first living thing that crossed the bridge."

"What happened?"

"That pig was very succulent, one of the best I've had. Now if you want me to tell you about the cathedral in Siena, or the one in Florence… Or maybe a few stories about my assassinations. I'm really good at that, if I say so myself."

Giancarlo didn't want to hear any more of these stories and wanted to get to the point.

"So why are you here? I'm not going to sell my soul if that's what you think."

"No, no. Been there. Done that. I'm here because I want you to win this battle."

"Why?"

"Because I don't want the Ghibellines to win. Dirty traitors. Cheats. Can't be trusted. The stories I could tell you. They rape, they steal."

"That sounds like things you'd enjoy."

"Not for the Ghibellines."

"And how will you arrange that they'll lose?"

"Arrange? My dear boy, things happen. That's all. Things happen. They don't have to be arranged."

"So why are you telling me this? What do I have to do?"

"Agree to my plan."

"Which is what?"

"Well, you go back to the battle. You win. Just like that. The Ghibellines run away. It's going to be a total disaster for them. Total disaster."

"What's the catch?"

"I wish you wouldn't use such a sophomoric term. I've been wanting to do this for a long long time. It's all so simple, and I should have tried it before. But now is a perfect time."

"What?"

"I cast a spell on your village."

"A spell? Are you a witch?"

"I'm going to ignore that. No, I'm going to make the village disappear for one hundred years. Then it will come back to life for a day. Then it will disappear for another hundred years, and come back for a day, and so forth and so on and so forth and so on."

"That's crazy! What would the people be doing all this time?'

"Well, they'd all be in bed asleep. For a very long time. A nice long, long sleep. The sleep of the dead, so to speak. I like that phrase. When they wake up it will be just another day for them. Look, I'm doing you, and them, a big favor. Do you know what's going to happen in Villaggio di Montagna and in the Garfagnana and in Italy and in all of Europe soon?"

"What? What's going to happen?"

"Come here. I'll tell you what's going to happen."

Giancarlo took a step forward, afraid to go any farther. The man began to whisper.

"This isn't known yet, Giancarlo, but in the next hundred years there's going to be a terrible plague spreading across Italy and the rest of Europe. I had so much fun planning this. I can't believe it's really going to happen soon. It's going to be huge! Huge!"

"What?"

"Well, picture this. Little rats from the East carrying a deadly disease are going to board ships bound for ports all over. Genoa, Pisa, Venice. Then the rats will come off the ships and attack people. And people will die, Giancarlo! Millions of people will die! The biggest disaster in history! The biggest! In Italy, three-fourth of the population will die. Three-fourths!"

Giancarlo hid behind a tree when he heard the man's fiendish laughter.

The man composed himself and continued. "But you can save the people of your village from this Black Death. They will be entirely safe in Villaggio di Montagna. Snug and safe and sleeping in their beds. They couldn't get up, and those walls you built will prevent outsiders from coming in. Those are great walls, Giancarlo, great walls! I love walls!"

"I can't believe this."

"And it would all be because of you, Giancarlo. You will have saved their lives."

"But what about in the future? What other things will happen?"

"Wars. Wars. Wars. And more plagues and pestilence and famine and poverty. Disasters! But in Villaggio di Montagna there will be no wars or plagues or pestilence or famine or poverty. The people will be sleeping."

"What about me? Am I going to go back and sleep and sleep and sleep?"

"My dear boy. Every bargain has a sacrifice, right?"

"You're going to kill me."

"Oh, how morbid you are. No, no, no, no, no. Look, I'll find you a very nice place where you can live out your days. Somewhere in the country. You can take your wife and kids. You'll be very happy."

"But I'd miss my people."

"Watch it, Giancarlo. This isn't a time to be sentimental. And it isn't as if I killed them off. Hell knows that I've done that so many times. They'll be perfectly healthy when they wake up. They'll just think it's the next day. They'll continue their chores and their boring lives. But they'd remember you, and every time they'd declare a special day and have a celebration to honor Lord Giancarlo di Villaggio di Montagna. There will be a big banquet and singing and dancing just like you have done. Even jousts! Don't you like the jousts in your village? You'll go down in history, Giancarlo. Centuries from now, when there are these things called books, little boys will read about you and want to be just like you. You'll be famous."

"I don't want to be famous."

"Yes, you do. Everyone does. Don't deny it."

"I don't believe this."

"Well, fine. Let the Ghibellines win the battle. Fine with me."

"No!"

"Let these barbarians come and burn all the houses and destroy your village."

"No!"

"Let them destroy your castle and tear down your beautiful walls."

"No!"

"And rape and murder all of your women."

"No!"

"And do unspeakable things to your children."

"No!"

"And, remember, Giancarlo, the Black Death!"

"No!"

"The blood will be on your hands, Giancarlo."

"No! No! No!"

Giancarlo walked toward a tree, banged his head on it, then went in another direction and smashed his sword against a metal pole.

It was a half hour before he returned to the man, who was now sprawled on the grass and appeared to be asleep.

"Wake up!"

"Oh, there you are. And I was having such a nice dream. It was about the time I eliminated Godfrey the Hunchback while he was shitting in the forest. That was so easy, and so much fun! Well, have you decided?"

"One more thing. If I agree to this, will the villagers ever escape this awful penalty? Will someone be able to free them and let them live normal lives again?"

"You're asking an awful lot, Giancarlo."

"Well, you're demanding an awful lot."

The man thought for a while.

"Well, all right. Only it will have to be someone from a land not yet known."

"Someone from a land not yet known? What the hell does that mean?"

"Someone from a land not yet known."

A SPECIAL DAY

SPRINKLED LIKE SNOWFLAKES, some stars were in clusters and others flickered alone in the sky when the twin bells of the Church of Sant'Agnese began to peal. It was only 4 o'clock in the morning. A special day for the people of Villaggio di Montagna was about to begin again.

Dogs, roused from their sleep, began to howl. Chickens cackled in their pens near the gardens. Cows in the barns started to moo and horses in their pastures to neigh. Sparrows stirred in their nests. A black cat clawed up a tree. Roses, lilies and peonies opened their petals. The village slowly came to life.

It had been asleep for a long time.

In the bedroom of their home on via del Mercato, Sergio Castellano woke with a start and poked his wife.

"Marcella," he whispered. "It is time to awaken."

She snuggled closer to him. "What, husband?"

"We are going to have another special day."

"No! It seems like just yesterday when we had a special day."

"In Villaggio di Montagna, time does not mean very much."

Marcella yawned and pulled her nightcap off. "You know, I had the strangest dream about a special day. Let me think on it."

"You always have strange dreams, wife."

"No, this was different. I can't remember what it was all about, but there was something in it that said this was going to be a day like we have never had before. It was sort of, perhaps, a premonition."

Sergio got up on his elbows. "A premonition? Like something bad is going to happen?"

"No…no…I do not think so. It is just that whatever would happen has never happened before. There was a man in it. A man we had never seen before. And a woman and two children."

Sergio stroked his wife's hair. "That is about the strangest dream you have ever had, my dearest. Let us just wait and see. Perhaps something will happen today. I think we should get up to find out. We need to make every minute count on a day like today. Please wake the children."

Marcella gently shook her daughter, who was lying on her other side. "Rosanna, wake up. It is today. And awaken your brother."

Rosanna stretched her arms in the darkness and poked her brother, next to her on the opposite side of the bed.

"Romero, wake up, wake up! Your hair is on fire! Your hair is on fire!"

Grumbling incoherently, he turned over on his side.

"Romero! Wake up! Now!" Rosanna pushed her brother off the bed and he landed with a thud on the earthen floor.

"Va? Via!" he cried. "Go away."

He tried to grab his sister's arm but she pulled away.

"It is time to get up, Romero," Marcella said. "We are going to have a lovely day."

Now all four were out of their big lumpy bed, which was actually just a pile of straw covered with blankets.

In the darkness, Sergio pulled on his clothes and walked barefoot to the window to open the heavy shutters. A full moon lit the church steeple, the castle on the nearby hill and the towers and stone wall that surrounded the village. Then, faint lights from tapers began to flicker in windows along via del Mercato. A window in a house down the cobblestone street, however, was already brightly lit by a dozen candles.

"Stupido! That wretched Rocco Tabussi just bounced out of bed when the bells rang and got all the candles lit and opened his shutters so he could tell everybody he was first. Tabussi will not let anybody get the best of him. *Bastardo!"*

"Forget Tabussi, Sergio," Marcella said. "Today of all days, forget about Tabussi."

"I will never forget him, wife," Sergio said. "*Bastardo.*"

"Husband, please."

"All right, all right. For you. For today."

Turning around, Sergio stubbed his big toe on a chair. "*Porca miseria!* I will go down and get some candles."

By the time he had lit a half dozen candles from embers still burning on the hearth, Marcella and the children were dressed and in the kitchen. Marcella and Rosanna wore plain brown dresses, tied with cords at the waist, and simple shoes made out of cowskin. Like his father, Romero wore a woolen tunic over breeches and heavy boots. Now that he was fifteen years old, he could wear some of his father's clothes.

Sergio stirred the ashes in the hearth and added a few sticks from the pile nearby. Soon, a blazing fire warmed the room on this chilly June morning. Rosanna, cheerful even this early in the day, hummed a nonsense song she'd made up as she went to the chicken coop in the back: *"Cows sing, horses fly/The moon is in the sky/Soon it will be morning/For my lover and I."*

Minutes later, she returned with a dozen eggs. Still trying to get the sleep out of his eyes, Romero trudged to the barn to milk Bianca, the cow. Marcella busied herself wiping off the dust that had somehow accumulated on the table, the chairs and the bench near the hearth. She pulled down the iron pan that always hung on the side of the fireplace.

"Today, we will have a *festa*," she said. "Fried eggs, barley bread with marmalade, and fresh milk!"

Sergio led his family to the nearby well, where they could wash their hands and faces with lye soap and fill their stone pitchers with water. They could hear their neighbors milling around in the darkness across the village.

"*Buongiorno!*" Sergio yelled, and soon everyone was calling back: "*Buongiorno! Buongiorno!*"

When they returned home Marcella fried the eggs and Sergio cut thick slices of barley bread. When the eggs were finished, she placed them on the bread. As always, they would eat with their hands.

"We should say a prayer before we eat," Sergio said. When all heads were bowed, he began, "Oh God, bless our family and bless this special day. Bless our little village. Bring peace and goodness to Villaggio di Montagna and let us refrain from any fighting today. And please take care of Lord Giancarlo and his family, wherever they may be."

THE SPECIAL DAY would not officially begin until Mass was said at the Church of Sant'Agnese. As usual, Marcella and the children sat on the wooden benches near the front, while Sergio joined the other men standing in the back.

No one spoke, and except for three candles in each of the six windows, the place was in darkness. Romero and Rosanna strained to see the painting of Santa Agnese on the wall behind the altar. It showed the saint holding a lamb in one arm, signifying her purity, and a sword in the other, a sign that she had been beheaded.

The colors were still fresh and vibrant.

"It is called a fresco," Marcella whispered. "Lord Giancarlo had it done. Just before…just before…"

The elderly priest, Father Enrico Lombardi, entered from a side room flanked by two young altar boys. One carried a holy water sprinkler, the other a censer with incense burning. The priest, looking as though he had just awakened from a long sleep, walked slowly around the altar, sprinkling it with holy water. Then he shuffled down the aisle and did the same for the congregation. Returning to the altar, he took the censer and incensed the altar, then the congregation.

Then he knelt before the altar.

"In nomine Patris, et Fílii, et Spíritus Sancti.
"Amen.
"Introíbo ad altáre Dei."

"In the Name of the Father, and of the Son, and of the Holy Spirit.
"Amen.
"I will go unto the altar of God.
"To God, Who gives joy to my youth."

The priest kept peering at the missal, as if he'd forgotten the words. His sermon was especially long, dwelling on the need for upholding church law and contributing to this church's upkeep. Seated nearby, the altar boys began a game of crossing and uncrossing their feet. On his bench Romero nodded and then succumbed to sleep. Rosanna fidgeted with the cord around her waist and Marcella fingered her rosary beads. In the back, Sergio nodded to friends he hadn't seen for so long.

The sermon was followed by two men passing collection baskets on long poles. Sergio dug into a leather pouch that hung from his belt and found two *soldi*. The man holding the basket made a face when he saw the amount, and Sergio made a face back.

At Communion, a few widows dressed in black tripped on the broken tiles as they approached the altar. They muttered something about the church needing more candles.

At the end of Mass, Father Lombardi returned to the pulpit for closing remarks. He blessed the people of Villaggio di Montagna and urged them to have a day of peace.

"We pray to have a day without arguing or dissension or fighting," he said pointedly.

And then he said, "And God bless Lord Giancarlo and his family."

The congregation ended with a song:

"Regina cæli, lætare, alleluia:
"Quia quem meruisti portare, alleluia,
"Resurrexit, sicut dixit, alleluia,
"Ora pro nobis Deum, alleluia."

"Queen of Heaven, rejoice, alleluia.
"The Son whom you deserved to bear, alleluia.
"Has risen, as He said, alleluia.
"Pray for us to God, alleluia."

Outside, the stars were fading and the sky began to brighten in the east. Everyone milled around the little piazza in front of the church.

"*Buongiorno!* It is good to see you again!"

"Did you sleep well?"

"Is this not a beautiful day?"

It had become the custom for everyone after the Mass to walk down the hill to the large Piazza del Popolo in the center of the village and to visit the merchants taking part in market day. Since Sergio was the village's *podestà,* a nominal position at best, he led the way.

At first, everyone seemed happy just to be together again, jostling along the cobblestones in the narrow streets. There were only two sections, or *contrade,* in Villaggio di Montagna, the *Drago,* or dragon, and the *Oca,* or goose. The villagers walked first through the *Drago* section, its blue-and-white flags flying on the houses as they passed, then made their way through the *Oca* section with its red-and-white flags.

There were a few catcalls between the two groups along the way, but mostly it was done in good humor. No one wanted a repetition of what happened on the last special day.

In the piazza, the aromas from Benedetto Santini's baked flatbreads, covered with eel, filled the air, while Nunzio, the deformed orphan with only one name, sold chestnuts from his stand of burning coals. Since Nunzio had no home, each night after a special day one villager or another let him sleep inside. In a corner, a small band of bagpipe, flute and drums played loudly, if not coherently, and children splashed in the fountain in the middle, ignoring their mothers' pleas not to get wet.

Luca the blacksmith was the first attraction.

"*Buongiorno,* Luca," Sergio cried. "How many horseshoes will you make today?"

"Not enough, Sergio. Never enough."

The crowd watched as he used a blower to kindle a fire among coals in a pit, then heated a length of iron and beat it into shape. A dip in a pail of water and it was ready, all in a matter of minutes.

"I will take four!" Sergio said.

"Come back in an hour," Luca replied.

Next to him, twin brothers Lorenzo and Luciano argued while painstakingly linking bits of wire into a chainmail vest, a task that had occupied them for as long as they could remember. Lorenzo rubbed his eyes, declaring that the work was making him blind.

Luciano shoved him. "Hurry up. We have to finish this today. We did not finish last time."

"And who will buy it?" Lorenzo asked. "There are no knights in this territory."

"You never know. Just finish."

Nearby, the ancient Massimo Montoni sharpened knives on a wheel, and Renzo Fortuno tested the strength of an arrow against a crossbow. Spread out around the piazza were stands for figs and dates and pomegranates and grapes and olives alongside tables with thick bottles of olive oil, beer and vintage wines.

The crowds lingered, examining the various pots and jars made by Franca Sporcozi and the woolen shifts displayed by Amelia Guidizi.

"Amelia," Marcella said, "your work gets better every time. I love the way you stitch the hems. *Molto bello!*"

"*Grazie,* Marcella. You are very kind."

"Sergio," Marcella said, "I would like to get a new one. Mine is getting so old."

"You deserve it," Sergio said, handing over a handful of *soldi*.

By far the most popular exhibit was at the corner of the piazza where three monks from the Abbey of San Joachim demonstrated the art of bookmaking. They had brought pages made from the dried hides of animals and cut into squares, and one brother showed how inks had to be mixed and pens prepared.

"Here," said Brother Alphonsus, "is a page copied from another edition. Notice the fine lettering and how the initial letters are illustrated. It took one of our monks a week just to do this one page."

Then he held up a completed book. Its cover was decorated with jewels, enamels and ivory carvings.

"Bellissimo!" the crowd whispered.

"Most of what we do are the sacred texts," the brother said, "but sometimes we will receive a commission from a prince or a lord to do a scientific text."

Rosanna got up the courage to ask a question. "Why do you make these books when nobody can read them?"

"Some people can read them," the monk replied.

"Only rich people. Poor people cannot read books."

"Perhaps not today," the monk said, "but in the future perhaps everyone will be able to read books."

"I do not think I can wait that long," Rosanna said.

Marcella hugged her daughter. "I am sorry, Rosanna. I am *molto dispiaciuto*."

"I really want to read, Mama."

"I know, dear. I am sorry."

As they moved from one stall to another, Rosanna noticed that her brother was no longer with them.

"Papa, Romero is not here."

"Damn," Sergio said, "where's that *ragazzo* off to now?"

They backtracked their steps until Rosanna noticed that Romero was in a corner behind the fortune teller's tent. He was not alone.

"Mama," Rosanna said, "he is with Giulietta Tabussi again."

Romero and Giulietta were in a close embrace, her head on his chest. He was kissing the top of her head.

Sergio stormed over to the couple. "Romero, come with us!"

Romero hugged Giulietta one more time, then reluctantly obeyed. Giulietta fled into the crowd. Sergio was grim, but silent, as the family came up to a display of flutes.

"Papa," Romero said, "can I get one of those? My pipe has only three holes. I cannot play anything on it."

"You think you deserve it?"

"Yes! Or maybe a drum? Mine is worn out. When I play with the other *ragazzi* they all laugh."

"I do not want to talk about it now."

Sergio started to lead his son away, and in doing so stepped on the boot of the man behind him.

"Watch it, Castellano," the man said.

"You're telling me to watch it, Tabussi?" Sergio said.

"Want to make something of it?"

Sergio's face was inches away from his accuser's. "You wouldn't dare."

Marcella grabbed Sergio's arm. "Husband, let us go."

She led the family to a display of willow baskets.

If this were not a special day, the villagers would have returned to their homes at noon for a light lunch and a nap. But today, there was work to do.

The men and boys returned to the church and entered the cavernous hall next to it. The women and girls went home and restarted the fires in the hearths. Each family was assigned a chore, one to roast chicken, another to make pasta, another to bake bread, and so on.

Everyone looked forward to the celebration of the life of Lord Giancarlo di Villaggio di Montagna.

THE MEETING

MARCELLA'S TASK WAS TO MAKE apple pies, as many as she could, and she and Rosanna sat at their table peeling the pile of apples before them.

"Mama, why do I always have to do girl things?" Rosanna asked.

"Perhaps because you are a girl?"

"Anyone can peel apples. Why doesn't Romero do this?"

"I do not know. Because he is a boy?"

"That is no reason. He does all the fun things. He chops wood. He goes hunting with Papa. He goes swimming. What do I do? I stay home and peel apples."

"I know, *cara*, I know. I wish it were different. I do not want to chop wood, but you know what? My own father, your grandfather, took me hunting once. And I actually killed a rabbit. But then when I saw it, I did not like what I saw. So I never went hunting again. But I think I would like to go swimming. That might be a *divertimento*. Papa and Romero go to the River Forno when it is hot and they come back all refreshed. Girls cannot do that. We would have to take most of our clothes off and we could not do that."

"Why not? Boys take their clothes off. Natalia and me hide behind trees and watch them."

"No!"

"Yes, we do. All the time."

Marcella smiled to herself. She remembered doing the exact same thing when she was a girl.

"Well, do not let them catch you. We must hurry, we have hundreds of apples left."

Meanwhile, Sergio and Romero had joined the other men and boys at the church hall to set up for the banquet. This meant placing long planks over sawhorses to create tables and covering them with strips of damask that were stored in a locked room.

It was in that storage room that the altercation started. Sergio had reached for a roll of red damask on a top shelf when it came tumbling down, right on the head of Rocco Tabussi.

"What the hell!" Rocco yelled.

"*Scusa*. It slipped."

"Slipped like hell. You deliberately knocked that on my head."

"I did not! It slipped. If your fat ass wasn't hogging all that room it wouldn't have hit you."

"Oh, yeah?"

"Yeah!"

"Yeah!"

"*Vaffanculo!*"

"*Vai a cagare!*"

Sergio invited Rocco to step outside.

"*Andiamo!*"

"*Andiamo!*"

No one quite knew when the feud between the Castellano and the Tabussi families had begun. Most people believed it started when Sergio's great-great grandfather mistakenly appropriated a sheep belonging to the Tabussi family when both clans lived on Monte Sumbra.

The elder Tabussi accused the elder Castellano of stealing the sheep. The elder Castellano replied that the sheep had strayed into his own herd. One thing led to another, blows were struck, their wives and children became involved, and for decades neither family spoke to the other even though they lived within spitting distance on the hillside.

And so it continued through the generations, even after Sergio and his family and Rocco and his family both moved to Villaggio di Montagna.

On the last special day, Sergio and Rocco had gotten into such a violent fight over a remark Rocco had made that Sergio suffered a sprained arm and Rocco a broken nose. It took dozens of men to separate them.

Now there was a new factor in the feud. Sergio's son Romero, who was fifteen, and Rocco's daughter Giulietta, who was thirteen, had begun talking to each other every chance they could. Even now, while their fathers were fighting over the roll of damask, they found each other and wandered off to the River Forno. They sat on the bank and talked. And talked. And got to know each other even better.

So when Sergio and Rocco left the storage room the first thing Rocco said was:

"And you better damn well keep that son of yours away from my daughter, shithead."

"My son? She's the one who keeps chasing him, *bastardo*!"

Rocco thereupon slugged Sergio, who slugged him back, and the two were soon rolling around on the grass outside the church hall, separated only when the elderly Father Lombardi threatened to excommunicate both of them.

Everyone else went home to get ready for the celebration. That meant exchanging their dark brown tunics and breeches and dresses for lighter brown tunics and breeches and dresses. Carrying all the food the women had made, they paraded through the village and deposited the pots and pans and dishes on the tables. There was so much food, the bright damask tablecloths could hardly be seen.

Pastas and meat and fish and vegetables and salads and fruit and desserts. The supply didn't seem to end and the joyful villagers laughed and talked and even began to sing as the afternoon wore on. This prompted Romero and two of his buddies to go to the small stage at the end of the room and set up their band, the "Princes." Romero was on drums and his buddies played flute and lute, an odd mixture but these were the only instruments they had. They formed what they called a "barn band," but they obviously had little time to practice with the cows and horses interrupting. And it showed.

They had just started to play when Giulietta left her table and sat entranced in front of Romero. He immediately began to sing a song he had made up, in a halting falsetto:

> *"When the sun rises in the morning,*
> *"When the sun goes to sleep at night,*
> *"You will always be my maiden*
> *"And I will be your knight."*

Giulietta blushed and Rocco rushed over and grabbed her shoulder.

"Giulietta! Come back here and eat!"

"I am not hungry, Papa."

"Yes, you are!"

"No, I am not. Papa, leave me alone. I'm thirteen years old."

"Right. You're thirteen years old."

Everyone watched as Rocco dragged his screaming daughter back to their table.

Fortunately, it was time for the joust to begin and a young man had been chosen from each *contrada* to engage in the historic battle. Dressed in metal armor that had become slightly rusty, the man from *Drago*, carrying a blue-and-white flag with a dragon on it, faced the man from *Oca*, who carried a red-and-white flag with a goose on it. They tried to look fierce beneath their metal helmets, but they knew this was all for show.

In earlier times, they would have ridden horses toward each other, but their horses had grown too old and tired, so the men simply walked fast.

On the sidelines, the villagers took bets on which man would be victorious. They put their money in separate pots, and the winning amount would go to the church.

On their first pass with their lances, the two jousters missed each other by yards. Laughing, they turned around and tried again. And again. On the fifth attempt, the man from *Drago* nicked his opponent slightly on the arm and was declared the winner.

As a resident of *Oca,* Rocco immediately challenged the verdict.

"This is fixed! I knew it was fixed!"

"How could it be fixed?" Sergio, who was a resident of *Drago*, asked. "Everyone saw what happened. Anyway, who cares who won?"

"It was fixed," Rocco cried. "I know it!"

More words were spoken and inevitably the two grown men were again rolling around on the ground like teenagers. The villagers cheered them on.

"Go *Drago!*"

"Go *Oca!*"

"Sergio!"

"Rocco!"

The shouting and yelling went on far longer than necessary and the afternoon was fast fading. People started to drift away, ready to go back to the church hall and the beer that awaited them. Then suddenly, as Sergio and Rocco continued to pummel each other, the crowd grew silent.

Four figures had appeared on the hillside above the church. A man, a woman, a boy, a girl. They didn't move.

"Look!" someone cried. "It's Lord Giancarlo!"

"It's Lord Giancarlo!"

"No! It can't be!"

"And his wife!"

"And their children!"

"And they're naked!"

THEY WERE NOT NAKED, OF COURSE, but since they were clad only in white T-shirts and shorts, and with the sun behind them, Carlo, Nancy, Andrew and Grace appeared to be badly in need of clothing. And they were shivering. Father Lombardi came to their rescue.

He poked the young man next to him. "Here's my key. Go into the sacristy and get my robes and surplices. *Fretta*!"

Waiting for the youth to return, the villagers edged their way to the newcomers. No one spoke, but everyone was sobbing. As *podestà*, Sergio was at the head of the group.

"Giancarlo?"

"My name is Carlo, yes. How did you know?"

At that, everyone got down on their knees on the muddy field. The clothing arrived just then and soon Carlo and Nancy had pulled chasubles over their heads while Andrew and Grace drowned in long white surplices. With Carlo in red and Nancy in green, they looked every bit like a lord and lady.

That prompted everyone to bow so low their foreheads got muddy.

"Lord Giancarlo," Sergio said, "we have so many questions. But first, *benvenuto*! You all look rather tired, but we understand that. Your children, my, in truth they have grown! Oh, we missed you so much!"

"Really?" Carlo said. "We didn't even know you were here, that your village was here. But our car stopped running and…"

"Your cart? Surely you are not traveling in a cart? You always loved riding horses, but never in a cart."

"Ah, no…"

"Can you tell us where you have been?"

"Oh, all over. We went to Lucca, we went to Florence…"

"We have never heard of those places. And we never leave here anyway. You must have enjoyed them, Lord Giancarlo."

"Yes, they were very nice. But tell me, are all of you ghosts? We heard you were ghosts."

What followed reminded Carlo of his lecture on vaudeville routines in his musical theater history course.

"No, I am not a ghost," Sergio said. "Who is a ghost? You must be a ghost."

"No, I'm not a ghost. You are a ghost."

"No, no, I am not a ghost. You are a ghost."

Nancy interrupted. "Sir, we are very tired, and also very hungry. Do you think we might have a little something to eat?"

At this, the crowd hurried to make a path for the four visitors to the church hall where they were seated at the head table and deluged with plate after plate of pasta and chicken and beef.

"Excuse me," Andrew said, "could we have some knives and forks?"

"Knaves and forks?" someone asked. "We have heard of knaves, but we do not have any here."

"No, *knives* and forks. To eat with."

The crowd of people, who were hovering over the visitors, tried to understand.

"Did you forget how to eat in all your travels?" a man said. "Here, I will show you."

The man pulled a bowl of beef stew in front of him, grabbed a handful and put it in his mouth. Grace looked like she was going to throw up.

"Oh," Sergio said, "perhaps you would like this."

He handed Carlo the lone wooden spoon on the table. Carlo let his wife try the stew first, then Andrew, and then took a few spoonsful himself. Grace declared that she wasn't hungry, but when Marcella offered each guest a piece of apple pie, even Grace could not refuse.

It was then that Sergio and the others noticed the bloody handkerchief around Carlo's hand.

"Oh my, Lord Giancarlo. That is still the wound from that old battle?"

"Um, no. it was just a flashlight."

"You are very brave, Lord Giancarlo."

Nancy flashed a black look at her husband.

"Excuse me," Carlo said, "but I wonder if there's a hotel or someplace where we might rest for the night. We've been driving all day."

"A hostel?" Sergio said. "Why, Lord Giancarlo, you know we do not have any hostels in Villaggio di Montagna. Remember when you made the piazza you were thinking about adding one but you felt this would bring in too many strangers."

"Oh."

"But you will stay in your castle, of course. No one has stayed there since you left, but our women go up there every special day and dust and make sure everything is in order for when you return. And now you have, and we are so happy."

"Castle?" Andrew asked.

"Of course," Sergio said. "Here, Marcella and I and our children will help you up there. I am certain you are all very tired."

"Yes, very tired. The castle would be nice," Carlo said. He could feel Nancy's eyes burning into the back of his head.

Sergio put his arm around Carlo's shoulder, Marcella held Nancy's hand, and Romero and Andrew and Rosanna and Grace trailed behind as they trudged up the hill.

"Careful not to trip on your gowns, kids," Carlo yelled back to his children.

When Sergio opened the heavy wooden doors, the Americans were led into the Great Hall: big heavy tables and chairs on the wooden floor, large paintings on the walls and the sun streaming through heavy curtains at the windows. Miraculously, the sun had stopped moving in the sky the moment Carlo and his family had entered Villaggio di Montagna. According to the villagers, it was a special day that was not ending.

"Certo," Sergio said, "I am certain you know the way, but I will lead you to your rooms just in case."

The main bedroom contained an ornate bed with a canopy, a heavy chest and a large chair.

"And you know that the chamber pot is underneath the bed," Sergio said.

"Um, yes, I know," Carlo said. Grace whimpered.

Rosanna showed Grace her room, and Romero pointed Andrew to his. They said good night to the villagers.

"Carlo!" Nancy said when they were alone, "what in the world are you doing? Why are you pretending that you're some lord from the Middle Ages? You have to tell them who we are. I'm so embarrassed."

"I will," Carlo said. "I will tomorrow. I don't know if this is a dream or if we're in some sort of time warp or if we've gone crazy, but I'm too tired right now to think about it."

"OK, first thing tomorrow. For sure."

They had never slept on a bed so soft, so comforting.

IF THE SUN HAD SET, people might have thought it was the next morning when everyone awoke. But the sun was still in its same position in the sky, and the villagers and the Americans were equally amazed.

"*Stupendo!*" Sergio told Carlo when he arrived at the castle. "We weren't even tired when we went to bed, and when we woke up it was just like last night. It is a miracle! *Miracolo!* We are having two special days."

Since the closets in the castle were empty (moths were blamed), Sergio had brought a change of clothing for the family—the "good" versions of their tunics and breeches and dresses while the villagers remained in their workday clothes. Carlo and Nancy and Andrew and Grace were almost the same size as Sergio and Marcella and Romero and Rosanna, so the outfits worked out almost perfectly.

"Sergio," Carlo said as he adjusted his belt, "there's something I want to talk to you about."

"I know, I know, we have a lot to catch up. But first, you must be very hungry. Come to our house. Marcella is making a wonderful breakfast."

Nancy glared at Carlo, but Carlo shrugged and they followed Sergio to his house. Marcella had indeed made what they considered an elaborate breakfast, fried eggs and toast. Without spoons, they followed their hosts' examples and dipped the bread into the eggs. Andrew was so hungry that Marcella made him a second batch. Grace tried unsuccessfully to keep her fingers clean.

"Now you will want to go around the village and see what has happened since you left," Sergio said.

"Sure," Carlo said, "but first I must tell you…"

"We can talk on the way. *Andiamo.*"

With Nancy still glaring at Carlo, they followed Sergio and his family through the village. Andrew and Romero found a reason to stop at the shop on the piazza that made musical instruments.

"I play the drums a little," Romero said.

"Really?" Andrew said. "I wish I could play. But I like to listen to music. Do you like rap?"

"Rap? What's that?"

"It's where they talk really fast. Like this:

"When he was ten, his father split, full of it, debt-ridden
"Two years later, see Alex and his mother, bed-ridden
"Half-dead, sittin' in their own sick
"The scent thick…"

"That's from a musical on Broadway called *Hamilton*," Andrew said.

"Musical on Broadway? *Hamilton*? Andrew, I do not know what you are talking about."

"Well, I think it's great. I listen to it all the time."

"How do you listen to it?"

"On my headset. I'd show you but it's in the car. Probably wouldn't play here anyway."

The two boys, both fifteen, were obviously not communicating about music so they turned to a mutual subject of interest.

"Do you have a girlfriend?" Romero asked.

"I like this girl at school," Andrew said. "Her name is Stacy. But I don't think she knows I exist."

"I am fond of a girl here," Romero said. "Her name is Giulietta. Maybe you will meet her. She is so beautiful! Her skin is real pale and she has the most amazing blue eyes. *Bellissima!* I could look at her all day."

"Cool," Andrew said. "Very cool."

"No!" Romero said, his fists ready to attack. "Why do you say that! She is nice! Do not insult her or I will…"

"No, no. I wasn't insulting her. Where I come from, saying 'cool' means nice, great."

"Oh. *Tutto bene.* Anyway, she likes me, too. I know she does. You know what I do sometimes? Sometimes late at night when my father is sleeping I go out of our house and go to her house and stand under her window. She comes to her window and we talk real soft. Sometimes I even sing a little. I cannot stay long but, what did you call it? It is very cool."

"That is very cool. I could never do that with Stacy."

"But we have this problem. My father and her father do not get along. In fact, they fight all the time. The two families have been fighting forever. Now our fathers have forbidden us to see each other. They yell at us if they catch us. I am so desperate, Andrew, I do not know what to do. Sometimes I think I will kill myself. Look, I have already tried."

He rolled up his sleeves and showed Andrew scars on his wrists.

"You're a cutter? No! You didn't!"

"I do not know what this is called, what we do. Giulietta did it, too. We did it together on the last special day, but it did not work. We just want to die, we just want to die!"

Romero stopped, sat on a big rock in the piazza and held his head in his hands. Andrew didn't know what to do. He patted his new friend on the shoulder.

"Oh, it can't be that bad, can it?"

"It is! It is terrible! *Terribile!* If we were old enough we would run away. We have talked about it. But we do not know where we would go. Nobody ever leaves Villaggio di Montagna."

Sullen, the two boys walked on, looking at the displays outside the shops but not really seeing anything.

Nearby, Grace and Rosanna were examining the old books that had been shown at the market day.

"I wish I could read," Rosanna said. "I told that fat old monk in the booth that only rich people were allowed to read and he said that maybe someday I would, too. I cannot wait until someday!"

"That's terrible!" Grace said. "I read all the time. I wish you could read the books I'm reading now. They're all about women having rights. Just like men have rights."

"Rights? I do not think I know what that means."

"Oh, it means things like jobs. Women doing the same kind of work as men."

"Like chopping wood?"

"Well, I don't know about that, but other jobs. And getting equal pay for their work."

"I do not know. I do not think even men get paid for their work here. I mean, they take care of the farms and the crops and the animals, and we all live pretty much the same."

Grace thought she should change the subject.

"Do you have a boyfriend?" she asked Rosanna.

"No. There is a boy that goes swimming with Romero, but I don't think he even knows I exist."

"I don't have a boyfriend either. I guess we're just too young."

"But we are thirteen. Giulietta Tabussi is thirteen and she and Romero are together all the time. At least until my father or her father catches them."

"I think," Grace said, "that girls should be able to go out with whoever they want. They should learn early that they control their own bodies."

Before Rosanna had a chance to respond, they ran into Sergio and Carlo and Marcella and Nancy and it was time for another gathering in the church hall. This was to celebrate, Sergio said, the return of Lord Giancarlo di Villaggio di Montagna.

NANCY GRABBED CARLO'S ARM just as they were about to enter the church hall and warned him that he could not delay telling the truth any longer. He should do it right now.

"Can we eat first? I'm starving."

"No."

But when they entered the packed hall they were greeted by cheers and whistles and stomping.

"Lord Giancarlo's back! Lord Giancarlo's back!"

Carlo and his family took their places at the head table and he tried to quiet the crowd with faint hand gestures. When that didn't work he tried a few broader ones and finally a few royal salutes. Andrew and Grace waved a little and finally even Nancy smiled and waved.

Carlo started to speak but Sergio announced that dinner would now be served. It was as elaborate as the previous day, even more so. Pasta and meats and vegetables and on and on.

After everyone had eaten dessert, Carlo rose to quiet the crowd but was preempted by Sergio, who went on at length about how pleased and excited Villaggio di Montagna was to welcome its leading citizen and benefactor back from, well, …wherever he had been.

"Tell us, Lord Giancarlo, about your journeys. As you know, not a single one of us has been outside the walls of our village. What is it like?"

Carlo knew he had to confess.

"Well, let me say that my family and I have come a long way, in fact from a country that is not even known to you. You see, we are from America."

Heads turned and questions were mouthed, but Carlo realized he didn't know how to explain "America." He hurriedly continued.

"We came to Italy to visit relatives who live in a village not too far from here. They told us about this part of Italy and so we came here and we first stopped in Barga."

No one had heard of Barga, though it was less than thirty miles away.

"We met a woman there who told us about Villaggio di Montagna, and of course we wanted to come here."

Carlo could feel Nancy poking him in the back. "Tell them you're not Giancarlo! Tell them!"

"Now," he continued, "I have something else to say. When we first arrived, you assumed that I was a man you have long admired and who I guess has somehow disappeared. Well, I am not that man. My name is Carlo, but it is not Giancarlo. I don't even know who Giancarlo is."

Across the room there were cries of "No! No!"

"I'm sorry that I deceived you. I should have made this clear right at the start. But I want to say that we, my family and I, are very grateful for the welcome you have given us. This has been the highlight of our trip and we will never forget all you wonderful people and the beautiful Villaggio di Montagna."

He sat down.

The crowd was obviously confused.

"Then who are you?" a man asked.

"We are just ordinary people," Carlo said. "My wife and I teach in a university in our country and our children go to school."

The villagers knew that when Lord Giancarlo was young he had gone to the University of Bologna, the oldest university in the world, so they were familiar with the term, but they didn't understand how this fair-haired man before them could teach there. He didn't look old and he didn't even have a beard.

"And did you say that your wife teaches there, too?"

"Yes, both of us."

A woman teaching at a university? This was beyond comprehension.

"What about your hand?" a man asked. "Giancarlo injured his hand in a battle and always wore a white bandage. You have a bandage."

"This? Oh, I cut it on a flashlight. I thought I told you that."

This was too confusing, and the crowd tried to make sense of these revelations.

At the back of the room a man stood up.

"Well, I know what this is all about. It is a hoax. This man is not Lord Giancarlo even though he pretended he was. I do not blame him. He did not know any better. But who do I blame? That man over there! Sergio Castellano. He's the one who let this man fool us. He lies, he cheats. Now he has pulled the biggest hoax of all."

"Sit down, Rocco!" someone yelled. "You know that is not true!"

"How do I know it is not true? The Castellanos have always been liars and cheats."

Sergio, of course, was offended by this and soon Rocco Tabussi and Sergio Castellano were face to face in the middle of the room, almost spitting at each other.

"Tell me that to my face, Tabussi!" Sergio yelled.

"I'm telling you to your face!"

"Cavolo!"

"Porca vacca!"

At the head table, the Americans were confused, embarrassed and worried.

"What's this all about?" Carlo wondered. Andrew leaned over.

"Romero was telling me about this, Dad. It seems the two families have been feuding for ages and ages and now it's worse because Romero

Castellano and Giulietta Tabussi have been seeing each other. It's serious, Dad. Romero and Giulietta even tried to kill themselves. Romero says he wants to die."

"That's terrible," Nancy said. "They've been feuding for ages and nobody has tried to stop it?"

As Sergio and Rocco started to exchange blows, Carlo cried out, "Wait! Stop!"

He banged his steel cup on the table.

"Listen up!" he said. He felt as if he was trying to calm down a bunch of unruly college students. "Listen up!"

The room eventually quieted, and their neighbors from *Drago* and *Oca* pulled Sergio and Rocco apart.

"Listen," Carlo repeated. "Let me tell you a story."

Silence.

"I'm told that the Castellanos and the Tabussis have been feuding for a long time. Well, I know about another feud like that so let me tell you about it. This is a famous story. Everybody knows it. They even wrote a play about it. There was a family called the Montagues and another called Capulets. They lived in another city in Italy called Verona. They had feuded for years, but neither family knew what caused it in the first place.

"Now the Montagues had a son named Romeo and the Capulets had a daughter named Juliet. In fact, their names are sort of like Romero and Giulietta here, aren't they? Juliet was thirteen years old and we think Romeo was a few years older.

"They were deeply in love but both of their fathers refused to let them see each other. They did everything they could to keep them apart. But the two lovers still got together. Sometimes Romeo went to Juliet's window and they talked."

Romero smiled at Giulietta, who was sitting close by.

"It got complicated," Carlo said, "but in the end, there was a tragedy. Both Romeo and Juliet died. They killed themselves. All because their parents wouldn't let them see each other. And it wasn't until then that their grieving families finally realized how foolish they had been."

Carlo paused to let all this sink in.

"So is this the story here? Are you going to continue with this feud forever and forever? And are you going to let Romero and Giulietta kill themselves because you are so stubborn?"

The room was quiet as Sergio and Rocco stared at each other.

"Well, are you?" someone yelled. "Are you going to let this *ragazzo e ragazza* kill each other because you are so stubborn?"

"Stubborn as mules!" someone else shouted.

Father Lombardi rose slowly to his feet. "It is time to call a halt to this," he said. "This has been going on for centuries. Perhaps this man isn't Giancarlo, but perhaps he was sent to us to teach us a lesson. Listen to him, Sergio and Rocco. For God's sake, listen to him."

No one spoke. Sergio and Rocco stopped glaring at each other and reluctantly shook hands. Sergio went back to his family and put his arm around Romero. Rocco hugged Giulietta. They led the two young lovers to the middle of the room, where they joined hands. Everyone milled around both families, cheering and laughing.

Carlo looked around the room and whispered to his family: "Let's get out of here."

After slipping out the back, they shed their tunics and breeches and dresses and left them in a pile at the door. The sun was still bright so T-shirts and shorts were fine. When they ran up to their car they saw a man dressed in armor on a horse next to it, but when he saw them, he waved and rode away. Carlo noticed that the man had a white cloth tied around his right hand.

Miraculously, the car started.

BACK HOME

THE FOLLOWING MAY Carlo opened his laptop and found two emails. One was from Ezio and Donna, who said they were fine, that there wasn't anything new in Sant'Antonio since they left, and that they were still waiting to hear about their trip. "We hope it wasn't too boring."

The other was from a name Carlo did not recognize.

"Clara Marincola? Who's that? Probably wants money."

But he opened the email. It was the longest one he had ever received.

"Dear Signor Mantucci: I'm so pleased that I just found the card you left me almost a year ago so I am now able to write you. It's been terribly busy here at the tourist office in Barga and my staff and I have barely been able to keep up with all the tourists who are coming to the Garfagnana now.

"But I know you will be interested in hearing about something that happened not long after we met last June. Remember that I told you about the legend of this mysterious village called Villaggio di Montagna that was supposed to appear every hundred years? Otherwise it was cloaked in mist and people didn't really believe it existed.

"Remember how I told you that there were reports that the village had been seen a couple of times over the centuries, but also that I said this was probably a story that the people in the Garfagnana wanted to use to attract tourists. Remember how we couldn't believe it?

"I don't know where you went from here, but I imagine you didn't look for Villaggio di Montagna. You wouldn't have found it anyway. Well, something happened last June, maybe just a few days after you left.

"It seems that one day people in the villages in the surrounding hills noticed that the mist had suddenly lifted from the valley and there was in fact a village nestled there. They couldn't believe it. They had never seen anything there before.

"Some brave men went down to the village and found that it looked like something straight out of the Middle Ages. The houses were all small and made of wood and mud, the streets, such as they were, were narrow and made of cobblestones. There was a piazza in the middle and there were some shops around it. And there was a little church."

Carlo stopped reading so that he could wipe his eyes with a handkerchief. He alternated between laughing and crying.

"And then people started coming out of the houses. They were rubbing their eyes as if they'd just awakened from a long sleep. They were all dressed like in the Middle Ages, too, with brown tunics and breeches.

"They didn't know how to answer the questions the other people asked. They seemed to have a strange dialect, and every once in a while the name 'Giancarlo' was heard, but the people from the other villages didn't know who that was."

Carlo was now sobbing amid his laughter.

"Well, anyway, that was then. And so much has happened since then I don't know where to begin.

"The people from this village, Villaggio di Montagna, knew that something had happened while they were sleeping, but that somehow they had survived some terrible periods and that they were now in the twenty-first century.

"It didn't seem to faze them. They just thought they'd missed a lot of wars and terrible things but they were now ready to start new lives.

"They couldn't live in those old houses, of course, but over the next months the Italian government, which as you know doesn't exactly act swiftly, provided a good deal of loans, and the people of Villaggio di Montagna built an entirely new village for themselves right next to it. Small but nice homes that have heat and electricity and running water. Even toilets!

"Just like, as I told you, when the village of Fabbriche di Careggine was flooded to make that lake and its residents were moved to the town of Vagli Sotto.

"They kept the same street pattern, but built real paved streets. They built a piazza in the middle of it, with shops all around. Only this time the shops sell expensive clothing and household goods. And there are fancy restaurants. People have big-screen television sets and the village is equipped with Wi-Fi and kids go around with headsets and iPhones. And cars! Almost everyone has a car. Or scooters.

"There is also a new church, very modern, with a very stark steel crucifix behind the altar. I'm told some people don't like it. And there's a school, and even a library!

"And they gave a name to the new village, Villaggio dei Sogni, the Village of Dreams.

"I should also tell you that two men from village, Sergio Castellano and Rocco Tabussi, who are apparently great friends, took charge of this whole project. They raised the money and supervised construction and I'm told there wasn't a single argument between them."

Carlo couldn't stop laughing.

"But here's the best part. The people of Villaggio di Montagna wanted to preserve their original village, so with Sergio and Rocco supervising, they made repairs to the houses and the shops and the streets. They made the old village look really nice. And now, every weekend, the people of Villaggio dei Sogni go over to Villaggio di Montagna and put on their medieval clothes and work in the shops. There's a man making horseshoes and a woman selling tunics, and some monks bring real old books to show how they were made. And they sell a lot of souvenirs, of course. We just made a film of this and it's going to be on YouTube. Watch for it.

"And there's a big banquet on Saturday afternoons followed by a joust between two men dressed as knights. They call it the Faire Medievale di Giancarlo, or Giancarlo's Medieval Fair. I don't know where they got the name. But you know what? It has become one of the most popular tourist attractions in the Garfagnana, bigger than Barga or Vagli Sotto. People come from all over and they pay goodly amounts to enter the village. The money is being used to repay those government loans and they're almost paid off.

"Oh, I almost forgot. They found the decomposed body of a man in the River Forno at Villaggio di Montagna. He was dressed in black and had black hair and a crooked nose. The people had never seen him before.

"So, Mr. Mantucci, I'm going to send you our new brochure, 'Step With Us Into the Past.' I want to invite you to come back and see Villaggio di Montagna. There really is one! You wouldn't believe it!"

Yes, Carlo thought, yes, I'd believe it.

Nancy called from the kitchen. "Carlo, why are you laughing so loud? I can hear you from here."

"Nancy! Come here! You've got to read this email I just got!"

"Can it wait, Carlo? We're late for rehearsals and the students are already upset with us because they think this musical is so preposterous. They think it's just fantasy and they want something more realistic. I'll read the email later. Let's go. We have to rehearse the second act of *Brigadoon*."

BEHIND THE CURTAIN

2018

THROUGHOUT THE LONG NIGHT, Sam tried not to move, afraid he'd awaken Nora. Sleepless, he was trying to come up with the answer to the question he knew he'd be asked that day.

He knew he was lucky. He'd been doing all right, but just all right, in the theater department's master's program, and a couple of months ago his professor had offered him a chance to improve his grade by researching and writing an extra-credit project.

"You can do it as an independent study," Professor Nancy Mantucci had said. "But it has to be good. And it has to be original."

The trouble was, he didn't know what to write about. He had rejected so many ideas. It was supposed to be almost the length of a book, but some topics were too superficial. Some were too broad. Some required research that was not available. And he just wasn't interested in some ideas.

And today he had to meet with the professor with a subject in mind.

"Shit!" It was barely a whisper but it was loud enough to cause Nora to stir.

"What? What?"

"Nothing," he said. "It's nothing. Go back to sleep."

Nora was soon breathing heavily. Normally, he liked to watch Nora sleep, the way her lips fluttered, but now he was too preoccupied.

He thought some more. Every subject has been done. Every single person has been researched. There's nothing left do. Maybe he wouldn't do it. He'd just take the grade, average though it was, and hope that Professor Mantucci would still write a letter of recommendation for him. Or maybe he'd drop out and try to get a job. But he couldn't go home and face his parents if he left college now.

Exhausted, his mind began to wander. Songs from musicals he had seen, songs on his playlist. As he often did during these times of stress, he started silently singing obscure songs from forgotten musicals.

"*You start to light her cigarette...*"

"*I'm so happy, I'm afraid I'll die here in your arms...*"

"*It's the being home together/When the shadows rise...*"

Sam began to hum aloud and Nora turned over and pulled a pillow over her head.

"*It's the going home together through the changing years...*"

"I love that song," he said aloud. "What great lyrics."

He could hear Nora grinding her teeth.

"*It's the talk about the weather and the laughter and the tears...*"

"What? What? What is it? Samuel, will you just go to sleep! I've got a major paper due tomorrow. Today!"

"Sorry, sorry. Go back to sleep. I'm getting up."

It was 5:45 and only the dimmest of light shone through the tattered blinds. Sam eased out of the bed, disturbing Bella, who was sleeping at the foot. He picked up Nora's leotard from the floor and pulled on the terrycloth bathrobe he had "borrowed" from a hotel on their vacation in Nantucket last year.

In the miniature kitchen, he poured a glass of orange juice, saving the last clean glass for his girlfriend, and plugged in the coffeemaker.

Staring at the chipped wooden table, he sang aloud. "*It's the talk about the weather and the laughter and the tears... It's the talk about...*"

He stared even harder at the table.

"*It's the talk about...*"

He sat down. His right knee was shaking.

"*It's the talk about the weather and the laughter and...*"

He stopped short and stared at the coffeepot.

"*the laughter and the tears...*"

"That's it! That's it!"

He poured coffee into a chipped mug that read "Eagles."

"I've got it! By George I've got it!" He was dancing around the kitchen now. "Professor Mantucci will be so pleased."

He dug out his phone and checked messages. The daily one from his mother, wondering what he'd finally chosen for the project and berating him for not texting her back. He found the score for the Red Sox. Beaten badly again. He found the weather report: More rain expected.

He got dressed, put the phone in his pocket, kissed Nora's head and ran down the stairs to his bike.

Another song popped into his head. *"Oh, it's grand to see my picture in the papers/I enjoy a life that has a dash of spice…"*

He passed another student on her way to the library.

"How's the project coming, Sam?" Anita yelled at him. "Did you ever think of an idea?"

"I'm fine! I'm fine! No problem. Thanks for asking!"

He thought Anita looked disappointed. Everyone on campus seemed to know that he hadn't been able to think of a project.

Central State's campus was only ten minutes away and, even though low clouds threatened rain, Sam liked the way it looked on this chilly mid-September morning. The ivy-covered old buildings, dating from the time when the university was a teachers' school, would never blend with the concrete newer ones, but there was a certain charm about it all, he thought.

He had chosen Central State because it was close, but not too close, to home. He could bring his laundry back every couple of weeks and enjoy his mother's cooking. He hadn't had many friends in high school so he mainly stayed home and played videogames. Short and skinny, with freckles and unruly blond hair, he often joked around to hide a deep insecurity.

Perhaps that was why Professor Mantucci and her husband, Carlo, paid a little more attention to him than other students. Unconsciously, they thought he needed some protection.

He had always been a musical theater geek. His mother played Broadway albums constantly. When he was young he and his younger sister and two cousins performed all the parts of *West Side Story* in their back yard. He was Rolf in *The Sound of Music* when he was a sophomore in high school and had the title role in *Oliver!* when he was a senior. At Central State, he was Doody in *Grease*, Benny Collins in *Rent* and Dieter in *Spring Awakening*.

He knew, because of his looks, it would be difficult to be cast as a lead, but he was going to try. If not, he could try for the second lead, the funny friend, the good buddy. Still not ready to look for a job after he received his bachelor's degree, he decided to go on for a master's.

And through the theater classes he had met Nora. He could never understand why this dark-haired, dark-eyed and petite budding actress chose to be with him. They'd met in their sophomore year. She was also from a small town and her parents were teachers. They'd broken up a couple of times, and Sam didn't think they'd have a long-term relationship. He didn't know what Nora thought. They didn't talk about it.

"Oh, it's grand to see my picture in the papers/I enjoy a life that has a dash of spice..."

Professor Mantucci's office was hidden in a corner behind the curtains in the theater building. Crossing the stage, he almost tripped on the cord leading from the lone floor lamp at the back.

"Stupid light," he muttered.

He found her bent over her laptop, typing away, her glasses on top of her black hair.

"Guess what?" he said.

"Let me guess. You've thought of an idea for your independent study project!"

"Right! Remember when you drove four of us to New York and we saw *The Golden Apple?* You said you wanted us to see it because it was an innovative musical and one of your favorites and it was hardly ever performed?"

"And they did a terrific job."

"I thought so, too. That story of Ulysses set in Washington State, the staging, the acting, but mostly the score. I had never heard such wonderful songs. Especially the lyrics. The lyrics are so witty and intelligent. And memorable. I can't get them out of my head. I've got the CD on my phone and I play it all the time."

"I'm so glad you liked it. Most people have never heard of it. Even theater people."

"Well, I was lying in bed this morning still trying to think of an idea for my extra-credit project..."

"…I'm glad you've been thinking. It's getting awfully late, you know. The deadline is September 15 for a proposal. That's a week from Thursday."

"Right. But then I started humming the songs that we heard in that show."

"I'm sure Nora appreciated that."

"Nora can sleep through a tornado. Anyway, I was humming along, especially to that song that Ulysses and Penelope sing together. It's so beautiful."

"Going Home Together."

"Yes, that's it. So I suddenly had the most brilliant idea. You'll never guess."

"Try me."

"John Latouche! Who wrote the lyrics! I'll write about him. And he's written other shows, too. You told us! And nobody's written a book about him, right? He's dead, I think, but he'd make a great bio, wouldn't he? I could do it. I could find the sources."

"Yes, yes, I suppose so."

Nancy Mantucci began to intently study the bust of Shakespeare on the shelf next to the door. He thought he heard her say, "Oh, dear."

"What's wrong, Professor?" Sam asked. "Isn't that a great idea? Remember when we were driving you said people didn't know much about him?"

"Yes, I remember that I said that. Then."

"So he'd make a good subject for a book, right?"

"Well…"

The professor dug through a pile of papers on a table behind her and pulled out a thick book with a gray cover and red lettering. She slid it across the desk.

"Oh, no," he said. "*The Ballad of John Latouche*. By Howard Pollack. Shit!"

"I'm so sorry. I just got this last week and haven't had a chance to look at it."

"Shit!"

"I'm sure you could have done a good job."

"Oh, sure. Howard Pollack. He wrote that book about Gershwin that you required us to read."

"Also books about Aaron Copland and Marc Blitzstein."

"Shit."

"You'll think of something else, Sam."

"No, I won't. I won't! There's nothing else. Nothing!"

Almost in tears, Samuel Peterson tore out of Nancy Mantucci's office and this time tripped on the cord from the lone light at the back of the stage and fell flat on his face.

"Goddamn it! Shit!"

Crossing the stage, two freshman girls happened to see the accident.

"Sir, are you OK?"

"Can we call someone?"

"No!" Sam shouted. "Leave me alone! And don't call me Sir!"

He tore back into his professor's office.

"Why the hell is that light on the stage all the time? Somebody could get killed!"

"You mean the ghost light?"

PROFESSOR NANCY MANTUCCI let her angry student settle down. She offered coffee from the pot on the hot plate behind her and took out the box of chocolate chip cookies she had made the night before. They were supposed to be for a faculty party this afternoon, but he could have a few.

She didn't say anything, just busied herself on her laptop. She remembered when her own son, Andrew, went into a rage over something or other. Fortunately, it was never very serious, and he got over it.

Sam had quieted down now, hunched over with his head in his hands. The professor waited it out.

"I'm sorry about the book, Sam. It's just bad timing. But there are lots of subjects out there. You'll think of something."

"No, I won't. This was the only idea I've had. The only one."

"And I'm sorry about the light. It must have been moved when we tore down the set last week. I'll have maintenance move it back."

"What the hell is that light doing there in the first place? It's always on."

"You don't know? Nobody has ever told you the story?"

"What story?"

"I can't believe you've been here six years and you don't know the story of the ghost light."

"Just dumb, I guess."

"No, Sam, you're not dumb. Let me tell you."

She poured herself another cup of coffee and offered Sam more cookies. He took two.

"Well," she said, "every theater that I've ever worked in—and you know I've worked in a lot of them—has had a light burning all the time on the stage. It's always just an electric light on a stand or a pole like we have here."

"Why is it always on?" Sam asked. "That's wasting electricity."

"It's mainly for safety. As you know, the stage area can be awfully dark. And we certainly wouldn't want anyone to fall into the orchestra pit."

"Safety? That cord almost killed me."

"Yes, I know, and I'm sorry. And we'll have to put the light somewhere where the cord isn't in the way."

Having gulped down both cookies, Sam took another one.

"So, OK, why is it called the ghost light?"

Professor Mantucci sighed.

"Afraid you'd ask that. We try to avoid talking about such things. Well, it's long been a tradition that every theater in the world has a ghost, and the light is supposed to appease them. There's a legend that the light is kept on so that the ghosts can perform on stage after everyone else has left."

"Come on. Really?"

"Well, it's just a nice tradition, I think. No harm done."

"Professor! That's stupid. There aren't any ghosts."

"Well, you know that actors are naturally superstitious. Why do you think we always call that play we did last year the Scottish play?"

"You mean *Macbeth*?"

"Shhhhh. Sam, you're not supposed to say that word!"

"Professor! This is weird. Why not?"

"Because the play is supposed to be cursed. Actors even avoid saying their lines out loud before the play, especially the witches' incantations. It brings bad luck."

"That's stupid!"

"Sam, it's all very innocent. Like saying 'break a leg' before an actor goes on. Everyone does that."

Sam eyed her suspiciously. "Professor, are you superstitious?"

"Me? No! Why would you think that?"

"Because—and I've always wondered why you did that—every time on opening night, before the curtain goes up, we form a circle and we say a prayer. Or at least some people do."

"That's not being superstitious. That's just hoping, well, praying, that we have a good performance."

"But there's something you do right after that. I've seen you! I've seen you many times!"

"What? What do I do?"

"You don't think we can see you, but you go off to the side and you turn around three times—three!—and you raise your arms. Why do you do that?"

If Professor Mantucci's face wasn't already sunburned from her summer at the Cape, one might have thought she was blushing.

"Oh, Samuel, it's nothing. I don't even know I'm doing it. It's just a habit. It's nothing. Really. It's nothing at all. I can't remember even doing it. Really."

"Right. You do it all the time. We've all seen you."

Professor Mantucci said she needed to get a glass of water and went into the hall. Left alone, Sam helped himself to a couple more cookies.

"I hate to say this, Sam," she said as she returned, "but I was hoping to save a few of those for the faculty party later."

"Sorry. They're very good, by the way."

"Thank you. Now, let's get back on track. Let's think about your project."

"Yeah, I guess so."

"You know, if Latouche has been done, what about the composer of *The Golden Apple*? Jerome Moross? I don't think anyone has written about him, and he did a lot of scores."

"No. I'm sick of *The Golden Apple*. I don't want to have anything to do with it."

"All right, all right. Just a thought. But remember. A week from Thursday."

Professor Mantucci turned the coffeepot off and noted that she had a class in a half hour. Outside her window the campus was filled with students. When Professor Mantucci was a student the scene would have been noisy, with students yelling and calling to each other. Now, it was almost completely silent. Every last one of them had an electronic device attached to a hand. No one said a word, except sometimes "excuse me" when one student crashed into another.

"OK," Sam said, "I'll go home and think about this some more. Not that it will do any good."

"Come back tomorrow and we'll talk, OK? I'll think, too."

"Will do."

Sam was almost out the door when he turned back.

"Wait. I just thought of something."

"So soon? What is it?"

"No, not that. But I just remembered something your husband told us when we were building the set for *Mac*...the Scottish play."

"Which was?"

"Carlo was telling us about the trip to Italy you took with your son and daughter a few years ago and you were in this rugged part of Tuscany—I think he said it was called something like the Garfagnana—and I guess you got lost or something and suddenly you were back in the Middle Ages."

"Carlo told you that?"

"Yes! Well, I guess he said that we shouldn't talk about it with you. Why not?"

"Samuel, I just don't want to talk about it."

"Why not? Oh, and he said you saw some ghosts. Really?"

"Samuel, this is silly. I don't want to talk about it."

"Why not? You believed you saw ghosts, didn't you?"

"Samuel, we were lost, it was dark, we couldn't see anything. Carlo has made up this whole story and he likes to blab it all over. I don't want to talk about it."

"Aw, Professor. So it's true. You and Carlo and the kids went into this rugged part of Italy and you were transported back into the Middle Ages and you think you saw some ghosts. Nora laughed so hard when I told her about it. She loves screwy stories like that."

"Please. Don't spread this around. It didn't happen. I don't want to talk about it."

"You *are* superstitious, Professor! I can't believe that someone with all your education and all your degrees would believe in ghosts."

"Don't you?"

"Are you kidding? Of course I don't believe in ghosts. They're just made up. And I don't believe in ghost lights either. Or saying Macbeth! There, I've said it."

SAM PARKED HIS BIKE and climbed the three flights of stairs to their apartment much slower than when he descended that morning. He tossed some Friskies into Bella's bowl and gave her fresh water. He wandered into the bedroom, made the bed, picked up Nora's pajamas and pulled the shades, then lowered them. He turned on the television and, finding only news of disasters and murders, turned it off. He threw himself on the couch and buried his face in a pillow that smelled, not surprisingly, of Bella.

He found a text from Nora saying she finished her paper and how did the meeting with Professor Mantucci go?

"Not well," he thought, but wanted to wait until Nora got home before discussing it.

Desperate, he Googled "Theater Research Projects," thinking that he might crib from someone else's topic. But he mostly found programs taught at other universities and a playwriting course.

There was no point. He decided he wasn't going to even try to think of an idea for his project. If he thought of one, fine. If he didn't, fine. He'd take his grade, such as it was. Or something.

Now bored, he played Street Pursuit for a while and then got more bored. He began Googling again. He wondered what he might find about ghost lights in theaters, and so he typed "Ghost Light Theaters."

Wikipedia immediately had a response. Only a few paragraphs. The first talked about safety, as the professor said. It also said they were sometimes called equity lights, perhaps because they were originally mandated by the Actors' Equity Association.

"Equity," he thought. "I hope I can join the union someday."

The Ghosts of the Garfagnana

He began to read the second paragraph, "Origin and Superstitions." Every theater has a ghost, according to superstitions, he read, and then something interesting: The Palace Theater in London "keeps two seats in their balcony permanently bolted open to provide seating for the theater ghosts."

"Aw, come on. Who's going to believe that? The British. They always make stuff up."

He continued his search. Next on the list was "Ten Theaters with Frequent Ghost Sightings."

"This should be interesting."

First on the list, the Belasco Theater in New York, where the producer David Belasco is said to haunt his theater wearing a monk's robes because when he was alive he was called the "Bishop of Broadway."

"Some women have even reported feeling a mysterious ghostly pinch, which theater folk attribute to (who else?) the randy producer."

"What? What? Come on!"

Next, the Palace Theater in New York, where Sam read that Judy Garland, who gave concerts there, is a resident ghost, with her own door.

"Judy Garland! I have to tell Nora. She loves Judy Garland. Now we can go and see her!"

Next, the Paris Opera. Sam knew that this was the setting for *Phantom of the Opera* and hoped he'd find something about a ghost swinging from a chandelier. But the description said only that a chandelier fell on a workman, and the ghost was that of an older woman who committed suicide in the 19th century and was said to roam the streets outside the opera house searching for the man who jilted her.

"Well, that's no fun. I like Andrew Lloyd Webber's version better."

Further down on the list, the Drury Lane in London. "One of London's most famous ghosts, the 'man in gray,' is regularly reported here, wearing riding boots, a powdered wig, and tricorn hat."

"I love this. Who'd believe all this stuff? It's crazy."

He skimmed the rest of the list. Memphis, Tennessee; Wellington, New Zealand; Ashland, Oregon; Los Angeles.

"My God, they're all over the place."

He tried another list, and another and another. At least, doing this, he didn't have to think about his project.

Many of the lists were similar, although one declared that the Drury Lane ghost was supposed to bring good luck.

"We could use a ghost in our theater," he thought. "Almost nobody came to see *Bye, Bye, Birdie.*"

On the tenth or twelfth list, Sam did see a new theater inhabited by a ghost.

"The Teatro Alfieri is a nineteenth-century theater and opera house in the town of Castelnuovo di Garfagnana in the region of Tuscany, Italy."

"The Garfagnana! That's where Professor Mantucci and her family were. I wonder if she knows about this. They said they saw ghosts. Maybe they're all over up there. This is so crazy. How can people believe in this stuff?"

Sam's left leg began to twitch. That happened every time he got excited. He read on.

"The theater was erected in 1860, commissioned by the local Counts Luigi and Giovanni Carli. The latter also aided in the design along with Antonio Vittoni. It was originally dedicated to King Victor Emmanuel II, and it acquired its present name, in honor of the playwright Vittorio Alfieri, following the establishment of the Republic after the war.

"At the long-awaited inauguration, a large crowd came from all over the area. On the evening of August 22, 1860, the curtain went up, beginning with Vincenzo Bellini's *The Alien* melodrama. Thus began an intense activity that saw the new theater becoming nationally renowned, bringing the Garfagnana fame far and wide. It is still a popular theater for concerts and ballets even to this day.

"There is, however, another reason why Teatro Alfieri is famous. Sometimes, during a performance, a short, chubby man wearing a black military uniform adorned with medals and a green sash has been said to appear somewhere on the stage. He has piercing eyes, a goatee and a mustache that stretches to his ears. He looks angry and is scowling, and stands there sometimes for a full minute, and then he is gone.

"Everyone knows that King Victor Emmanuel II was not pleased that the name of the theater was changed."

"King Victor Emmanuel II? Who's that?"

Another search online.

Full name: Vittorio Emanuele Maria Alberto Eugenio Ferdinando Tommaso.

"Really? Is that how he signed his checks?"

"King of Sardinia from 1849 until March 1861. At that point, he assumed the title of King of Italy and became the first king of a united Italy since the sixth century, a title he held until his death in 1878. The Italians called him the 'Father of the Fatherland.'"

Sam turned off his phone.

"So he was still the king of only Sardinia when the theater was built and then he became king of all of Italy. No wonder he's mad that they changed the name of the theater. What a stupid story."

NORA ARRIVED THEN, breathless not only from the stairs but also because one of her professors had just offered her a part-time job helping him write a book.

"Sam, it's about Lin-Manuel Miranda!" she exclaimed. "Imagine! He wants to go into his background, especially about how he spent his summers in Puerto Rico and how that influenced *Hamilton*. Maybe we'll have to go to Puerto Rico! And he said we might have to see *Hamilton*! Can you imagine! I've been dying to see it for so long!"

"Nora, don't plan on it. It might not happen."

Nora threw her book bag on a chair. "I know, but I really really want to see it, don't you?"

"I guess. But you know what happened to me today?"

"The professor liked your idea? Great! Anyway, Professor Alexander said I could start next week."

"Actually, she didn't think my idea was very good," Sam said as he began to wash the breakfast dishes. "I'm supposed to meet with her again tomorrow."

"And I could pick my own hours. I'm free Wednesdays and Fridays, so that would be good."

"And I still don't have another idea."

Nora returned from the bedroom pulling a sweatshirt over her head. "And he said I could sit in on interviews with Mr. Miranda. I'm so excited! Imagine!"

"And did you know there are supposed to be ghosts in theaters?"

"Well, sure, everyone knows that. The first interview is the second week of October. I need to do a lot of reading before that."

"Well, I didn't know about ghosts."

"Maybe he'll let me ask some questions. Oh, I just can't wait!"

"And I read that Judy Garland's ghost is in a theater in New York."

"Really?" She began drying the dishes. "Everyone says Mr. Miranda is such a nice guy so I don't think that would be a problem. I know I'd be nervous, though."

Needless to say, Sam didn't talk much during dinner. Or during the long evening. He fed Bella twice and decided to go bed early. Nora talked nonstop about the bloody interviews she was going to have with Lin-Manuel Miranda.

She was still excited in the morning and Sam left early. His mind wandered all day, from "Advanced Scene Study" to "Medieval Minstrels" to "New Theater in China," and at 7 o'clock he stumbled into the graduate students' lounge. His friends had ordered beer and pizza, and the smells overpowered even the cast-off imitation leather couches and musty shag rugs. "Please Clean Up. You're Not at Home" read a large sign in red ink.

Professor Mantucci had offered only two other graduate students the opportunity to raise their grades by doing an independent study project. Paul had finished his research for a study of Isabella Andreini and her husband, Francesco, who had starred in sixteenth-century *commedia dell'arte* plays. Monica had begun writing her project on satiric references in Moliere's *Tartuffe*.

"And you, Sam?" Monica asked. "How's your project coming?"

Sam confessed that he had not started on a project, and in fact didn't even have an idea for one.

"Then what have you been doing?"

"Oh, just thinking. Say, do you know about ghost lights in theaters?" Everyone had.

"I guess I'm the only one who hadn't," Sam said. "And did you know we're not supposed to say the name of that play, you know the one about the king of Scotland who…"

"Don't say the name!" everyone shouted. "It's bad luck."

"Good grief," Sam said. "Why are you all so superstitious? I suppose you believe in ghosts in theaters, too."

This prompted every one of the students to relate a theatrical ghost story. There was the Belasco, of course, and the Paris Opera, but others as well.

"There's a ghost dressed in white at the New Victory Theater in New York," one student said. "It's still there."

"And one of the Ziegfeld Follies girls—I think her name was Olive Thomas—is still running around the New Amsterdam Theater in her beads and flirting with stagehands," another said. "She's supposed to have died from swallowing mercury pills and the question is whether she did it on purpose or whether her husband did her in. There's even a YouTube video about her!"

"But it's not only in New York," a third said. "We went to the Strand Theater in Lakewood, New Jersey, and people there said that there was a woman in a flimsy gown who was in the mezzanine. We got seats on the first floor."

"There's another New Jersey theater," a fourth said. "The Grange, in Howell. It's a six-year-old girl named Rachel. She steals props and costumes and turns lights on and off. One woman left her T-shirt on a couch and it vanished."

Sam put down his bottle of Bud and grabbed the last slice of pizza. "That's crap. People just like to make stuff up and then they like to scare other people. It's just good publicity. 'Come and see our ghost!' There aren't any such things as ghosts."

"Well," Paul said, "if you saw a ghost you'd believe it."

"Have you ever actually seen a ghost, Paul?" Sam asked.

"Well, no."

"There, you see." Sam got up to get another bottle of beer. "I rest my case."

For the next half hour everyone talked over one another, telling various ghost stories they'd heard or read about. Then Agnes said:

"Sam, if you're so sure that there aren't ghosts in theaters, why don't you go to one and prove that there isn't a ghost there. Put your money where…"

"And how am I supposed to prove that?"

"Well, just hang out a lot and see if one turns up."

Sam slapped his leg to stop the twitching. "That might take months."

"But it might be fun," Paul said.

"What am I supposed to do? Yell out, 'Come out, come out, wherever you are, ghost?' Come on."

"Well," Veronica said, "maybe one will come out right away and then you won't have to wait for months."

Everyone except Sam thought this was very amusing.

"I know," Paul said. "Let's have a bet. Let's bet Sam that if he doesn't see a ghost in a theater in, say, two months, we'll each give him $25."

"And if he does see a ghost," Amy asked, "what then?"

"Then…then he has to take us all out to dinner at Francesco's, the most expensive restaurant in town."

"Yes!"

"Yes! I've always wanted to go there."

"I can't even afford to walk past it."

There were fourteen students in the room and each pledged $25 if Sam could prove that a certain theater didn't have a ghost.

"That's $350, Sam. Think about it."

Since Nora paid the rent, Sam existed on at best $45 a week from his savings, so he didn't have to think long.

"OK, I'll do it. I know I'm not going to find any ghosts, and anyway, while I'm there I can be thinking about what to write about for my project."

He dropped his beer bottle in the pile with the others and prepared to leave.

"Wait!" He smacked his head just like an actor in a play. "I can use *this* for my project! I'll go to some theater and sit there every night and take notes and make sure I don't see a ghost. And then I'll write it all up and turn it in and Professor Mantucci will give me an A."

"What theater?"

"I don't know. I'll think about it."

PROFESSOR NANCY MANTUCCI was not pleased with Sam's idea when he told her about it the next morning. She was certain that the project's committee would feel that it was too "iffy" and lacking a real thesis. She said it would take months to research and God knows how long to write, and the project was due on September 1 of next year. And mostly, she feared that the committee would find that it was, in her words, "not academic."

Sam tried to argue his case and said that he'd write a proposal and show it to her the following day.

"All right, you can do that, but remember," she said, as he picked up his backpack, "the deadline for the idea is a week from today."

Sam spent the rest of the day and well into the night at his laptop. Nora came home at one point, found cold mac-and-cheese in the refrigerator, and left for a dance class. They barely spoke.

At 2 a.m., Sam had written and rewritten and rewritten until he finally had a three-page single-spaced proposal. He read what he'd written:

"Ghosts in the Theater: A Case Study"

The first part was mainly history on the evolution of the idea of theatrical ghosts, going back to Seneca the Elder in Rome. He was so excited when he found that reference that his leg started to shake. Then there was a section on the use of ghosts in plays, featuring Shakespeare's *Julius Caesar*, *Richard III* and the Scottish play. Sam didn't know if it was all right to write the name or if it was bad luck only to say it out loud. He left it blank. He also included more modern plays like Noel Coward's *Blithe Spirit* and its musical version *High Spirits.* He was very pleased with himself for remembering that from his Modern Musicals class.

The next section was a listing of various theaters in which ghosts were alleged inhabitants today. The list was very long. Teatro Alfieri was near the end.

And the last section was Sam's plan to visit a theater, spend two months there, attend every performance, and report his findings.

"The only problem," he thought as he put the pages in a folder, "is that I don't know what theater to use. I know I'm not going to find any ghosts so it doesn't make much difference."

Bleary-eyed, he found the professor talking to her husband when he arrived at her office at 9:30. Professor Mantucci and Carlo were going to leave for New York this afternoon to spend the weekend seeing shows.

"Look, I've brought you my proposal. See what you think."

"OK," the professor said, "I'll read it on the train but you know I still have doubts about this. Is this complete now? Any loose ends?"

She told her husband about Sam's plan for his project and made it clear that she had great reservations. Carlo, however, thought it was an excellent idea. Married for twenty-eight years, they didn't often disagree and had long settled into life in the theater department at Central State, where Nancy was now chair. Carlo did set design and taught two courses.

"Well," Sam said, "the big thing I'm missing is what theater to use. I want to spend two months in one to prove there isn't a ghost there, but there are so many I don't know where."

"You could pick one of the obvious ones," Carlo said, "like the Belasco in New York or the Paris Opera."

"I'd rather not use one of those. They all have legends and people wouldn't believe what I found. Anyway, I could never afford going to Paris or somewhere and live there for two months."

"Nancy," Carlo said, "doesn't the department have a fund for research that we can use for graduate students? Remember that kid from Kansas who spent weeks at the New York Library for the Performing Arts looking up material on early operetta?"

"He spent more time in bars than in the library," Nancy said. "But, yes, we do have a fund, and it's actually quite solvent at this time."

"So I could go to Europe or some place?" Sam asked.

"Perhaps. It depends where."

They thought for a while until Nancy and Carlo began to put their things away.

"Well," she said, "we'd better be going. It's a long train ride and it's supposed to rain in New York and we'll have trouble finding a cab. Give some serious thought to this, Sam, and we'll talk about it again on Monday. Let's go, Carlo."

"Wait," Sam said. "When I was looking up ghosts in theaters I found out about one in a theater in a town in the Garfagnana region of Italy. That's where you went a few years ago, right? And didn't you say you saw ghosts there?"

"No...no, we didn't," Nancy said. "Carlo made that up."

"Nancy!" Carlo said. "How can you say that? You know we were lost and suddenly we were back in a town in the Middle Ages!"

"Really?" Sam said, "just like *Brigadoon*?"

"No, not just like *Brigadoon* or anything else," Nancy said. "I think Carlo was hit on the head or something. He's made this all up."

"Nancy!"

"Let's go, Carlo."

"Listen," Sam said, looking at a piece of paper on which he had written notes, "I found that there's supposed to be a ghost in something called Teatro Alfieri in Castelnuovo di Garfagnana."

"I remember we stopped in that town," Carlo said. "We went to a castle and Andrew was very bored. We didn't go to a theater."

"Sam, you know what I think about this whole idea," Nancy said. "Oh well, let me know so we can arrange the finances. Carlo, we have to go."

Nancy grabbed her purse, threw her jacket over her arm and went out the door. Carlo followed behind but not before winking at Sam. "Go to the Garfagnana," he whispered.

Sam had no idea where the Garfagnana was. Except for Rome, he didn't know much about the landscape of Italy. Back in the apartment, he went online and discovered that the Garfagnana was a region north of Lucca, so he found a map and located Lucca.

Like most college students, he didn't read newspapers and depended on Twitter and Reddit for whatever news he obtained. Now, he had to do a crash course on Italy. He dug out his phone. Lots about the pope. Anti-establishment forces gaining power. Opposition to migrants. Another change in leadership. There seemed to be a lot of that. Not too much positive, he concluded.

Sam was searching the Cheapflights site when Nora returned from her Pilates class.

"Wasting more of your money, Nora?" he said. "Pilates is just another fad."

"I'm not listening to you." She kissed the top of his blond head. "I'm enjoying Pilates. What are you doing?"

"I'm going to Italy."

"Oh! For?"

"My independent study project."

"Which is about?"

"Ghosts in theaters."

"Oh. And you're going to go to Italy to find them? There are lots in the United States, you know."

"Yeah, sure. Look, here's a flight from New York to Florence."

"And from there?"

"The Garfagnana. Remember Carlo talking about it?"

"And how they got lost and wound up in the Middle Ages?" Nora said. "It's a fun story."

"Anyway, there's a theater there that's supposed to have the ghost of a king, so I'm going to go sit there for two months and prove that he doesn't exist."

"Sam, you said that *I was wasting money?*"

"You'll see."

TWO WEEKS LATER, all twenty-eight of the other graduate students gathered in the two-bedroom apartment shared by Chuck and Sandy and Milly and Phil and Anton and Boris on the other side of town. They were giving a surprise "ghost" party for Sam. Having received the extremely reluctant approval of Professor Mantucci as well as a generous grant, and having gotten permission from his other professors, he was ready to go to Italy.

They'd all raided the theater's makeup supplies for white paste for their faces. James had somehow borrowed a monk's habit from the local Franciscan parish and wore a sign on his back saying "David Belasco." Molly, dressed in black, was "Mysterious Lady." Nora, who had made an excuse to arrive early, wore a long white gown as "Ziegfeld Girl."

Most of the others were in white sheets. They would have cut out the holes for eyes, nose and mouth but with the price of sheets the way they were, they just wrapped them around themselves.

When Sam arrived, the rooms were dark except for dozens of candles, and the partygoers greeted him with "Ooo-ooo-ooo."

"Very funny," he said, trying to go along with the gags.

On the table were an enchilada dip with potato chips standing up representing tombstones; slices of tomatoes with black olives looking (somewhat) like eyes; crescent rolls that appeared to be witches' hats and, of course, deviled eggs.

Empty cans and bottles of Bud and Miller and Coors began to stack up next to the sink, and the party became more rowdy.

"Be sure to take your camera, Sam. Oh, wait, ghosts don't like to have their pictures taken."

"Can you get his autograph? Maybe with invisible ink?"

"Tell us what he smells like. I heard ghosts smell like mushrooms."

"Or sulfur."

"Or death."

"How do you know the ghost is a man?" Ruth asked. "There are plenty of lady ghosts."

Later, they sat on the bedraggled couch, the recliner, the footstools and mainly the floor.

"Can't wait until you get back, Sam. I can taste Francesco's lasagna already."

"I'm going to order the *tortellini primavera* chicken Parmesan. It's their specialty."

"No, veal *scallopini*."

"No, lobster *fra diavolo*."

"All right, all right," Sam said. "Let it go. You're not going to Francesco's because I'm not going to see any ghosts. There's no such thing as ghosts."

"Ooo-ooo-ooo," they all replied in unison.

"Sam," Paul said, "how can you say there aren't any ghosts when they've been seen in so many theaters for so many years?"

"Publicity, I keep telling you! That's all. Legends. Somebody makes something up and everyone believes it. And it goes on and on and on. And it takes a life onto itself."

Sam was getting angry and defensive. "You're not going to be very happy when I come back and you have to give me $25 because I didn't see a ghost."

"Oh," Emma said, "I guess I'd better start saving my pennies right now."

Sam got up. "Well, I have to pack. Thanks for the party. See you in a couple of months."

"*Buon viaggio!* Say hello to the king!"

It didn't take long for Sam to pack, mainly because he didn't have much to pack. He'd checked the weather in Italy and it looked good. Four light shirts, three pair of jeans, underwear, shaving stuff, chargers for his electronics. It would all fit in his backpack. He checked his phone to test the iTranslate app he'd installed. He knew there were problems with it, but he desperately needed something. Having coughed up almost $200 for an expedited passport, he was ready. He texted his mother, thanking her again for the unexpected large loan. She wasn't happy about all this.

"Why in the world do you have to go to Italy for your project? Couldn't you have gone to some nice theater in the States?"

She worried about his safety, his inability to speak Italian, whether he'd eat well, whether he had enough clothes. And especially Italian girls because she had seen too many movies.

Nora returned from the party, having had a little too much Zinfandel and still going on about the interview she and the professor were going to have with Lin-Manuel Miranda. Sam tuned her out, dozed off only a little that night and left her—and Bella—still sleeping in the morning. He texted her a note: "Have fun, will write."

He wasn't sure where his relationship with Nora was going. It was better to keep it cool.

SAM WISHED HE'D SLEPT BETTER because he was already napping on the bus and then on the train to JFK. He'd never been to JFK before and was in New York only that one time when Professor Mantucci took the group to see *The Golden Apple*. He'd flown only once before, freshman year when he went with three friends to London on spring break. He was terrified.

He got through security without losing his passport or his boarding pass. In the middle of the thirty-fourth row of the plane, the elderly woman next to him couldn't help noticing that his left leg was twitching.

"Are you all right, young man?"

"Yes. Sorry. Just nervous. Second time flying."

"It'll be fine once we've reached altitude. I've flown so many times. Where are you going?"

"Florence."

"Florence! That's where I'm going. You're going to love it there. By the way, my name is Rosella."

"I'm Sam."

"Sam. Such an American name. Uncle Sam!"

Rosella said she had moved from Italy but was going back to visit an older sister who was celebrating her seventy-fifth birthday.

"We grew up near the church of Santa Croce. We took classes at the Accademia d'Arte."

"Really? Isn't that next to where the David statue is?" Sam remembered this from the Michelangelo section of an art history class, and for the first time he was getting excited about going to Italy.

"Of course. I used to walk past that building going to and from class."

"Really? That's so cool."

Rosella went on about other museums and churches and walks along the Arno and the artisan shops in the Oltrarno. Sam wished he had scheduled more time in Florence.

She asked why he was going to Italy. For some reason, he was vague, simply saying that he was a college student and doing some research in the Garfagnana.

"The Garfagnana is such a beautiful area, very rugged, though. My sister and I loved to go with our husbands to Barga. They used to have these huge dinners out in the open called the *sagra*. I don't know if they have them anymore, it's been so long. Those were such good times. It's thinking about all this that makes me miss Filippo so much."

She took a violet handkerchief out of her purse and wiped her eyes.

"Be careful, though," she said. "Strange things have happened there."

"Really? Like what?"

Rosella just smiled. "Oh nothing. Do you want to tell me anything else about your research?"

"No, I'd rather not."

She rested her hand on his. "Young people can be so mysterious."

Dinner arrived, and they managed to get through the hot pasta, the cold roll and the frozen fudge.

Rosella folded the tinfoil over her plate. "And where are you staying tonight?"

"I don't know. I've got this guidebook and it lists some places for students."

"No, no, no," Rosella said. "No! Those places are terrible. You're staying with us. My sister will love to have you."

There was no point in arguing, and Sam felt very relieved.

"We have a very nice place and you'll be comfortable."

With the plane's lights turned off, Sam stretched out and promptly fell asleep. When he woke, breakfast was on his tray. Rosella had finished hers and was applying her lipstick. Transfixed, he looked out the window as they flew over the Alps and then at the rolling hills as they approached Florence. He really was in Italy.

"You're going to have a wonderful time," Rosella said. "Everyone does."

Rosella's sister Maria was waiting outside the tiny Florence airport in a sleek silver Mazzanti, and Sam settled back into the soft leather. The trip took them along a winding highway into the hills above Florence and then into a long driveway to a three-story eighteenth-century villa.

"My husband and I lived here for many years," Maria said. "I haven't changed a thing since he passed away."

Sam thought he must be dreaming. Marble floors, chandeliers, antique furniture, gold fixtures.

"Now, you can freshen up in the guest room upstairs to your right," Rosella said. "We'll have dinner in an hour."

Over pasta and crusty bread and fruit and wine on the patio overlooking the city, Sam couldn't help noticing how much Rosella and Maria resembled each other with their short wavy white hair, tanned complexions and ample bosoms. Their pearl necklaces and blue dresses were almost identical.

"Some people think we're twins," Maria said, "but you can see that Rosella is much taller than I am."

"Oh, at most two inches," Rosella said. "So, Samuel, what do you think of Italy so far?"

"I think I'm in a movie," he said.

"No, no," Maria said. "This is just Italy. You really should stay and see more of it."

"Sam says he's going to the Garfagnana to do research," Rosella said, "but he's being very mysterious."

"Why is that?"

Perhaps liberated by the wine, Sam told them how he was going to the

Garfagnana to make sure there wasn't a ghost in a theater there because he was going to write a project for extra credit on the fact that there aren't ghosts in theaters.

Once he said this, he felt very stupid.

"How interesting," Rosella said. "What theater will you be observing?"

"Teatro Alfieri in Castelnuovo di Garfagnana."

"Really?" Maria said. "Remember when we went there, oh, ten years ago, and we saw the wonderful ballet based on *Macbeth*?"

Sam was too embarrassed to tell them not to say that word.

"There's supposed to be a ghost there of a king, Vittorio Emanuele," Sam said.

"Oh yes," Rosella said, "everyone talks about the ghost. Sometimes they talk more about the ghost than what they've seen on stage. He's not there all the time and he's supposed to be there just for a minute, then he disappears."

"Come on," Sam said. "Did you see the ghost?"

"Oh, you young people are so suspicious of everything. Well, we won't talk about it anymore, will we, Maria?"

"No," Maria smiled. "We won't."

"But," Rosella said, "if you're looking for ghosts you should let Brother Renato help you."

"Yes, yes, of course!" Maria said.

The sisters explained that Brother Renato was their nephew and that he was certified as an exorcist. Sam had seen the movie *The Exorcist*, so they didn't have to explain that an exorcist was supposed to have the power to drive demons from someone who was possessed. Sam tried hard not to grin.

"It's true," Maria said. "The Catholic Church said he had the power to do this and he's done it countless times, hasn't he, Rosella?"

"I think about eight."

"But," Sam said, "I'm talking about ghosts, not devils. What does he know about ghosts?"

"Oh, a lot I'm sure," Maria said. "Ghosts, devils. It's all in the realm of the supernatural."

Rosella found a piece of paper and wrote a phone number on it. "We're going to ask him to meet you in Castelnuovo di Garfagnana, but if he's late or something, call him. I'm sure he'll be happy to help you. He's a very nice man."

"He's at the Abbey of Saint Gaudentius, what's left of it," Maria said. "It was bombed during the war."

"It's on top of a mountain not far away," Rosella said.

"I'm afraid I'm not Catholic," Sam said. "Who was Saint Gaudentius?"

"Not even Catholics know about him," Rosella said. "He was a bishop. He goes way back, to about the year 300, I think. They named the abbey after him when they built it in the 1300s. It took forever to build."

"It was filled with monks when it was first built," Maria said, "but now, well, you know what's happening in the Catholic Church. There are only twenty or thirty monks there now. Not many young men want to be monks."

"Or priests," Rosella said.

Maria sighed, "Or girls wanting to be nuns."

"Come," Rosella said, putting her hand on Sam's arm. "You must be exhausted."

It was not until Sam crawled into bed that he realized he hadn't texted Nora.

"Oh, well. Tomorrow."

He slept soundly in the soft bed, waking to find sunlight pouring through the handmade embroidered curtains. In the kitchen, modernized with stainless steel fixtures and granite countertops, Rosella was frying eggs while her sister sliced fresh bread and put pots of jam on the table.

"We normally don't have this big a breakfast but we know Americans like this," Maria said.

Rosella ignored Sam's plan to take a taxi to Florence and drove him instead.

"And if you have any questions, any problems, anything at all, be sure to call us," she said as they arrived at the bus station. He kissed her on both cheeks, something he saw other Italians doing.

Before he closed the car door, she added, "And be sure to connect with Brother Renato. I know he'd love to help you."

"Thanks. I will."

"And one more thing. Don't be afraid of any ghosts you see! They're quite harmless."

The trip to Castelnuovo di Garfagnana took four hours and Sam slept all the way. Adjusting his backpack when he descended from the bus to the sidewalk, he felt a hand on his shoulder. The middle-aged man wore a black robe that stretched over a rotund belly down to bare sandaled feet. He wore a heavy rosary around his waist.

"Sam? I'm Brother Renato. My aunts said you'd probably arrive on this bus."

AFTER SHAKING HANDS, Sam couldn't help staring at his visitor's hair, or rather the lack of it. The bald head was surrounded by a fringe of red hair.

"It's called a tonsure, Sam. All of us Benedictines have it. You can tell us a mile away."

"Oh. It kind of looks like a halo."

"Well, I'm afraid sainthood does not come with it. And, yes, I know English. My order sent me to Boston to study but maybe just to get me out of the way for a few years. But how was your flight? Did you have a nice bus trip from Florence? Aren't my aunts delicious? Look, you must be starving. Shall we go someplace?"

It wasn't until now that Sam realized he hadn't eaten anything since breakfast with Rosella and Maria.

"Yes!"

"My favorite place is Trattoria Bonini. It's a little out of town but it's very good."

The brother was using the abbey's ten-year-old Fiat, with dents on the doors and hood, but in no time they parked alongside a three-story stone building with a red sign and a green-and-white awning.

The place was crowded, but an empty square wooden table with a white tablecloth hid in the corner. Most of the other customers appeared to be from the vicinity and knew each other. With all the shouting and hugging and kissing, it was rather loud.

"Since this is your first day in Italy," Brother Renato said, "you must have something very Italian."

Sam's experience with Italian food had consisted of an occasional dish of Nora's overcooked spaghetti and a football night sausage pizza from

Angelo's. He poured over the menu, which fortunately had an English translation.

"Um, I don't know. It all seems very, um…"

"Foreign?"

"Yes."

"Well, you're hungry. Let's skip the appetizers and go right to the main course. I suggest wild boar stew with polenta. It's their specialty and I've had it so many times. I love it."

"Um…"

"Wild boar isn't popular in America?"

"I've never even heard of it."

"Trust me. You'll love it."

"This is an animal somebody shot?"

"Well, yes. I suppose that's how it got here. You'll love it."

The waiter was ready to take their order. Sam hesitated, but Brother Renato took charge and submitted the order for two in Italian.

"And we'd like a red wine. How about the Sant'Agnese Piombino?"

"Very good." The waiter smiled at Sam sympathetically.

Not being Catholic, Sam didn't know what a brother was. "Is it like a junior priest?"

The monk's laugh filled the crowded room.

"No, afraid not. I'm not ordained as a priest, or even a deacon, but I've taken vows of poverty, chastity and obedience. I live in the Abbey of Saint Gaudentius with twenty-four other brothers and six priests. Well, I should say what remains of the Abbey of Saint Gaudentius. It was bombed by the Allies during the war and we stay in just a part of it. We've given up the farms and the olive oil business but we make a little money on the wines from our vineyard."

He played with his knife and fork.

"That's too bad," was all that Sam could say.

"Well, it's life. We go on."

"Your aunts said you were an exorcist. You mean like Father Damien? Nora, she's my girlfriend, loves that movie. She gets so scared. I have to hold her tight. You should see us."

"Perhaps not. No, I'm not like Father Damien. That movie did more harm to exorcism than, well, the devil himself."

"But you can drive the devil out of someone? That's so cool!"

"I'm not sure if that's the word for it. Anyway, the church has authorized me to perform the rites of exorcism. Normally, it's a priest, but as I've just indicated, there aren't as many priests around here anymore so sometimes brothers are allowed."

Sam was getting very interested. "So how do you do it?"

Brother Renato sighed. He'd been asked this so many times.

"We don't start the process until we are absolutely certain that the person is possessed. Then, in brief, I pray over the person using what's called a sacramental. I use a rosary. I invoke the name of Jesus Christ and the Archangel Michael, and we visit the person maybe three times a week. Sometimes this takes years."

"Years?"

"The devil is very persistent."

"How many times have you done it?"

"Five. Well, actually four because the devil came back in one case. I thought I'd had him, too."

"I don't know if I believe in devils," Sam said.

"Most people don't. That doesn't make them less real."

Before Sam could ask another question, the waiter was at their side with their dinners.

"Oh, my, this looks very good," Brother Renato said. "Excellent!"

Somewhat in horror, Sam looked down at his plate.

"Try it. You really will like it."

And he did, and he did. The boar, he thought, tasted somewhat like chicken, and the polenta wasn't as gritty as he remembered from the one time his grandmother had made it. Anyway, he drowned out both with the red wine.

"But enough about me," the monk said. "My aunts tell me that you're looking to interview King Victor Emmanuel II at Teatro Alfieri."

"Right. No, I'm going to prove that his ghost isn't there."

"Good luck."

Sam explained that he was in a theater program at a university and he had decided to prove there wasn't a ghost in at least one theater to show that the whole concept of theater ghosts was false.

"It's really insane," he said. "People really believe this. There's a whole list of theaters that say they have ghosts. It's all for publicity."

Brother Renato wondered how Sam would prove this, but Sam clearly hadn't thought this through.

"Well," Sam said, "I think I'll go to the theater every night and sit in the audience and see if I see this ghost."

"Every night?"

"Every night that there's a performance."

Brother Renato said he had seen the schedules for Teatro Alfieri and was impressed. There were symphony concerts, quartets, soloists, dramas, musicals, operas, ballets. Usually they were single events, but plays often ran for a week.

"You're going to get quite an education. There's such variety, classical, modern, everything, and you know you'll have to sit through the entire performance because the king could show up anytime. He's been rumored, in fact, to join the cast at a curtain call."

"Come on."

"Well, that's the story. Anyway, you can't nod off or fall asleep or you'll miss him."

"I won't. I'll stay awake. Have you been to the Teatro Alfieri?"

"I'm sorry, but I have never been to that theater. Benedictines have such archaic rules. But of course I've heard about the ghost. Everyone has."

"I imagine it's a fun story for people to talk about. Maybe they like to scare their kids."

Brother Renato drained his glass and poured another for both of them.

"Sam, when you're as old as I am, you've learned not to question everything. There is probably some truth in every tale, no matter how odd and unbelievable it may be."

"But ghosts?"

"Even ghosts."

"Come on."

Most of the original crowd at the restaurant had dispersed, but others had taken their place and it was still boisterous. There seemed to be a waiting line. Brother Renato signed the check and summoned the waiter.

"And where do you plan to stay while you're proving that there isn't a ghost at Teatro Alfieri?"

"Could you drive me back to town? I think I'll be able to find something."

"Oh, you think you'll be able to find something? Just like that? At 9 o'clock at night you're going to be wandering the streets of Castelnuovo di Garfagnana and asking people if they know if there's a hotel or some place you can stay?"

"Um…"

"Thought so. Well, it just happens that even in the ruins of the Abbey of Saint Gaudentius we have an extra room, though we call it a cell. The bed is hard and the water's cold, but there's excellent hard bread for breakfast. In fact, you can have the cell where our ghost visited."

"What?"

"Come along, Sam. It's late."

SINCE IT WAS NOW DARK, Sam didn't see much of the countryside as they drove up the hill to the Abbey of Saint Gaudentius. He could see the shell of the main building, and Brother Renato led him to the small area in the back that had been spared by the bombs. All of the other monks were praying or had retired for the night and there was an eerie quiet in the dark halls. Brother Renato took Sam to the end of a row of cells and used a rusty iron key to unlock the door.

"When the place was built there were only candles, of course," he said, "but now, at least sometimes, we have electricity. It's very temperamental."

He flipped a switch and a small bulb on a wall flickered to light, went off and came back on. The small room contained only a bed, a desk and a chair.

"We're glad this cell was saved from the bombs," Brother Renato said. "This was the cell where one of our monks beat himself with a whip in the Middle Ages and was visited by a ghost. All right, go to bed. You'll hear bells at 2 o'clock and again at 7, and you can sleep through them, but breakfast is at 8:30. Join us."

"But? But?" Sam couldn't believe his ears.

"Good night, Sam." Brother Renato left.

Sam felt very alone after the monk left. Central State seemed so far away. He missed his family. He missed Nora. He even missed Bella, though he still had her scratches on his hand. He was in a strange country where he didn't know the language and people talked too fast. Brother Renato was the only person he knew. He desperately wished he had someone else to talk to.

"A stranger in a strange land," he thought.

He undressed, clicked off the light and crawled under the crisp white sheets. He was exhausted. He had awakened early at the sisters' villa outside of Florence, took that long bus ride to Castelnuovo di Garfagnana, had a dinner of wild boar—wild boar!—and then came to this monastery where he was sleeping in a cell once occupied by a monk who whipped himself and was visited by a ghost. Right. He should text Nora, but it would have to wait. He wasn't even sure if his phone would work here.

Sam woke when the 2 a.m. bell sounded and saw the light on the wall come on, go off, then flicker for about five minutes before going off.

"What the...?"

He turned over and, after tossing and turning, went back to sleep. The same thing happened at 7 a.m. Sam got up and made sure the bulb was tight. He dozed off again and barely got to the dining room in time for breakfast. The small group of priests and monks huddled in a corner, and since this was one of the few times they were allowed to speak during the day, they were apparently telling jokes because they were laughing a lot.

"Welcome, Sam!" Brother Renato cried out. "Join us."

A cook brought scrambled eggs, hard bread, jelly, milk and coffee. Sam devoured it all.

Told of the reason for Sam's visit to Castelnuovo di Garfagnana, the other monks didn't understand.

"You came all the way from America to see a ghost?" one elderly monk asked. "Don't they have ghosts in America?"

"No," Brother Renato said, "he came all the way from America so he *wouldn't* see the ghost. I know, I know, it's hard to explain. He's young. Let him do his thing. Right, Sam?"

Red-faced, Sam could only stammer, "Thanks."

After breakfast, Sam cornered Brother Renato in the hall.

"Brother Renato, what's this about a monk who lived in my cell and a ghost?"

"Ah yes. Well, I guess I should tell you. Come outside and we'll go for a walk."

Because Sam hadn't seen the countryside last night, he was now overwhelmed by the stretches of craggy mountains, the green valleys, the little towns and villages. He really was in Italy. Central State, and Nora, seemed so far away. Which reminded him. He needed to text her. He wondered why he was putting this off.

"Well, Sam," Brother Renato said, "stories change radically over the years, not to mention the centuries. All I know is that there was a crazed monk named Brother Ludovico who whipped himself and got into trouble because of it."

"Why would he whip himself?"

"It sounds very odd now, but there were people called Flagellants then who thought that the Good Lord wanted them to beat themselves to atone for their sins."

"That's sick."

"Well, yes. The abbot and the other monks tried to get him to stop, but he wouldn't. But then there were reports that the monk was visited by a ghost. Soon after, the monk changed his life and went out into the countryside and helped the poor."

Sam had to think about this.

"Just like that? Because of this ghost? I don't believe in ghosts, but who was the ghost?"

"Well, now we go back centuries before. In the early days of this monastery there was a young monk who was, it was believed, murdered by another monk in revenge. This young monk was only twenty-one years old."

"Weren't people scared of this supposed ghost?"

"Actually, not. He was never threatening. In fact, he had a kind of warm presence. The monks called him a friendly ghost."

"Well, forgive me, Brother Renato, but I don't believe any of this."

"Sam, it gets a lot more interesting. The ghost started to perform miracles and he was canonized a saint and a shrine was built and there was a statue of him that performed more miracles."

"Come on."

"But during the war the Allies destroyed the shrine. Look, see that big pile of rubble and marble near that hill? That's the chapel. Or where the chapel was."

"Come on."

"I know this is hard to believe."

"Hard to believe?" Sam said. "Only some bad fiction writer would make up a story like that."

"You're right."

"Oh, did this ghost, or now a saint, have a name?"

"Giacomo."

"Giacomo. Sounds like some bad writer made up that name, too."

"Probably."

Sam was starting to have a headache.

"Oh, Sam, one more thing. It's rumored that Giacomo likes to comfort men who are lonely."

IN THE LATE AFTERNOON, Brother Renato found Sam wandering around the monastery grounds and told him he had good news.

"Since I have a lot of free time now that there aren't any devils lurking around, I've decided to join you on your adventure. We'll go to the theater tonight and every night there's a performance, and my job will be to make sure you stay awake, and when I see King Victor Emmanuel, I will poke you and be sure that you take notes. OK?"

"That would be great. And you really think we're going to see this guy, don't you? You think I'm being foolish."

"As I said, it's good not to question everything."

Sam expressed his gratitude for all the time Brother Renato would spend with him, for giving him rides and for letting him stay at the abbey. This was working out far better than he expected. It might not even take as long as he had planned. If he hadn't seen the ghost in, say, a month, maybe two—and he was certain that he wouldn't—he could go home and write his paper, hand it in and happily accept his degree.

At 6 o'clock, after a small meal of soup and sandwiches, Sam and Brother Renato climbed into the Fiat and descended the winding road from the mountain to Castelnuovo di Garfagnana. They drove along in silence until they reached the village. Brother Renato turned onto via

Vecchiacchi and then via Enrico Vermi and finally via Marconi. And there was Teatro Alfieri.

Sam had been in at least fourteen theaters since he developed a serious interest in musical theater, but he had never experienced anything like the magnificent Teatro Alfieri at Castelnuovo di Garfagnana. Three stories high, the golden exterior glowed in the setting sun. An ornate carving of theatrical and musical symbols decorated the top floor, and twin statues stood in arches at the sides.

They stepped past the arched entry and into the theater. Besides the two long rows of red velvet seats on the main floor, five galleries rose to a ceiling painted with delicate flowers around a circular light at the center.

"Impressed?" Brother Renato asked.

"Wow! Wow! Look at that ceiling! The paintings! They must be more than a hundred years old. This is so awesome!"

"And the lights. They're using more electricity here tonight than our abbey does in a month."

Sam had paid for the tickets, expensive ones on the main floor. He realized how much money he was saving by living in the abbey and felt he owed Brother Renato something.

"Thanks, Sam. I didn't know I was going to see King Victor Emmanuel II for free. I can't wait. This is quite a treat."

The program that night was by a visiting Russian soprano, Irinushka Dobrolyubov, who had brought along her own pianist, Victor Zhigunov. The theater was now filled, and as the lights dimmed, Brother Renato nudged Sam. "Now stay awake."

"I will, I will."

He tried to see if there was a ghost light somewhere on the stage, but it was too dark.

The pianist came on first, bowed to the audience, flipped his tails and sat down on the piano bench. To thunderous applause, Madame Dobrolyubov glided to the center of the stage and stood before the lone microphone. She wore a golden gown that almost reached the floor and a diamond tiara in her yellow hair. She was not petite.

Sam tried to read from his printed program, but since it was in Italian, he let Brother Renato translate it out loud.

"*Vado, ma dove* by Mozart. This aria, like *Chi sa, chi sa,* was written as an insertion aria for Martin y Soler's opera *Il Burbero di buon core*, with a libretto by Lorenzo da Ponte, who, of course, wrote the librettos for *Don Giovanni, Cosi fan tutte* and *Le Nozze di Figaro*. Many of the da Ponte librettos contain very serious moments in otherwise comic operas, such as *Come scoglio* from *Cosi*, or *Porgi Amor* and *Dove* from *Nozze*."

For someone whose most serious musical knowledge lay somewhere between *Guys and Dolls* and *The Pajama Game*, this was too daunting.

"Just close your eyes and appreciate the sounds," the monk said.

That was bad advice. Three minutes after the soprano began to sing, Sam was gently snoring. Brother Renato nudged him again.

"I'm sorry I said that. You're supposed to stay awake, remember?"

Sam came back to life, and it was not difficult remaining awake during the powerful *Pace, pace mio Dio!* from *La Forza del Destino* and the virtuosic Bolero from *I Vespri Siciliani*.

"You see," Brother Renato said as the soloist took her bows, "concerts by sopranos aren't that bad. And she was very good. Even I knew that."

Madame Dobrolyubov took even more bows, and as the applause died down and the audience drifted toward the doors, Sam and Brother Renato realized they had been so wrapped up in the concert that they didn't remember why they had come.

"He didn't show!" Sam said. "I didn't see the king, did you?"

"No. I'm sure I would have. Well, he isn't supposed to appear every night, you know."

"Right. As if he ever does."

Sam took out his notebook and gleefully began to write: "September 25. Concert by Russian soprano." Using Brother Renato's guidance with the program, he went into detail about the selections and also about the staging and the lighting. He would need specific details for his report. He ended with: "No show by the king."

"I'm going to sleep well tonight," he said as they drove back to the monastery.

Except that he didn't.

The light bulb came on, and then blinked for a maddening four or five minutes, almost every hour and then just as suddenly went off. Sam kept tightening it, but found that it was loose every time.

"Maybe I should have found a place in town," he thought. "At least I would have gotten some sleep."

He didn't allow himself to think about the cause of this abnormal annoyance.

The next night at Teatro Alfieri was a recital by a young French pianist, Francois Boucher. He had received enthusiastic notices throughout Europe in the last year and was eagerly anticipated. There was much chatter as Sam and Brother Renato took their seats.

"I love piano recitals," Brother Renato said. "My sister used to play the piano."

"I've never been to one," Sam said, realizing he hadn't been to a lot of things.

Indeed, Sam found himself nodding off during Beethoven's Sonata No. 32 in C minor and again in Liszt's Transcendental Etudes. But after intermission, he was wide awake for Chopin's Sonata No. 3 in B minor, Op. 58.

"Well, if nothing else," Brother Renato said, "at least you're learning about some of the greatest classical compositions of the last two hundred years."

Throughout the concert, they kept their eyes focused on everything on the stage. Perhaps the ghost would stand over the pianist's shoulder, perhaps he would float above the piano, perhaps he'd glide out from the wings.

Again, Sam carefully described the concert, noting at the end that "King Victor Emmanuel II failed to appear."

"I knew it!" Sam exclaimed as he put his notebook away. "I knew there wouldn't be a ghost here."

Perhaps it was because he was so excited, but Sam couldn't sleep well that night. He waited for shenanigans from the light bulb, and they started about 2 a.m. There was also a new twist. The shutters on the lone window began banging at 4:30 a.m. even though there was not a trace of wind. Sam got up and closed them, but found that the latch had been broken, and the banging continued intermittently through the rest of the night.

"Hello?" he shouted. "Is anybody there?"

Silence.

"Hello?"

Silence.

"I'm not even going to think about this," he thought as he tried unsuccessfully to go back to sleep. "There must be a breeze somewhere, and Brother Renato said this place has bad electricity."

BECAUSE THE CONCERTS in Castelnuovo di Garfagnana were in the evening, Sam asked the monks if he could be helpful during the day. Brother Renato suggested that he work in the winery, the lone enterprise that was supporting the monks financially. Since the monastery's other attempts at selling produce—cheese, olive oil, sausage—had failed, and the dwindling number of monks desperately needed financial stability, wine was now their only marketable commodity.

"I think," he said softly, "Brother Xavier and Brother Constantine may be partaking of too many samples. Keep an eye on them."

The monastery had been making wine for more than two centuries, first for its own sacramental use during Mass and then making it a profitable venture. Indeed, its red wine, Vino Rosso Benedettino, was sold as far away as Lucca and Pisa and sometimes even in Florence.

It took Brother Xavier only one look at Sam to decide where to put him.

"Take off your shoes and socks."

For hours on end, the American college student stomped and stomped, his feet crimson and his legs aching.

"At least I don't have to pay rent," he thought. "Or for meals. Or for rides into town for the concerts. Nora is not going to believe this."

He had Brother Xavier take a picture of him stomping grapes.

The work was mindless, and Sam's thoughts drifted back to Nora and Central State. He wondered if she had interviewed Lin-Manuel Miranda again. He wondered if their relationship would change when he returned. He wondered if the other graduate students—Paul and Monica—had finished their projects. Strangely, he missed them.

He thought about next spring's musical, *Pal Joey*, and how he would love to play the lead. He realized, though, that there were a few problems. He couldn't act. He couldn't sing. And he couldn't dance. He also knew that he wasn't handsome, but Joey didn't have to be, just have some charm.

Frank Sinatra wasn't so handsome in the movie, he thought, just acted like a charming heel. He could act like a charming heel, and he was going to try out. So he hummed the songs in time to his stomping.

"*Sound the happy hunting horn/There's new game on the trail now...*"

And

"*If my heart gets in your hair/You mustn't kick it around...*"

Night after night, he and Brother Renato continued to journey to Teatro Alfieri for successive concerts by an American string ensemble, an Austrian folk duo and a French chanteuse. After each, Sam filled his notebook with details, always ending with the fact that there was no ghostly visitor at any of them. Then they saw a poster for the following week's attraction.

"Look," the monk said, "it's *Theater für ein neues Zeitalter*. I wouldn't think they'd come to a small town like this."

"What does that mean?" Sam asked.

"It's 'Theater for a New Age.' They're an avant-garde company from Munich. They're known for taking classics and turning them into, well, plays that maybe a monk should not be seen attending."

"Why?"

"They're known for absurdist theater. A lot of thunder and lightning. A lot of noise. A lot of sex and a lot of nudity. Naturally, they draw big crowds. Even we at the monastery have heard stories. Last year, they did *Doctor Faustus*. The two angels were naked and Mephistopheles didn't have much more on. There was a lot of simulated sex before Faustus was dragged off to Hell. I'm sure Marlowe was turning over in his grave, but the audiences loved it."

"What are they going to do here?"

"Let's see. It's such fine print and my eyesight isn't very good anymore. Oh, yes, Shakespeare. *Macbeth*."

"Mac...the Scottish play?"

"No, *Macbeth*."

Sam was too excited to attempt an explanation. If ever the ghost was going to appear, it would be during this production. Of course, he wouldn't appear. Because there wasn't any such thing as a ghost.

At night, he wasn't bothered when the bulb on the wall went on, then off, then on again, or when the shutter bounced at the window, or when he heard some gentle humming.

That was something new. It took several nights, but Sam finally recognized it as a hymn he'd heard the monks singing in the chapel.

"Hello?" he shouted. "Who is that humming?"

Silence.

The humming resumed.

"Hello? Who are you? Is that a hymn?"

Silence.

The humming resumed.

"Look, I don't care if you hum, just do it quietly so I can sleep."

As soon as Sam put his head on the pillow, he fell asleep.

The next morning, he told Brother Renato about this and even hummed a little. The monk said it sounded like an ancient hymn about Saint Bede, an English saint who had been appropriated by the Benedictines.

"You heard humming?" Brother Renato asked.

"Yes, but I'm sure it was from the chapel."

"What time was this?"

"After midnight, maybe 12:15 or so."

"Sam, nobody was in the chapel at that time."

"OK, so maybe a monk was humming in his cell?"

"I doubt it. Monks go right to sleep after Compline. And you're not near any other monk."

"Well, I heard it."

Brother Renato smiled. "Of course you did."

Sam didn't tell Brother Renato about a couple of other things that he'd noticed recently. One time, he was walking down the hall to the refectory when he thought that something—or someone—was walking along with him. It wasn't threatening, but it did keep the same pace as he did. When he arrived at the refectory, whatever it was vanished.

The other time, he was just drifting off to sleep when he felt a warmth all around him. At first he thought it was Nora's arms, then realized she wasn't there. Also, he noticed a gentle fragrance, sort of like the jasmine outside his mother's house, and he was sure Nora wouldn't wear it. Smiling, he went to sleep and in the morning felt more rested than at any time during his trip.

"Nothing," he thought. "Just my imagination. Nothing. Nothing!"

Oddly, he wasn't concerned about these strange happenings. Rather, he was somehow comforted by them, and, remarkably, he didn't feel so alone anymore. While he didn't want to think about the source, he did ask Brother Renato again the name of the ghost who had been around so often centuries earlier.

"Giacomo."

"Giacomo. That's a nice name."

"So was he."

After that, Sam felt that he had a new, if ethereal, friend.

Because Brother Renato thought the play by the *Theater für ein neues Zeitalter* might be sold out, he drove Sam to Castelnuovo di Garfagnana early. Having heard Sam's explanation, even he was now calling it "The Scottish Play."

They knew it was going to be different as soon as they entered because the auditorium was totally dark and they had to grope their way to their front-row seats.

"We'll be able to see the king up close," Brother Renato said.

"There's no such thing as the king," Sam said.

A half hour after the play was supposed to start, cymbals crashed, drums rolled and fog filled the stage and spilled into the audience.

"Great," Sam said, covering his ears. "We're not going to be able to see the king after all. If there is a king."

Then the witches, ancient hags, naked with long stringy hair that almost covered their private parts, came from the back and slithered down the aisles.

"*When shall we three meet again/In thunder, lightning, or in rain?*" the first one screeched.

"*When the hurlyburly's done,/When the battle's lost and won,*" the second witch squealed.

They scrambled onto the stage and the play began. The audience soon realized that it had been drastically cut. Macbeth, played by a naked diminutive youth, spoke in an incomprehensible dialect. Lady Macbeth, well over six feet tall, traveled on roller skates. Whenever there was a murder—and there seemed to be more than usual—a stagehand appeared to throw a pail of red paint at the victim. The drunken porter assumed a major role, wandering among the actors and making lewd gestures. Then Banquo's ghost appeared, and Brother Renato nudged Sam, who was now visibly shaking.

"Look, Sam, a ghost."

"Not the right one."

When the witches reappeared, they chose to dance with everyone else on stage amid ear-splitting music. During Lady Macbeth's sleepwalking scene—also done on roller skates—all the lights were turned off save for a dim spot that followed her around the stage. Then floodlights turned on so that everyone in the audience could witness Macbeth being murdered. That took about ten minutes.

Finally, with bodies littering the stage, it was over. At first, there was no reaction from the stunned crowed. Suddenly the place exploded with yells and cheers and a standing ovation that lasted twelve minutes.

Sam thought he was going to throw up, so Brother Renato hurried him out into the cool night.

"Still no ghost, Sam."

"He was probably afraid to come anywhere near that stage."

MORE WEEKS WENT BY. It was now late November and Sam had been in Castelnuovo di Garfagnana for almost two months. The hills and valleys had been beautiful before but now they were spectacular. Reds and purples, golds and yellows—a master painter had covered the countryside. Even Sam, who rarely noticed the fall colors in Pennsylvania, was fascinated, and he had Brother Renato stop a half dozen times so he could take pictures. He sent some to Nora.

As they continued their theatergoing, they saw a Chinese ballet troupe, a rock band from Brooklyn, Scottish Highlanders, Brazilian folk dancers, and many more. After each, Sam made detailed entries in his notebook, only now he was just using ditto marks for the last line.

Didn't he need more than his observations?

"Perhaps you should talk to other members of the audience," Brother Renato suggested. "They could talk about their experiences."

Sam knew the monk was right. His project would need what Professor Mantucci called "primary sources," so he decided to talk to audience members during the program intermissions and ask what they knew about this alleged ghost.

Being basically shy—especially for a theater major—Sam had to rehearse a half dozen times before going up to someone in the lobby and saying, "*Buonasera.*"

With Brother Renato at his side translating, he approached a gentleman of about seventy to see if he could ask a few questions. The man sighed and seemed to agree.

"Sir," Sam began, "I am doing some research about Teatro Alfieri and I wonder, have you been coming here for a long time?"

"Oh yes, ever since I was very young, probably younger than you are."

"And you enjoy the programs?"

"I especially enjoy the ballet. We get companies from all over the world but the ones from Russia are the best, of course. There was a magnificent *Giselle* last season, and also a *Firebird* that was just enchanting. Of course, I also adored the *Coppélia,* and *La Sylphide* may be a trifle silly but I always look forward to it. And then there's…"

"Sir, I wonder if I could ask you a question about something that I've heard sometimes happens during a performance."

"And what is that?"

"I've heard, and this may only be a rumor but it's so ridiculous that I'm almost embarrassed to ask it, but anyway, there's a story that sometimes there is an apparition on the stage, something that doesn't belong there."

"You're talking about the ghost of King Victor Emmanuel II, of course."

"Yes! Have you seen him? Often?"

"Young man, why are you asking this?"

"As I said, I'm doing some research. And I…"

"Doing research on King Victor Emmanuel II? Well, how interesting. Oh, I see my friend over there. Good luck to you."

"Yes, but…"

It was too late. The man had walked away and was hidden in the crowd.

"Damn!" Sam said.

Brother Renato took his arm and led him away. "Odd. I wonder why he didn't want to talk about it."

"I didn't even get his name."

"Well, he wouldn't have added much, would he?"

It was too late to find someone else so they went back inside and found their seats.

The next time, Sam approached a pair of women who looked as though they were sisters, sort of like Rosella and Maria. They seemed flattered to be asked questions by such a polite young man.

Sam knew this time that he should get their names first. Flora Bendetti and Clara Ostenzi. He also knew that he should avoid preliminary questions.

"I wonder if I may ask you if you have ever seen the ghost of King Victor Emmanuel II?"

"Oh my, oh my," Flora said.

"What a question," Clara said.

"So you have seen him?"

"Oh my," Flora said. "Come sister."

And with that they walked away.

"This is so strange," Sam said. "Why don't people want to talk about the ghost?"

"Maybe they're afraid he'll retaliate?"

"Or maybe he doesn't exist and they don't want the world to know."

And so it went. Sam tried to question five more audience members and never got past the first questions. Then he attended a musical theater night. Four singers had prepared a program of Rodgers and Hammerstein, Kander and Ebb, Cole Porter and Kurt Weill. Sam thought the singers were presenting the songs too operatically, but he generally enjoyed the program.

In the lobby, he spied a couple who looked like college students.

"Hi! I'm from America. Where do you go to school?"

"Really? All the way from America? We're from Bologna. We go to the Bernstein School of Musical Theater, but we come here all the time. My name is Franco."

"And I'm Natalia."

"Happy to know you! I go to a school in the States and I'm doing some research here. Say, have you seen the ghost of King Victor Emmanuel II?"

"The Bernstein School of Musical Theater is the only musical theater school in Italy," Natalia said.

"We were so glad to get in," Franco said. "It's very competitive. But the training is so good, acting, singing, dancing."

"When you come here," Sam said, "have you ever seen the ghost of King Victor Emmanuel II?"

"And we put on a big musical every year," Natalia said.

"Just recently we did *Jersey Boys* and *Spamalot*," Franco added.

"But I wonder, since you come here often, have you ever seen the ghost of King Victor Emmanuel II?"

"I wish you had time to come to Bologna," Natalia said. "It's a fascinating city."

Brother Renato nudged Sam and whispered in his ear. "They're not going to say anything. Let's get out of here."

After more tries, and with an empty notebook, Sam was ready to give up. "I guess I won't have any primary sources."

"Wait," Brother Renato said. "We should talk to somebody in management. See what they have to say."

Three nights later, they found the manager in the lobby sharing drinks and conversation with some obviously wealthy patrons. Sam waited until he could attract the man's attention, and, breathlessly, cut to the quick.

"Sir, I'm from the United States and I'm doing research on the legend of ghosts in theaters and can you tell me if there is a ghost of King Victor Emmanuel II in Teatro Alfieri?"

"Ah, you're the young man I've heard so much about. I hear you've been to so many performances in our little theater in the last weeks. Thank you so much for coming. And all the way from America! Have you enjoyed them? We try to put on a diverse schedule every year while at the same time honoring our past."

"I can appreciate that very much. But can you tell me if there is the ghost of King Victor Emmanuel II sometimes in Teatro Alfieri?"

"Oh, my young man, so many people have asked me that question."

"But does he come here? Have you seen him?"

"You know what I always ask them?"

"What?"

"Would your eyes deceive you? Thank you for coming. *Buona notte!*"

He rejoined his friends in conversation.

"What the hell does that mean?" Sam asked Brother Renato as they returned for the second act of *Nutcracker*.

"Well," the monk said, "remember what I told you. When you're as old as I am, you've learned not to question everything. There is probably some truth in every tale, no matter how odd and unbelievable it may be."

"But has the ghost of King Victor Emmanuel II really been seen in Teatro Alfieri? And why don't people want to talk about this? What's going on?"

They drove back to the monastery in silence. Sam was now talking to this "Giacomo," who manifested himself as a warm presence near his bed.

"Giacomo, Giacomo, what am I going to do? I really believe now that there isn't a ghost of the king and I can write about that. But Professor Mantucci will want to know how the legend started and why people don't want to talk about it. And I've got to wrap this up soon. I'm supposed to go back home next week."

Suddenly, Sam felt better, calmer, and he noticed a gentle waft of something sweet. He fell asleep.

The next morning, Brother Renato stopped him in the hall. "Sam, I made a phone call. I want you to meet somebody today."

DRIVING DOWN TO CASTELNUOVO DI GARFAGNANA, Brother Renato explained how Nicola Tagnolini could answer his questions.

"Nicola Tagnolini is one of the most famous journalists in Italy. He has won many, many prizes. He has worked for years for the newspaper *La nazione*. It's a regional paper out of Florence but covers all of Tuscany. Over the years many important people have written for it. Mario Luzi? A poet and novelist. Giovanni Spadolini? Prime minister of Italy in the 1980s.

Carlo Collodi? Pen name for Carlo Lorenzini. He wrote *The Adventures of Pinocchio*."

"Really? He wrote *Pinocchio*? I loved that book. My mother read it to us every night. My sister used to take it to bed with her."

"So now we will meet the famous Nicola Tagnolini. You will see, he is a fine gentleman. I have known him for years."

They met the famous journalist in the piazza in front of the Duomo, and if Hollywood needed to cast a distinguished Italian, he would have easily won the role. Well over six feet, with a neatly trimmed beard, long white hair and a monocle in his left eye, Nicola Tagnolini wore a three-piece Armani suit and obviously expensive Italian-made shoes. His maple cane was topped with the golden head of a lion.

Sam gave Brother Renato his phone so he could take a picture of him and Nicola Tagnolini, and then Sam took a picture of the journalist with Brother Renato.

The piazza was crowded with tourists taking selfies, so they adjourned to a nearby *bar* and ordered espresso. In the weeks Sam had been in Italy, he had become obsessed by Italian coffee and knew when it was proper to order cappuccino (before 10 a.m.) and when to ask for espresso (after that). He couldn't wait to go to Starbucks with his friends and say, "I'd like an *espresso doppio*, please. Oh yes, I had this so often when I was in Italy. They make it so much better over there."

Declining to answer Brother Renato's questions about his most recent exposé on drug dealing in Barga, Nicola Taglonini asked instead about Sam's visit.

"How do you like Italy, Samuel? Are you impressed?"

"I can't believe I'm here. It's all so beautiful. I know I'll want to come back."

"The next time you come you should contact me, and I will point out some out-of-the-way places to visit. Now, Brother Renato said you have seen many performances at Teatro Alfieri."

Sam described everything he had seen, saying he had learned so much about theater, music and dance.

"Your favorite?" Tagnolini asked.

"Probably the jazz band from Norway. They were awesome."

"And your least favorite?"

Sam didn't hesitate. "That theater group from Munich! I couldn't believe it. Have you seen them?"

"Oh yes, several times. What can I say? They play for the masses, and who can account for taste? But Brother Renato says you have some questions about Teatro Alfieri?"

Sam described his project and said that after more than two months, and after seeing everything at the theater during that time, he had not seen the alleged ghost of King Victor Emmanuel II a single time.

"So how did this legend start?" he asked.

Tagnolini drained the last of his cappuccino.

"Over the years, I have talked to many people about this, including the management of the theater. The story apparently started in 1924 during a performance of *Richard III*. Are you familiar with this play?"

"Oh, yes." Sam thanked God he'd taken a Shakespeare class and tried to remember details.

"You know, then, how bloody this is, with the mad king killing his enemies right and left. In 1924, a group similar to *Theater für ein neues Zeitalter* came to the village and performed Shakespearean plays in repertory. The *Richard III* was particularly gruesome, with loud thunder and lightning and many pails of red paint thrown around.

"Even at that, the murders were more vivid than one would expect, and by the end Richard had killed twelve people, or at least was responsible for twelve deaths. As you know, of course, all those people appear to Richard in a dream. Prince Edward, King Henry VI, King Edward the IV, Clarence, Lady Anne, Rivers, Gray, Hastings, Vaughan, Buckingham, the two young princes. They're all there, and they tell him, 'Despair and die!' and shortly after, he is indeed killed by Richmond.

"But here is where the story gets more interesting. Amid all those ghosts—and who was going to keep count?—there appeared to be an added figure. He was a short, chubby man wearing a black military uniform adorned with medals and a green sash. But while the other ghosts stayed, this one remained for less than a minute, and then disappeared."

"King Victor Emmanuel II?" Sam asked.

"Some people immediately thought that, and the buzz and consternation in the theater was so loud that the rest of the play was canceled."

Afterwards, Nicola Tagnolini said, this supposed ghost was the subject of conversation throughout the village. They couldn't wait to see if he would appear again. Since the group was performing in repertory, the next night was *Romeo and Juliet,* followed by *The Merchant of Venice,* and then *Richard III* again.

"And of course all the performances were sold out. But no ghost of a king appeared."

Sam was so excited he almost fell off the wooden stool.

"The following week they were doing *Richard III* again, and the figure appeared at the same point and then disappeared. The audience was so aroused that again the rest of the play was canceled. The management of Teatro Alfieri seemed as surprised as anyone and denied any knowledge about the supposed ghost. The director of the theater company, however, declined to comment."

"So I'm guessing that the theater company planted someone there?" Sam asked.

"Who knows? People don't remember this, or don't want to remember, but the stage was barely lit at the time. It would have been easy for an actor to slip on stage and then off again."

"But have people seen him again over the years?"

"In 1933, an opera company from France was doing *Aida* and he was supposedly seen during the Grand March, again for only a minute and way in the background, but enough so that people were aroused and the legend grew. There were no sightings until after the war, but in 1953, a Russian group was doing *Ivanov* and the figure supposedly appeared in the second-act party scene. Again, the stage was dimly lit.

"In 1974, during a performance of *Julius Caesar* by a classical theater group from Greece, it was allegedly seen during the 'Friends, Romans, Countrymen' speech. The last time was in 2002, when an adventurous theater company from Stockholm did Sondheim's *Sweeney Todd*. Now there's a show with a lot of blood. It was not until the final 'Attend the Tale of Sweeney Todd' song that the figure was purportedly seen in the crowd on stage."

Sam thought about these examples. "There doesn't seem to be any relationship between all these plays. Was there?"

"This is what I think after talking to many people," Tagnolini said. "In each case, the management of Teatro Alfieri vehemently denied any knowledge, and I believe them. But also in each case the company that was visiting was having serious trouble selling tickets. I can only assume that they had heard of the response when the alleged ghost appeared even decades earlier and wanted to—how do you say this in America?—cash in on it. Also, in each case, the stage was dimly lit and it would have been easy for an actor to slip on and then off.

"And it worked. In every case. The remaining performances were always sold out. And so the legend was continued and even grew stronger. It didn't matter that there weren't any more sightings for so long."

Sam still had a question.

"If people thought this might be a con job, why don't they want to talk about it? That seems very strange."

In typical Italian fashion, Tagnolini answered with a story.

"Samuel," he said, "in America, you have the legend of Santa Claus, right?"

"Yes, sure."

"Well, in Italy, we have the legend of the Befana. This is an old woman who also delivers gifts to children, only she does it on the eve of the Epiphany, January 6, because that is the last day of our Christmas celebrations.

"Unlike your jolly Santa Claus, however, Befana is portrayed as an old hag wearing a black shawl and riding a broomstick through the air. Like Santa Claus, she enters the children's homes down through the chimney, and even though she is rather ugly, she is often smiling as she distributes her candy and gifts.

"Your Santa Claus supposedly was inspired by the good Saint Nicholas, from the fourth century in Greece. The legend of our Befana is that the Three Kings visited her before the birth of Jesus and asked for directions. They asked her to join them, but she said she was too busy with her housework. But later, apparently realizing what she had missed, she began searching for the Baby Jesus. And she's been doing it ever since."

Sam wondered what this had to do with theater ghosts, but tried to look interested.

"Samuel, when you were little, I suppose you believed in Santa Claus?"

"Oh yes, of course. Every kid does."

"And when you found that he was only a legend, and that your parents actually gave you your gifts, I imagine you were disappointed."

"Oh, I cried for weeks! My sister told me, and she was a year younger than me! I was so mad we had a big fight. I don't think I'll ever forgive her."

The journalist leaned forward. "This is what I think. Theater people, and those who go to the theater, are really hopelessly romantic at heart. They want to believe what happens on that stage is real. So if there is a legend, like a ghost who suddenly appears at a performance, they like to believe that it could happen. And, more important, they hope they themselves will see the ghost sometime. It gives them comfort. And if they don't see a ghost, they can still hope that someday they will. People believe what they want to believe."

Sam thought about it and fiddled with his paper napkin.

"But, Signor, why don't they want to talk about the ghost? Every time I asked a question they would change the subject."

"Sometimes, talking about something as intangible as a ghost makes it more realistic, and people want to keep their fantasies to themselves."

"Sir, do you think this is the same reason why people say there are ghosts in other theaters?"

"I only know about Teatro Alfieri, but I imagine the same kind of legends have started and been preserved elsewhere. Again, I can only repeat what I said. People believe what they want to believe."

The *bar*, which had been crowded, was now nearly empty, and most of the tourists had taken their cameras and left the piazza at the Duomo. Sam thanked Nicola Tagnolini.

"I wish you much success in your project and your career," the journalist said. "Please send me a copy of what you have written. I am most interested in reading it."

Sam and Brother Renato rode back to the monastery in silence. In his cell, Sam was pleased to again feel a warm sweet-smelling presence. He sat on the bed and, unmindful of what his friends back home might have thought, went on for hours with "Giacomo," describing everything that had happened that day and what Nicola Taglonini had said. Then he got ready for bed.

"Anyway, Giacomo," Sam told his friend, "now I know that there aren't ghosts in theaters. I can go back home now and write this."

BACK AT CENTRAL STATE, Sam was warmly greeted by Nora, so warmly, in fact, that Bella was very upset that they hogged the bed for so long. Nora actually seemed interested in his trip and what he found, and he was fascinated by her work with the professor about Lin-Manuel Miranda.

Although he was jet-lagged, he met with Professor Mantucci the next day. She still had lingering doubts, but told him to start writing. That night, in the graduate student lounge, he described to his fellow students what had happened and showed off the dozens of pictures he'd taken. He also demanded the $25 they had pledged so that he and Nora could plan an expensive dinner at Francesco's.

The next morning, he got out his laptop, poured a cup of coffee as he remembered how much better it was in Italy, and began writing: "Ghosts in the Theater: A Case Study of Delusion and Deception."

He thought the title was "awesome."

In late January, he had completed the writing and turned it in to Professor Mantucci. He had hurried because auditions were starting for *Pal Joey*. He knew his limitations, but Nora had helped him with the lines, the songs and even the tap dance.

He knew exactly what he would wear: black pants, a black shirt and a white bow tie. He would be the coolest Joey ever.

He got the pants out of the closet and the shirt from the lower drawer of the dresser. He hadn't taken the shirt on his trip because it was too heavy for Italy.

Unfolding it, he thought he detected something, and then it became more and more apparent. A sweet-smelling jasmine.

"Giacomo! This was months ago and you're four thousand miles away. How did you do this?"

He put the shirt on and he could feel a warmth envelop his entire body. The scent only grew stronger.

"Giacomo, Giacomo, Giacomo!"

He was grateful that his fellow students had asked only if he still didn't believe there were ghosts in theaters. They hadn't asked whether ghosts could be friends.

CPSIA information can be obtained
at www.ICGtesting.com
Printed in the USA
BVHW072224160321
602717BV00005B/48